# User
# Interface
# Software

# TRENDS IN SOFTWARE

---

**User Interface Software**
ed. Len Bass and Prasun Dewan

*In Preparation:*

**Computer Graphics**
ed. John Amanatides and Don Mitchell

**Configuration Management**
ed. Stuart Feldman and Walter Tichy

# User
# Interface
# Software

*Edited by*

**Len Bass**
*Carnegie Mellon University, USA*

and

**Prasun Dewan**
*Purdue University, USA*

JOHN WILEY & SONS
Chichester · New York · Brisbane · Toronto · Singapore

*Other Wiley Editorial Offices*

John Wiley & Sons, Inc., 605 Third Avenue,
New York, NY 10158-0012, USA

Jacaranda Wiley Ltd, G.P.O. Box 859, Brisbane,
Queensland 4001, Australia

John Wiley & Sons (Canada) Ltd, 22 Worcester Road,
Rexdale, Ontario M9W 1L1, Canada

John Wiley & Sons (SEA) Pte Ltd, 37 Jalan Pemimpin #05-04,
Block B, Union Industrial Building, Singapore 2057

*Library of Congress Cataloging-in-Publication Data*

User interface software / edited by Len Bass and Prasun Dewan.
      p.   cm.
    Includes bibliographical references and index.
    ISBN 0 471 93784 3
    1. User interfaces (Computer systems)   2. Computer software-
-Development.   I. Bass, Len.   II. Dewan, Prasun.
QA76.9.U83U84   1993
005.1—dc20                                    93-9748
                                              CIP

*British Library Cataloguing in Publication Data*

A catalogue record for this book is available from the British Library

ISBN 0 471 93784 3

Produced from camera-ready copy supplied by the authors
Printed and bound in Great Britain by Redwood Books Ltd, Trowbridge, Wilts

# Contents

## 4 A Multi-threaded Higher-order User Interface Toolkit    61
*E. R. Gansner and J. H. Reppy*

## 5 Animation in User Interfaces: Principles and Techniques    81
*J. T. Stasko*

## 6 Virtual Reality: Perspectives, Applications and Architecture    103
*C. Esposito*

# Series Editor's Preface

During 1990, the twentieth anniversary of *Software Practice and Experience*, two special issues (one on UNIX Tools and the other on the X Window System) were published. Each issue contained a set of refereed papers related to a single topic; the issues appeared a short time (roughly nine months) after the authors were invited to submit them. The positive experience with the special issues resulted in *Trends in Software*, a fast turn-around serial that devotes each issue to a specific topic in the software field. As with the special issues of SPE, each *Trend* will be edited by an authority in the area.

By collecting together a comprehensive set of papers on a single topic, *Trends* makes it easy for readers to find a definitive overview of a given topic. By ensuring timely publication, *Trends* guarantees readers that the information presented captures the state of the art. The collection of papers will be of practical value to software designers, researchers, practitioners and users in that field.

Papers in each *Trend* are solicited by a guest editor who is responsible for soliciting them and ensuring that the selected papers span the topic. The guest editor then subjects each paper to the rigorous peer review expected in any archival journal. As much as possible, electronic communication (e.g. electronic mail) is used as the primary means of communication between the series editor, members of the editorial board, guest editor, authors, and referees. A style document and macro package is available to reduce the turn-around time by enabling authors to submit papers in camera-ready form. During the editorial process, papers are exchanged electronically in an immediately printable format.

We aim to produce three *Trends* each year. Topics to be covered in forthcoming issues include computer graphics, and configuration management.

The editorial board encourages readers to submit suggestions and comments. You may send them via electronic mail to bala@research.att.com or by postal mail to the address given below. Please clarify if a communication is intended for publication or not.

I would like to thank the editorial advisory board as well as the staff at John Wiley for their help in making *Trends* a reality.

**Balachander Krishnamurthy**
*Room 3D-570*
*AT&T Bell Laboratories*
*600 Mountain Avenue*
*Murray Hill, NJ 07974*
*USA*

# Preface

The design and implementation of the user interface have become both the primary determinants of user satisfaction and the primary cost drivers for software. User interface design and implementation are closely related—novel user interface designs cannot become commonplace unless effective techniques and tools are developed to support their implementation. The traditional focus on teletype-based user interfaces is a direct consequence of the fact these are the only kind of user interfaces supported by input/output routines offered by traditional computing systems.

In the last ten years, a new discipline has emerged to research both novel user interface designs and techniques and tools to make it easier to construct these designs. Several different but related lines of research have emerged in this area. This issue of *Trends in Software* identifies and explains these new research directions. The papers are written by leading experts in the field.

The first four papers provide a context that is relevant to all user interfaces. The next five papers provide the axes in which the field will grow. We begin by focusing on evaluating the design of the user interface. High quality user interfaces are designed by evaluating proposed or actual designs. The paper by Hix and Hartson discusses techniques for doing this evaluation.

The work in implementing graphical user interfaces has produced a large variety of tools and techniques and it has become difficult to compare and contrast them. Research in user interface software architectures is addressing this problem by defining the fundamental concepts and principles in this area and producing a set of requirements that user interface software must meet. The paper by Bass describes software engineering principles and a particular architecture that meets these principles.

The actual construction and execution of the user interface is performed by tools that fit within the system framework. Perhaps the most well-accepted tools today for constructing graphical user interfaces are window systems and user interface toolkits, which are considered essential parts of a contemporary computing system. The paper by Linton describes one, particularly interesting such tool.

The vast majority of current windows systems and toolkits today are based on a sequential, object-oriented programming paradigm. Is this programming paradigm fundamental to these tools? In their paper, A Multi-threaded Higher-order User Interface Toolkit, Gansner and Reppy argue that concurrent, higher-order functional programming is a more appropriate programming paradigm for these tools. They defend their position by describing in-depth a radical, experimental system based on this programming paradigm.

Given that every user interface needs to be evaluated, fit within some software architecture and be constructed with some tool, there are still several axes along which the field will develop in the future: the dynamic behavior of the interface, the number of people sharing the interface, the amount of immersion the user has in the interface and the technology used to present the interface. The next five papers describe these axes.

Graphical user interfaces represent only one of the exciting new advances in user interfaces. More recent and experimental, animation, virtual reality, multiuser interaction, multimedia interaction, are other such advances which address four orthogonal issues in user interfaces.

Initially used mainly for code understanding, animation is now being used as a part of the user interface. In his paper, Animation in User Interfaces: Principles and Techniques, Stasko gives an overview of this area. He discusses the various ways in which animation can improve human-computer interaction, identifies the properties of effective animation, and surveys tools and techniques for implementing both 2D and 3D animations.

Virtual reality allows the use of metaphors from some real life scenarios to interact with applications that simulate these scenarios. Virtual reality has become so popular so quickly that it is difficult to distinguish the technical issues from the promotional claims. The paper by Esposito provides an overview of the state-of-the-art in implementing virtual reality systems.

Multiuser user interfaces have the potential for solving the problems raised by today's distributed organizations and laboratories. Isolated multiuser interfaces developed in the early 1980s have been replaced by a new discipline exploring general design and implementation concepts in this area. In their paper, Designing Software for a Group's Needs: A Functional Analysis of Synchronous Groupware, Olson *et al.* describe a multi-dimensional design space of multiuser interfaces. In Tools for Implementing Multiuser User Interfaces, Dewan complements their paper by identifying, over-viewing, and comparing tools that make it easy to implement these user interfaces.

Multimedia interaction allows users to interact with the application and each other using media other than text and graphics. The paper by Stevens discusses multimedia not only in technical terms but also in terms of how multimedia will allow different types of interaction.

Predicting the direction of the diversity in user interfaces and designing a software system to be able to accommodate the diversity are both very difficult problems. This issue identifies the relatively mature trends towards addressing this problem.

**Len Bass**
*Software Engineering Institute*
*Carnegie Mellon University*
*Pittsburgh, PA 15213*

**Prasun Dewan**
*Department of Computer Science*
*Purdue University*
*West Lafayette, IN 47907*

# List of Authors

**Len Bass**
Software Engineering Institute
Carnegie Mellon University
Pittsburgh
PA 15213
USA
ljb@sei.cmu.edu

**Chris Esposito**
Boeing Computer Services
P.O. Box 24346
Mail Stop 7L-64
Seattle
WA 98124
USA
chrise@atc.boeing.com

**H. Rex Hartson**
Department of Computer Science
Virginia Polytechnic University
Blacksburg
VA 24061
USA
hartson@vtopus.cs.vt.edu

**Eiji Kuwana**
NTT Software Laboratories
1-9-1 Kohnen
Minato-Ku
Tokyo 108
Japan
kuwana@ntt-twins.ntt.jp

**Prasun Dewan**
Computer Science Department
Purdue University
West Lafayette
IN 47907
USA
pd@cs.purdue.edu

**Emden Gansner**
Room 3C-532B
AT&T Bell Laboratories
600 Mountain Avenue
Murray Hill
NJ 07974
USA
erg@research.att.com

**Deborah Hix**
Department of Computer Science
Virginia Polytechnic University
Blacksburg
VA 24061
USA
hix@vtopus.cs.vt.edu

**Mark Linton**
2011 N. Shoreline Blvd
M/S 7U-005
P.O. Box 7311
Mountain View
CA 94039
USA
linton@sgi.com

**Lola McGuffin**
Cognitive Science and Machine Intelligence
University of Michigan
701 Tappan Street
Ann Arbor
MI 48109-1234
USA
lola@csmil.umich.edu

**Gary Olson**
Cognitive Science and Machine
    Intelligence
University of Michigan
701 Tappan Street
Ann Arbor
MI 48109-1234
USA
gmo@csmil.umich.edu

**Judy Olson**
Cognitive Science and Machine Intelligence
University of Michigan
701 Tappan Street
Ann Arbor
MI 48109-1234
USA
jso@csmil.umich.edu

**Johnathan Reppy**
Room 2A-428
AT&T Bell Laboratories
600 Mountain Avenue
Murray Hill
NJ 07974
USA
jhr@research.att.com

**John Stasko**
Graphics, Visualization and Usability Center
College of Computing
Georgia Institute of Technology
Atlanta
GA 30332-0280
USA
stasko@cc.gatech.edu

**Scott Stevens**
Software Engineering Institute
Carnegie Mellon University
Pittsburg
PA 15213
USA
sms@sei.cmu.edu

# 1

# Formative Evaluation: Ensuring Usability in User Interfaces

**Deborah Hix & H. Rex Hartson**
*Department of Computer Science*
*Virginia Tech*

## ABSTRACT

Ensuring usability has become a key goal of interactive system development, as developers have begun to realize that it matters little how effectively an interactive system can compute if human users cannot communicate effectively with the system. In response to this need for increased usability, interactive system developers have realized the necessity for techniques to evaluate user interface design - to determine existing levels of usability and to identify problems to be solved in order to improve usability. In this paper we will discuss what we have found to be two main types of *formative user interface evaluation*: analytic and empirical. Both these types occur as part of the development process. We do not attempt to survey all approaches to either of these types of formative evaluation, but rather to offer a sampling of some approaches that have been found (by us and by others) to be useful in ensuring usability. We give only an overview of analytic methods, and then focus on empirical methods. We conclude with some of our observations on future trends in user interface evaluation.

## 1.1 Introduction

Stories abound about how not to evaluate a user interface. One of our favorites came from an undergraduate student telling us about her summer job. She was hired by a major government contractor to do some implementation on a portion of a huge interactive system. On her first day, the module of the project she was to work on was not quite ready for her to begin. In an attempt to find something for her to do for the week or so until the module was ready, her supervisor decided, on the spur of the moment, that the student could evaluate the user interface! Her instructions were to "Go play around with this thing and tell us what to fix." This

*User Interface Software*, Edited by Bass and Dewan
© 1993 John Wiley & Sons Ltd

company had planned no evaluation of the user interface for a multi-million dollar interactive system. In fact, the only evaluation the first version had (before it got to people who had to use it) was from this rising junior computer science major who knew absolutely nothing about human-computer interaction design and evaluation. She knew little about what the system was supposed to do, and even less about evaluating an interface. We were relieved (and not a little amused) to hear that the contractor did formally include interface evaluation in its development plan for subsequent versions, because the first release of this system was such a disaster in terms of its usability.

Only a decade ago, evaluation of most interactive systems was much like the scenario just described: ad hoc at best, nonexistent at worst. Users typically saw the system for the first time when it was fully implemented and often all the way to being the "final" deployable product. This method produced the horrifying, unusable user interfaces that proliferated into all application areas. Now, however, developers are finally realizing that the bottom line is: *Users are going to evaluate the interface sooner or later-* either correctly, in-house, using the proper techniques and under the appropriate conditions; or after it is in the field, when it is probably too late to make many effective modifications. For everyone's benefit, the sooner evaluation is done, the better.

Ensuring usability has become a key goal of interactive system development, as developers have also begun to realize that it matters little how well an interactive system can compute if human users cannot communicate effectively with the system. In response to this need for increased usability, interactive system developers have realized the necessity for techniques to evaluate user interface design - to determine existing levels of usability and to identify problems to be solved in order to improve usability. In this paper we will discuss what we have found to be two main types of *formative user interface evaluation*: analytic and empirical. Both these types occur as part of the development process. We do not attempt to survey all approaches to either of these types of formative evaluation, but rather we offer a sampling of some approaches that have been found (by us and by others) to be useful in ensuring usability. In Section 1.2, we will explain in more detail what our context for this paper is, and what is meant by formative evaluation. In Section 1.3 we will give only an overview of analytic methods, and then focus, in Section 1.4, on empirical methods. In Section 1.5, we summarize, and in Section 1.6 conclude with some of our observations on future *trends* in user interface evaluation.

## 1.2   Setting the Context

### 1.2.1   Formative vs. Summative Evaluation

The origins of the terms formative and summative evaluation are traced by Carroll, Singley, and Rosson [CSR92] to Scriven's [Scr67] methodological framework of goals and processes for performing evaluation of instructional materials. Dick and Carey [DC78] also used these terms in the same context. The terms have since been adopted in the human-computer interaction (HCI) literature (e.g., [HH89, Wil84]).

Summative evaluation is evaluation of a design after it is complete, or nearly so. Summative evaluation is often used during field or beta testing, or to compare one product to another. For example, a summative evaluation of two systems, A and B) is based on a linear sequence of development phases. However, there are implicit feedback paths from later phases to earlier ones, resulting in cycles that some consider iterative. The spiral life cycle [Boe88] features explicit cycles, but they are large cycles, passing several times through the same sequence of development phases. On the other hand, user interface development requires more frequent and less global cycling. Often, numerous tight, localized cycles of iteration are required just to achieve the desired level of usability for a single interface feature. In response to the need for this focus on iteration, and correspondingly on evaluation, we have developed a life cycle concept we call the star life cycle [HH89], shown in Figure 1.1.

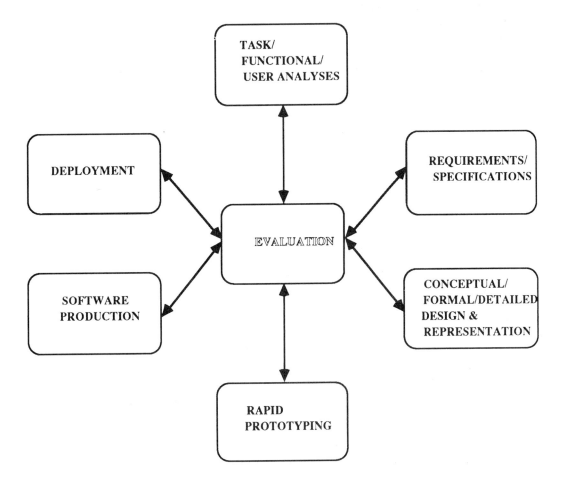

**Figure 1.1**    Star life cycle

The structure - or lack of it, compared to other life cycles - of this star life cycle shows that evaluation (of a kind appropriate to each activity) is to be applied to every user interface development activity (e.g., task/functional/user analyses, requirements/specification), not just to design. It also shows that there is not a single starting point, nor is there a prescribed order for development activities. Simply, each development activity should be followed by evaluation of some sort.

From our own experiences, and in talking with numerous other developers, we have found a rule of thumb to be that an average of three major cycles of formative evaluation, with every cycle followed by iterative redesign, will be completed for each significant version of a design. As we said above, there are also additional very short cycles, to quickly check out a few small issues. Most data generally come from the first major cycle of evaluation. If the process is working properly and the design is improving, later cycles will generate fewer new discoveries and will generally necessitate fewer changes in the design. The first cycle can generate an enormous amount of data, enough to be overwhelming. In Section 4, we will discuss how to collect and analyze these data in order to meet interface usability goals.

People sometimes mistakenly say that formative evaluation is not as rigorous or as formal as summative evaluation. The distinction between formative and summative evaluation is not in its formality, but rather in the goal of each approach. Summative evaluation does not support the iterative refinement process; waiting until an interface is almost done to evaluate it will not allow much, if any, iterative refinement. It is important that members of the development team, and especially managers, understand this difference. Otherwise, because formative evaluation is not controlled testing and usually does not require many participants (subjects), results of formative evaluation may be discounted as being, for example, too informal, not scientifically rigorous, or not statistically significant. Formative evaluation is, indeed, formal in the sense of having an explicit and well-defined procedure and does result in quantitative data, but is not intended to provide statistical significance. Formative evaluation is a technique used by developers to address the needs of users, and thereby to ensure high usability in an interface.

### 1.2.2   Evaluation of What and for What?

An interactive system can be viewed simplistically as shown in Figure 1.2.

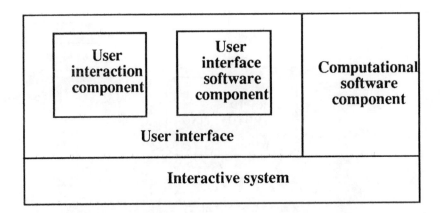

**Figure 1.2**   Components of an interactive system

Well-known techniques from software engineering are appropriate for developing the computational (non-interface) software component. Software evaluation can have many goals, including fidelity of implementation to the design, reliability (freedom from bugs), reusability, and so on. Since the user interface software component is, obviously, also software, these same goals apply. Usability is not on this list of goals.

So, surprising as it might be to those who have not thought about the distinction, it is not user interface software that is evaluated for usability. Rather, the *interaction design* - what the user sees and hears and does while interacting with the system - is evaluated for usability. The user interaction component includes the icons, text, graphics, audio, video, and devices that are presented to the user and with which the user interacts. User interface software might be the medium through which an interaction design is implemented, executed, observed, and evaluated, but an interaction design might also be manifest by means of a WYSIWYG rapid prototyping tool that does not necessarily produce user interface software in the usual sense. In fact, the user interface could be constructed in firmware or hardware, but it does not matter for our purposes here, since *it is the interaction design that is evaluated for usability.*

Thus, software evaluation techniques are not appropriate for evaluating user interaction designs; to ensure usability, different methods of evaluation are required, and those methods are the topic of this paper.

To further delineate our scope, we mention an attribute of interactive systems that can be measured very early in the development cycle and that is closely related to usability, namely, *user acceptance*. Davis [Dav89] shows that perceived usefulness and perceived ease of use are fundamental determinants of user acceptance. However, user acceptance metrics, which combine metrics for both usability and functionality of a proposed system, appear to have more direct benefit to management and marketing organizations than to development teams. For example, such metrics do not serve the formative evaluation process because they lack the kind of specific feedback about usability problems necessary for iterative development and design improvement. Therefore, we do not emphasize user acceptance within the scope of this paper.

### 1.2.3 Types of Formative Evaluation

As we mentioned earlier, there are (at least) two main types of formative evaluation: analytic and empirical. Many *analytic techniques* use descriptions of the behavioral or user's view of interaction designs based on tasks and/or grammars. These design descriptions are analyzed to detect usability problems early in the development process, perhaps before any implementation, or even prototyping, has been done. Thus, these techniques are often built on predictive models of user behavior and/or performance. These predictive models are sometimes validated by comparing predicted user performance with empirically measured performance (e.g., Reisner's work on Robart [Rei81], discussed below). Scriven [Scr67], as described in [CSR92], uses the term *intrinsic evaluation* for this kind of evaluation technique that studies the inherent structure of a design. These techniques usually involve a very detailed analysis of the design, and often the design rationale, in terms of goals and subgoals.

*Empirical techniques* for formative evaluation of interaction designs are based on data taken during observed performance testing with users. Typically prototypes are used as the medium for evaluation, in order to identify usability problems early in the development process. Scriven refers to evaluation for rapid detection of design problems as *pay-off evaluation*. This is an appropriately descriptive term for purely empirical approaches to formative evaluation in the area of human-computer interaction, because developers seek an immediate pay-off in terms of design improvements. This is in contrast to some other kinds of empirical work, such as controlled experimentation that may add to our theoretical and principle-based knowledge a little bit at a time.

Both analytic and empirical evaluation in the context of HCI have the same goal: to ensure usability in a user interaction design. However, they are very different techniques for reaching that goal, as we will discuss in the remainder of this paper.

## 1.3    Analytic Formative Evaluation

### 1.3.1    Some Examples of Analytic Evaluation

Before we concentrate on empirical approaches to formative evaluation, we offer a brief overview of some representative approaches to analytic evaluation, including the GOMS model [CMN83] the work of Kieras and Polson [KP85], the Command Language Grammar (CLG) [Mor81], the keystroke-level model [CM80], the Reisner Action Language model (1981), and the Task Action Grammar (TAG) [PG86]. These models all are the basis for some sort of analytic evaluation of a user interaction design.

The analytic approach to evaluation of user interaction design is generally based on examining and/or manipulating an abstract representation of that design. The result is a prediction of what would happen if usability were measured empirically with human participants; thus, an analytic approach can be used to compare two alternative designs or two different versions of the same design. As such, analytic techniques are sometime considered a substitute for empirical evaluation, at least at some point in the development cycle. However, *analytic methods must be considered complementary to, and not a complete substitute for, empirical evaluation* [Rei83]. When analytic evaluation is used, it is often used early in the evolution of a design, followed up later with empirical evaluation. By necessity, for the credibility of the prediction, each analytic method must be validated with empirical measurements of human performance.

The GOMS (Goals, Operators, Methods, and Selection rules) model [CMN83] supports predictive evaluation through task analysis of an interaction design. GOMS provides a foundation based on psychological theories for purposes of predicting user performance. A goal identifies a task and a method describes how the task is performed, in terms of operators and selection rules. Complex cognitive tasks can be encapsulated within the operators to simplify the modeling. The amount of detail generated in a GOMS interface description allows for a thorough evaluation at a very low level of detail, but the GOMS description can be an enormous, difficult, and often tedious undertaking to produce. As a practical matter, it requires a trained cognitive psychologist exercising expert judgement to produce these details. Knowing the difficulty of producing GOMS descriptions and that different GOMS analysts can produce quite different representations, Kieras formulated a practical approach to producing more standardized GOMS descriptions, one that can be used by non-specialists [Kie88]. Despite the complexity of the GOMS approach, there are numerous indications in the literature that it is used, at least to some extent, for developing and evaluating user interfaces.

Using the GOMS model as a basis, Kieras and Polson [KP85] have built a formal model to describe user knowledge required for performance of a task and for use of a device. This is a model of cognitive complexity - complexity of interaction as viewed by the user - that results in user performance prediction. This work is sometimes referred to in the literature as cognitive complexity theory. User knowledge is represented in the form of IF-THEN production rules, with the GOMS model providing the content, essentially converting user task performance into a computer program. Complexity measures (e.g., a count of the number of production rules) can be applied to the "programs" to measure the amount and complexity of knowledge required for performing specific tasks. Additionally, generalized state transition networks (GTNs) are used to represent the behavior of devices [KP83]. GTN representations for devices, along with production rule representations of users, can be executed together as a single simulation representing both user and devices. The results of simulation are the performance predictions.

The Command Language Grammar (CLG) approach to user modeling [Mor81] hierarchically decomposes system functions into objects, methods, and operations. The psychological hypothesis underlying the CLG is that ". . . to design the user interface is to design the user's model" [Mor80], (p. 296). Idealized user knowledge is represented with a somewhat complex grammar having the appearance of a high level programming language. System structure has three components - conceptual, communication and physical - and two different levels within each component. The assumption is that users form a layered mental representation of systems, and these components and levels are intended to mirror the layers of representation. Essentially, the CLG is a design tool to separate the conceptual model of a system from its specific command language and to reveal the relationship between the two ( [WBGM88], (p. 53), quoting Moran [Mor81], (p. 5). The CLG formalism offers a thorough and broad framework for describing many aspects of a user interface. Like GOMS, however, creating a CLG description is complicated and time-consuming. While the CLG concept has received much discussion and acceptance in human-computer interaction literature over the past decade, there seems to be some doubt about its utility in evaluation of real interaction designs [WBGM88].

The keystroke-level model ( [CM80], as discussed in Reisner, [Rei83]), models user-system interaction at - as the name implies - the level of keystrokes, and also includes other simple physical actions (e.g., mouse clicks) at that same level of granularity. A model of the user, derived from a structural representation of a command language system, is intended as a system design tool to predict expert user task time for routine tasks [Rei83], (p. 21). A method for performing a task is specified as a series of commands. Predictions of user performance are made by counting keystrokes and other similar actions such as pointing (e.g., cursor movement), homing (e.g., moving hands to the keyboard), and simple drawing actions. Another parameter includes mental preparation (e.g., deciding to make a particular keystroke). Like GOMS and the CLG, the level of detail in a keystroke analysis can be overwhelming.

The Reisner Action Language Model (1981) provides a technique for comparing predicted user performance associated with alternative designs, and for identifying design decisions that might cause user errors. Physical actions of the user are viewed as expressions in the language of the user. Complexity measures are applied to formal grammars of the user's language, revealing inconsistencies (e.g., more grammar rules are required for exceptions to a consistent description). Reisner applied this model to the Robart graphics system interface, describing its interface in the Action Language and then applying metrics to predict user performance to make comparisons of alternative designs and to identify design choices that could cause users to make mistakes. Like the CLG, the Action Language models computer and user as two cooperating and communicating information processors.

The Task Action Grammar (TAG) [PG86] is another formal user model - specifically, a cognitive competence model - with a command language orientation. A metalanguage of production rules encodes generative grammars that convert simple tasks into action specifications. As in Reisner's work, a goal of TAG is to capture the notion of consistency. Marking of tokens in production rules with semantic features of the task allows representation of family resemblances, a way of capturing generalities of which the user may be aware [WBGM88], (p. 58). Complexity measures taken on the production rules are predictors of learnability.

More recent work in cognitive modeling for analytic evaluation has largely been in the area of extensions to the original GOMS-related approaches (e.g., [Joh90]), combining GOMS-like models with other cognitive models for problem-solving. Some examples include Soar, a theory of cognition that provides an integrated architecture for exploring different user behaviors [PJ92]; and other areas such as documentation [GE90] and graphic machine-paced tasks [JV92].

## 1.3.2 Usability Inspection Methods

Researchers have recently begun exploring new approaches to user interface design evaluation, seeking ways to increase the efficiency of the process. A goal of their work is to find techniques for identifying at least major usability design errors without the cost and time consumption of empirical testing, specifically to find methods for usability evaluation that are more accessible to system developers and that will, accordingly, be used more often in real world development projects. These techniques are based on *inspection* of interfaces, with core tasks being inspected by expert evaluators typically using design representations or early interface prototypes. We include them in this section on analytic evaluation, because the essence of their approach is analysis.

One type of usability inspection method includes interface design *walkthroughs*, an evaluation concept adapted from software engineering and other design-oriented disciplines. A well-known type of these walkthrough techniques is the cognitive walkthrough [LPWR90], a theory-based evaluation technique focusing on an evaluator's expectations of a user's cognitive activities. The design is inspected, through a structured list of questions, for a match to users' goals and knowledge. Forms are used to guide the evaluator through the steps of the process. Success of the technique has been variable, depending on the cognitive science knowledge and skills of evaluation team members [WBJF92].

Nielsen's work on heuristic evaluation [NM90] is another example of an inspection method. Here the focus is on design guidelines rather than cognitive activities. Usability of an interface design is judged informally, based on intuition and opinions of evaluators, against heuristics that are a small set of general usability guidelines. While individual evaluators using this approach did not tend to find large percentages of existing usability flaws, aggregating over a set of several independent evaluators effectively solved this problem. This approach was validated by separate empirical studies [Nie92] in which he found that non-usability-specialists were not particularly effective at uncovering usability design problems, usability experts were better, and experts in both usability and the application domain performed best. Heuristic evaluation, along with scenarios (partial prototypes [Nie87]) and small thinking aloud studies [Nie88], constitute what Nielsen calls "usability engineering at a discount" [Nie89]. The advantages he states for this general approach are low cost, intuitiveness, ease of motivating developers to do it, and effectiveness early in the development process.

Walkthrough methods generally fare well in comparisons with conventional empirical usability evaluation [JD92, KCF92, LPWR90]. However, there are some contradictions among results, and we are warned [JD92] that such results are not to be taken as indications that inspection methods can replace empirical evaluation; there are many additional qualitative benefits from usability testing with users. In fact, Lewis et al. [LPWR90] explicitly state they do not wish "to claim that the cognitive walkthrough methodology will eliminate the need for evaluating prototypes of the interface." Their finding, based on empirical studies, is that cognitive walkthroughs are inexpensive (about one hour per task that is inspected), yet detect nearly half the usability problems found by empirical evaluation with users of a design. In contrast, Karat et al. [KCF92] found that empirical testing required the same or less time to identify each usability problem when compared to walkthrough methods.

Another example of a usability inspection method is claims analysis, a method developed by Carroll, Rosson, and Kellogg within their task-artifact framework [Car90, CKR91]. The task-artifact framework is based on a view of the world that contains user tasks, which are the context for artifacts (interface objects that interface developers build). In order to bring theory to bear on the interaction design activity, they propose the task-artifact cycle to formalize and speed up the connection between theoretical analysis and design. Their underlying hypothesis is that interface artifacts represent theories of the designer, containing claims about potential users and how they use the interface. The task-artifact cycle is a kind of instance of the classical epistemological cycle of theory formulation and observational validation. The design rationale is inferred from the design and stated in terms of cause-and-effect relationships between artifacts and psychological consequences of their use [CSR92], (p. 4).

### 1.3.3   A Brief Critique of Analytic Evaluation

Since the focus of this paper is not analytic evaluation, we will not give a detailed critique of the analytic approach to user interface evaluation. However, we will list some of the more common comments encountered in the relevant literature. For further reading, we suggest, for example, Carroll and Rosson [CR85]. General criticism of analytic evaluation methods, which we have gleaned from a variety of sources and our own observations, revolves around the following issues:

- Because these methods support analysis but not synthesis, they are not directly supportive of interaction design. To improve an existing interaction design, a developer must try some (random, unless supported in some other way) new design idea, build a large representation model, conduct the analysis, and see if the predicted performance is better.
- Empirical evaluation gives much more useful data - including qualitative data that can help identify specific problems in an interaction design - in terms of directly affecting usability.
- Almost all analytic approaches assume error-free, expert task performance. But error-free performance is obviously is not the typical experience of a user of an interactive system. And it is, indeed, study of error-related situations that often reveals the greatest indicators of usability problems.
- While most of the analytic approaches mentioned above produce a representation that includes a task structure, none deal with the temporal relations necessary to provide a complete user-task-oriented representation of a design.
- Most analytic approaches require that the design be complete and a full global model built for the entire interface before analysis, at any level, can proceed. An approach supporting local analysis - analysis of one area of design problems independent of the overall design - would be more cost effective.
- Many of these approaches are based on an open-loop model of command sequences wherein the user enters a command, then the system executes it. The model we seek is a model of highly interactive direct manipulation, involving incremental user actions concurrent with perception and reaction in a closed-loop feedback cycle.

While analytic evaluation of user interfaces has been, and continues to be, an open area of human-computer interaction research, we find that the sorts of issues just presented limit the efficacy of many of these analytic evaluation techniques. Because of these limitations, we do not foresee analytic formative evaluation replacing empirical formative evaluation.

However, in all fairness, GOMS-based analytic evaluation has been shown to be effective for real world problems within specific classes of tasks (e.g., constrained and repetitive tasks such as those of a telephone assistance operator). In such an application, CPM-GOMS, which is GOMS analysis combined with the critical path method of project management, was shown to be remarkably accurate in predicting performance, allowing analysts to sort out the complexity of parallel operator activities (e.g., [GJA92, GJS+90]). In this method, cognitive, perceptual, verbal, and motor actions for a task, plus response time of the system, are represented on a critical path timing chart. This supports determination of the effect on user performance of a given change in task procedures or in keyboard layout. This method supports prediction of the effect of, for example, adding voice recognition to the system, or changing system response time. The effect may be greater or smaller, depending on whether the part of the task affected by the change is on a critical path. This provides an explicit connection between design and user performance. The usefulness of GOMS, at least in this application domain, was indeed validated by a series of studies [GJA92]. Olson and Olson [OO90] give a good review of the current status of GOMS-related analytic modeling.

## 1.4   Empirical Formative Evaluation

Now we focus our discussion to the class of formative evaluation techniques based directly on empirical, observational data from user testing without a strong component of modeling or analysis (except for analysis of collected observational data, of course). Much of what we will say about empirically based formative evaluation is now part of what is generally called *usability engineering*, coming from the work of, for example, [GSWG86, Nie89, WBH88].

### 1.4.1   Types of Empirical Formative Evaluation Data

There are several types of data that are produced during empirical formative evaluation, to be used in making decisions about iterative redesign of the user interface. These types of data include:

- *Objective* - These are directly observed measures, typically of user performance while using the interface to perform benchmark tasks.
- *Subjective* - These represent opinions, usually of the user, concerning usability of the interface.
- *Quantitative* - These are numeric data and results, such as user performance metrics or opinion ratings. This kind of data is key in helping monitor convergence toward usability goals during all cycles of iterative development.
- *Qualitative* - These are non-numeric data and results, such as lists of problems the user had while using the interface. This kind of data is useful in identifying which design features are associated with measured usability problems during all cycles of iterative development.

Even though objective evaluation is often associated with quantitative data and subjective evaluation with qualitative data, subjective evaluation (e.g., using user preference scales or questionnaires) can also produce quantitative data. Also, objective evaluation activities (e.g., benchmark task measurements) can produce qualitative data (e.g., critical incidents and verbal protocol, discussed in Section 4.4.2 on Qualitative Data Generation Techniques, below).

## 1.4.2 Steps in Empirical Formative Evaluation

There are several major steps in empirical formative evaluation, including:

- Developing and conducting the experiment
- Generating and collecting the data
- Analyzing the data
- Drawing conclusions
- Redesigning and implementing the revised interface

We do not intend, in this paper, to give details on each step; we will present an overview to give the reader an appreciation for developing an experiment that allows collection of data that can be analyzed to determine usability of the user interface - the formative evaluation process. In-depth coverage of each of these steps, including hands-on exercises and solutions, can be found in [HH93].

While many members of an interface development team may be involved in performing any or all of these steps at various times, we will refer to the person who is primarily responsible for these activities as the user interaction design evaluator, or simply the *evaluator*.

## 1.4.3 Developing and Conducting the Experiment

Developing and conducting an experiment to be used for formative evaluation involves three main activities, not necessarily strictly in the order given:

- Selecting participants to perform tasks
- Developing usability goals and experimental tasks
- Directing an experimental session

### 1.4.3.1 Selecting Participants

Participant selection involves determining appropriate users for experimental sessions. ("Participant" is the term that most recent human factors literature now uses to indicate a human subject taking part in an experiment.) The evaluator must determine the classes of *representative users* that will be used as participants to evaluate the interface. This kind of user should be somewhat knowledgeable of the interactive system application domain (e.g., word processor, spreadsheet, graphics drawing application, process control system, airline reservation system, or whatever), but not necessarily knowledgeable of a specific interactive system within that domain. These participants should represent typical expected users of the interface being evaluated, including their general background, skill level, computer knowledge, application knowledge, and so on.

In addition to representative users, the *human-computer interaction expert* plays an important part in formative evaluation. Evaluators sometimes overlook the need for critical review of the interface by a human-computer interaction expert when developing a formative evaluation plan. Such an expert is broadly knowledgeable in the area of interface development, has extensively used a wide variety of interfaces, knows a great deal about interaction design and critiquing, and is very familiar with interaction design guidelines. An expert will find subtle problems that a representative user would be less likely to find (e.g., small inconsistencies, poor use of color, confusing navigation, and so on). More importantly, a human-computer interaction expert will offer alternative suggestions for fixing problems, unlike the representative user who typically tends to find a problem but may not be able to offer suggestions for solving it. An expert can draw on knowledge of guidelines, design and critiquing experience, and familiarity with a broad spectrum of interfaces to offer one or more feasible, guideline-based suggestions for modifications to improve usability.

The number of participants needed for each cycle of formative evaluation is surprisingly small. Each cycle needs a few carefully chosen representative users, and one or maybe two human-computer interaction experts. In fact, the purpose of formative evaluation is not to focus on a large number of experiments with a large number of participants for each one. Rather it is to *focus on extracting as much information as possible from every participant* who uses any part of the interface [CR85, WBH88]. Some empirical work [NM90] has shown that the optimum number of participants for a cycle of formative evaluation is three to five per user class. Only one participant per user class is typically not enough. But more than ten participants per class is not worth the diminishing returns obtained; after about five or six participants, they tend to cease finding new problems, and mostly reiterate the ones already uncovered by prior participants. Often three participants per well-defined user class is the most cost effective number. Empirical work by [Vir92] corroborates these suggestions, and, in fact, found that 80 percent of usability problems are discovered with four or five participants, and that additional participants are less and less likely to uncover new and/or severe problems.

### 1.4.3.2   Developing Usability Goals and Experimental Tasks

We have said that a key to determining usability in an interaction design is quantifiable usability goals. These are operationally defined criteria for assessing usability. Typically called *usability specifications*, they are established by the development team, and are the comparison point for actual observed user performance.

Usability specification tables are a convenient way to record established usability metrics. The concept of formal attribute specification in tabular form, with various metrics operationally defining success, was developed by Gilb [Gil]. The focus of Gilb's work was use of measurements in managing software development resources. Bennett [Nor84] adapted this approach to usability specifications as a technique for setting planned levels and managing development to meet those levels. These ideas were refined and integrated into the usability engineering concept in [GSWG86] and [WBH88]. *Usability engineering*, as defined in [GSWG86], is a process through which usability characteristics are specified, quantitatively and early in the development process, and measured throughout the process. Carroll and Rosson [CR85] also stressed the need for quantifiable usability specifications, associated with appropriate benchmark tasks, in iterative development of user interfaces. Without measurable specifications, it is impossible to determine either the usability goals of a product or whether the final product meets those goals.

We have, through years of working with real world developers and from our own evaluations, adapted the format in [WBH88], revising it into the form shown in Table 1.1. The example used in this usability specification table is a graphical drawing application on which we performed a complete formative evaluation for a client.

Let us briefly explain the usability specifications shown in Table 1.1. An important usability

| Usability Attribute | Measuring Instrument | Value to be Measured | Worst Acceptable Level | Planned Target Level | Best Possible Level | Current Level |
|---|---|---|---|---|---|---|
| Initial use | "Create a line drawing" benchmark task | Length of time to create line drawing on first trial | 30 secs. | 15 secs. | 5 secs. | 10 secs. |
| First impression | Questionnaire | Average rating (range -2 to 2) | 0 | 0.5 | 1.25 | 1.0 |

*where:*

**usability attribute** *is the usability characteristic to be measured; some common attributes include initial use, learnability, retainability, first impression, long-term user satisfaction, and so on*

**measuring instrument** *is a description of the method for providing a value; for example a benchmark task is an objective instrument and a questionnaire is a subjective instrument*

**value to be measured** *is the metric for which data values are collected (using the measuring instrument) during an evaluation session with a user; for example, length of time or number of errors in performing a benchmark task, or a rating on a questionnaire*

**worst acceptable level** *is the lowest acceptable level of performance for the attribute; the border of failure for usability*

**planned target level** *is the target indicating attainment of unquestioned usability success for the current version; the "what we would like" level*

**best possible level** *is a realistic state-of-the-art upper limit; the inspiration level*

**current level** *is the currently known level of the value to be measured for the attribute (when available)*

**Table 1.1** Examples of usability specifications for a graphical drawing application

attribute for virtually any interface is how quickly users can perform tasks the first (initial) time they use it. Thus, in the first attribute, user performance during initial use of the interface for the specific benchmark task to "create a line drawing" will be measured. This is a common task that users of such a system would probably want to perform frequently, quickly, and easily.

For each benchmark task cited in a usability specification table, a specifically worded benchmark task must be written telling the user what to do (but not how) during an evaluation session. For example, for the "create a line drawing" benchmark, the task description might be: Produce a line drawing similar to the approximate size and shape of this sketch:

As shown in Table 1.1, for this simple example, we state that initial use time to perform the task to "create a line drawing" must be, at the longest (worst level), 30 seconds. The expected (planned) length of time to perform this task the first time is 15 seconds, while the very best time to perform it is estimated at 5 seconds. A similar example, for the usability goal desired for "first impression" of the graphics application, is also shown.[1] The first usability attribute is associated with collection of objective data, specifically by measuring performance of the user on a particular benchmark task. The second usability attribute is associated with collection of

---

[1] There are heuristics for determining usability attributes and values of the various levels [WBH88]; however, we will not present a tutorial on establishing usability specifications in this paper

**Figure 1.3**   Line drawing for benchmark task

subjective data, measuring the user's opinion of the interface based on a questionnaire. Both measures are quantitative.

In addition to benchmark tasks developed for the usability attributes, the evaluator may also identify other *representative tasks* for participants to perform. These tasks will not be tested quantitatively (that is, against usability specifications) but are deemed, for whatever reason, to be important in adding breadth to evaluation of the user interaction design. These additional tasks, especially in early cycles of evaluation, should be ones that users are expected to perform often, and therefore should be easy for the user to accomplish. In early cycles of evaluation, these representative tasks, together with the benchmark tasks, might constitute a core set of tasks for the system being evaluated, without which a user cannot perform useful work. All task descriptions should, in general, be written down rather specifically and should state what the user should do, rather than how the user should do it.

In addition to strictly specified benchmark and representative tasks, the evaluator will usually find it useful to observe the user in informal *free use* of the interface, without the constraints of predefined tasks. Benchmark tasks, other representative tasks, and free use are all key sources of critical incidents (see Section 1.4.4 on Generating and Collecting the Data, below), a major form of the qualitative data to be collected. Free use by the participant is usually performed after some or all predefined tasks have been completed, especially those related to the initial use attribute. To engage a participant in free use, the evaluator might simply say to the participant, "Play around with the interface for awhile, doing anything you would like to, and talk aloud while you are working." We will discuss verbal protocol taking during an evaluation session in Section 1.4.4 on Generating and Collecting the Data, below. Free use is valuable for revealing user and system behavior in situations not anticipated by designers - often situations that can "break" a poor design.

### 1.4.3.3   Directing an Experimental Session

In order to properly direct an experimental session, the evaluator must produce training materials and determine experimental procedures - exactly what will happen during a test session with a participant. The evaluator must decide on whether laboratory testing or field testing, or both, will be performed. *Laboratory testing* involves bringing the user to the interface; that is, users are brought into a usability lab setting where they perform the benchmark tasks, performance measures are taken as appropriate, free use is encouraged, and so on. *Field testing* involves bringing the interface to the user; that is, the current version is set up *in situ*, in the normal working environment in which the user is expected to use the interface, and more qualitative, longer-term data are often collected.

Obviously lab and field testing each have pros and cons. In a laboratory setting, the evaluator can have greater control over the experiment, but the conditions are mostly artificial. On the other hand, in a field test, the evaluator has less control, yet the situation is more realistic. Laboratory testing is typically more appropriate for earlier cycles of formative evaluation, when major problems with an interaction design are typically discovered. Field testing works well for later cycles, when data on longer-term performance with the interface may be desirable. A combination of the two is the ideal circumstance for formative evaluation, but, in real life, true field testing may be limited or even impossible. In this case, laboratory testing may have to suffice.

In conjunction with developing experimental procedures, the evaluator should prepare *introductory instructional remarks* that will be given uniformly to each participant. These remarks should briefly explain the purpose of the experiment, tell a little bit about the interface the participant will be using, state what the user will be expected to do, and the procedure to be followed by the user. It is also important to make very clear to the participants that *the purpose of the session is to evaluate the system, not to evaluate them.*

Finally, an *informed consent form* must be prepared for each participant to sign. This form states that the participant is volunteering to participate in the experiment, that the data may be used if the participant's name or identity is in no way associated with the data, that the participant understands the experiment is in no way harmful, that the participant may discontinue the experiment at any time, and so on. This is standard protocol for performing experiments using human participants, and is to protect both the evaluator and the participant. The informed consent form is legally and ethically required; it is not optional.

When benchmark tasks have been developed, the setting and procedures have been determined, and the types of participants chosen, the evaluator must perform some *pilot testing* to ensure that all parts of the experiment are ready. The evaluator must make sure that all necessary equipment is available, installed, and working properly, whether it be in the laboratory or in the field. The experimental tasks should be completely run through at least once, using the intended hardware and software platform (e.g., the interface prototype) by someone other than the person(s) who developed the tasks, to make sure, for example, that the platform supports all the necessary user actions and that the task instructions are unambiguously worded.

During an evaluation session, the evaluator gives the participant appropriate instructions, has them sign the informed consent form, and administers the tasks. When the participant has performed the desired tasks, including completion of any questionnaire or survey, it is common practice for the evaluator to give the participant some sort of "reward" (e.g., money, mug, t-shirt, cookies). While it is often necessary to offer compensation in order to recruit participants, some practitioners believe monetary rewards can bias results. For example, it is possible that paid participants with greater financial need could be more motivated than participants without a financial need to perform for pay in a study. A possible misconception by a participant could be that good performance will lead to approval and therefore more "employment."

## 1.4.4  Generating and Collecting the Data

We have already mentioned qualitative and quantitative data. There are methods for generating and collecting both kinds, discussed in the following sections.

### 1.4.4.1   Quantitative Data Generation Techniques

Quantitative techniques are used to directly measure observed usability levels in order to compare against usability specifications. There are two kinds of quantitative data generation techniques most often used in formative evaluation, namely:

- Benchmark tasks, and
- Questionnaires.

We have already discussed development of *benchmark tasks* (in Section 1.4.3.2, above). During the experiment each participant performs the prescribed benchmark tasks, and the evaluator takes numeric data, depending on what is being measured. For example, the evaluator may measure the time it takes the participant to perform a task, or count the number of errors a participant makes while performing a task, or count the number of tasks a participant can perform within a given time period.

The second quantitative data generation technique is *questionnaires*, or user preference scales, for different features that are relevant to usability of the interface being evaluated. This kind of questionnaire or survey is inexpensive to administer, but is not easy to produce so that it is valid and reliable. It is the most effective technique for producing quantitative data on subjective user opinion of an interface. The Questionnaire for User Interface Satisfaction, or QUIS, survey [CDN88] is the best of these validated questionnaires.

### 1.4.4.2   Qualitative Data Generation Techniques

Qualitative data are extremely important in formative evaluation of a user interaction design. The kinds of techniques that are most effective for generating qualitative data include the following:

- Verbal protocol taking,
- Critical incident taking, and
- Structured interviews.

Perhaps the most common technique for qualitative data generation is *verbal protocol taking*, also called "thinking aloud." Here, the evaluator asks a participant to talk out loud while working, indicating what they are trying to do, or why they are having a problem, what they expected to happen that didn't, what they wished had happened, and so on. This technique obviously is invasive to the participant, so it should be used sparingly with benchmark tasks where timing is important. But it is immensely effective in determining what problems a participant is having and what might be done to fix those problems. The verbal protocol technique is best employed during free use of the system or during other non-timed predefined task performance by a participant. The evaluator will find that some participants are not good at thinking aloud while they work; they will not talk much and the evaluator will constantly have to prod them to find out what they are thinking or trying to do. It is perfectly acceptable for the evaluator to query and prompt such reticent talkers, in order to produce the desired information. Remember, one of our goals in formative evaluation is not to have a large number of participants, but rather to extract as much data as possible from each and every participant. Evaluators become more skilled at this as they work with more participants. The key to effective prompting is to give the participant helpful hints (e.g., "Do you remember how you did this before?", "What do you think the so-and-so menu is for?", "What did you expect to happen then?", and so on), but to refrain from telling them exactly what to do.

Another kind of qualitative data generation that works well, often in conjunction with verbal protocol taking, is *critical incident taking*. A critical incident is something that happens while the participant is working that has a significant effect, either positive or negative, on task performance or user satisfaction, and thus on usability of the interface. A bad, or negative, critical incident is typically a problem the participant encounters - something that causes an error, something that blocks (even temporarily) progress in task performance, or something that results in a pejorative remark by the participant. For example, an evaluator might observe a participant try unsuccessfully five times to enlarge a graphical image on the screen using a graphical editor. If it is taking the participant so many tries to perform the task, it is an indication that this particular part of the design should be improved. Similarly, the user may begin to show signs of frustration, either with remarks or actions.

An occurrence that causes the user to express satisfaction or closure in some way (e.g., "That was neat!", "Oh, now I see", "Cool!", and so on) is a good, or positive, critical incident. When a first-time user immediately understands the metaphor of how to manipulate a graphical object, that can also be a positive critical incident. While negative critical incidents indicate problems in the interaction design, positive critical incidents indicate metaphors and details that, because they work well or participants like them, should be considered for use in other appropriate places throughout an interface. Critical incidents can be observed during performance of benchmark tasks, other representative tasks, or when a participant is freely using the system.

*Structured interviews* provide another form of qualitative data. These are typically in the form of a post-experiment interview, a series of preplanned questions that the evaluator asks each participant. Such a post-session interview might include, for example, such general questions as "What did you like best about the interface?", "What did you like least?", "How would you change so-and-so?", and so on.

### 1.4.4.3  Data Collection Techniques

There are several recommended techniques for capturing both qualitative and quantitative data from participants during a formative evaluation experimental session, including:

- Real-time notetaking,
- Videotaping,
- Audiotaping, and
- Internal instrumentation of the interface.

We have found, through our own experience and numerous conversations with other evaluators, that *notetaking in real time* is still the most effective technique to use for data capture during a usability evaluation session. The evaluator should be prepared to take copious notes, either with pencil and paper or using a word processor, as activities proceed during the session. Because a multitude of simultaneous activities can happen fast in a session, when an evaluator is directing a test session for the first few times, it is a good idea to have a second evaluator observe the session in order to help take notes.

To collect quantitative data, the required equipment is minimal: a stop watch for timing participants performing tasks, and some kind of tally sheet for noting and/or counting errors. To collect qualitative data, the evaluator(s) should write down all observed critical incidents, as well as any other observations, as a participant performs each task or uses the interface freely.

*Videotaping* is a well-known and frequently-used data collection technique. Videotaping has many advantages, including detailed capture of what occurs during an experiment. A camera aimed at the participant's hands and the screen is the most important, and a second, if available, should be aimed for a broader view, including the participant's face.

However, the problem with analysis of videotape is two-fold. First, it can take as much as eight hours to analyze each one hour of videotape [MD89]. The chances of laboriously going back through several hours of videotape from half a dozen evaluation sessions is therefore very slim. Second, with multiple views and/or tapes of the same test session, there is a problem of synchronization of the tapes. The main use of videotape should be as a *backup* for what happened during a test session, not as the main source of data to be captured and analyzed. For example, in case of confusion, uncertainty about a specific detail, or some missed part of a critical incident that occurred during an evaluation session, the evaluator can go to a specific point on the videotape and review a very short sequence to collect the missing data.

We have also found that a few carefully selected videoclips (say, of five minutes each or less) can be of great influence on a design team that is resistant to making changes to what they believe to be their already perfect design. We have seen programmers who had the major responsibility for an interaction design watch videoclips in awe while a bewildered participant struggled to perform a task with an awkward interface. These same clips are also useful in convincing management that there is a usability problem in the first place.

Finally, *internally instrumenting the interface* being evaluated is a useful way to capture the kinds of data we have been discussing. For example, data on user errors or frequency of command usage, or automatically computing elapsed task times from start/stop times, can be automatically gathered by a fairly simple program. There is, however, a potential problem with this technique. Evaluators may think "the more data the better" but find themselves inundated with details of keystrokes and mouse clicks. A fairly short session can produce a several megabyte user session transcript file. Manual analysis of a file dump is totally untenable. But the difficult question is: what analysis should be done once such data are extracted from a transcript file? How can, for example, any of these keystrokes or cursor movements be associated with anything significant - either good or bad - happening to the user, and therefore related to usability? The only feasible way in which such data might be useful is if their analysis can be automated, and we know of very few viable techniques for analyzing (either manually or automatedly) user session transcripts. We will briefly discuss tools, including those for analysis of user session transcripts, in Section 6 on Future Trends, below.

## 1.4.5  Analyzing the Data

After all evaluation sessions for a particular cycle of formative evaluation are completed, the data collected during those sessions must be analyzed. We will not, in general, be performing inferential statistical analyses, such as analyses of variance (ANOVAs) or t-tests or F-tests. Rather, we will be using some data analysis techniques to help us determine if we have met our usability specification levels, and if we have not, how to modify the design to help us converge toward those goals in subsequent cycles of formative evaluation.

The first step in analyzing the data is to compute averages and any other values stated in the usability specifications (timing, error counts, questionnaire ratings, and so on). The evaluator can then enter a summary of the results into an Observed Results column added on to the usability specification table. By directly comparing observed results with the specified usability goals, the evaluator can tell immediately which usability specifications have been met and which have not been met during this cycle of formative evaluation. If all worst acceptable levels have been met and enough planned target levels have been met to satisfy the development team that usability of the current version of the design is acceptable, then the design is satisfactory and iteration for this version can stop. The one exception is if, for whatever reason, there is suspicion that the usability specifications may be too lenient, and are not therefore a good indicator of high usability. Then, obviously, the development team should reassess the usability specifications to see if they should be more (or less) stringent.

If usability specifications have not been met (the most likely situation after the first cycle of testing), then more in-depth data analysis should be performed. Our goal in further data analysis - much of which will be qualitative data analysis - is structured identification of the observed problems and potential solutions to them. We will then address solving those problems in order of their potential impact on usability of the interface. The process of determining how to convert the collected data into scheduled design and implementation solutions is essentially one of negotiation in which, at various times, all members of the development team are involved.

Table 1.2 shows a form that we have found to be useful in enumerating and organizing the multitude of problems that will inevitably be uncovered during a cycle of formative evaluation. We will use some data from our own formative evaluation of the graphical drawing application mentioned earlier, as an example to explain each column in this table.

| Problem | Effect on User Performance | Importance | Solutions(s) | Cost | Resolution |
|---------|---------------------------|-----------|--------------|------|-----------|
| Too much window manipulation | 10 to 35 minutes | high placement automatically but allow user to reposition it | fix window | 6 hrs. | |
| Black arrow on black background | ? | low | reverse arrow to white on black | 1 hr. | |

*where:*

**problem** *is an interface problem observed as users interact with the system during evaluation; usually identified from (negative) critical incidents*

**effect on performance** *is data about the amount of time spent by the user dealing with a specific problem*

**importance** *is a subjective indication, produced by the development team, of a problem's overall effect on user performance and interface usability; generally rated as high, medium, or low*

**solutions(s)** *is one or more proposed design changes to solve a problem*

**cost** *is the resources - usually time and/or money - needed for each proposed solution*

**resolution** *is the final decision made to address each problem*

**Table 1.2**  Example of cost/importance table for organizing and analyzing observed problems

Let us briefly explain the first interface problem shown in Table 1.2 for the graphical drawing application. In this application, whenever a new window appeared, it remained connected to the cursor, and therefore wandered around on the screen following mouse movement, until the user clicked a mouse button to purposefully place the window. The evaluator, during evaluation of several tasks, observed that users intensely disliked this design feature, because it distracted them from whatever task they were trying to do when a "wandering window" appeared, stuck to the cursor.

After all evaluation sessions, the evaluator makes a complete list of observed *problems* - potentially hundreds of them - and, as with usability specifications, a team decides on appropriate values for the other columns for each problem listed. In the graphical drawing application interface, after about four hours of the first cycle of evaluation sessions, we had a list of 54 problems to tackle, ranging from serious to trivial. Two of those problems are shown in Table 1.2. As we have already mentioned, the earliest cycles of formative evaluation typically give the most data and therefore result in the longest lists of problems. Later cycles generally produce fewer changes, especially if the process is leading to convergence toward a more usable design.

The *importance* rating results from a dialectic decision-making process among the entire development team (possibly including some users), and can take into account many factors, including impact on overall system integrity and consistency, intuition, and judgement about pragmatic development concerns. First candidates for high importance ratings are those that, as revealed by impact analysis (see below), have the greatest effect on meeting the established usability specifications. The wandering windows was definitely of high importance, because of the constantly mounting irritation it caused users and the amount of time it distracted them from their tasks.

The development team must also propose one or more possible *solutions*, that is, changes to the design to solve each of the observed problems on the list. Ideas for these proposed design solutions can come from a variety of places, including design principles and guidelines, suggestions by participants, known available technology, and study of other similar designs. More than one possible solution is often appropriate, and different solutions may have very different costs associated with them. That is, implementing one solution to a problem may be estimated to take two hours, while a different solution to the same problem may be estimated to take two days of coding time. When, in a later step of data analysis, decisions are made about which problems are most critical to fix, it may be useful to have alternative solutions with different costs, so that at least some sort of solution can be offered for a problem that might otherwise have to be ignored because the cost of the first choice solution is too high. For our wandering windows problem, the solution was to fix window placement automatically at the center of the screen when a window first appears, but allow the user to move and reposition it anywhere on the screen at any time. We then retested this redesign in future formative evaluation cycles.

For each proposed solution, a *cost* of implementing it must be estimated. This cost is usually the amount of resources, typically time (sometimes money) needed for making the indicated change. Typically it is measured in terms of the number of hours needed to modify a prototype, or to modify existing source code or to write new code. To fix the placement of a window, the programmer on the development team estimated that six hours of recoding would be necessary. Lower costs here are typically obtained when changes are made to a prototype, rather than to a version of the interface that has been coded. This reinforces the need to select good prototyping tools and to get a prototype running and testable as early in the development process as possible.

Finally, after cost/importance analysis and/or impact analysis (see below) of all problems in the list, a *resolution* - a final decision - is made for each problem in the list. This is an indication of how each problem will be addressed (e.g., "do it"; "do it, time permitting"; "postpone indefinitely") and which solutions will be implemented. After our general analysis of the graphical drawing application, we decided that the wandering windows had to be modified, along with more than a dozen other serious problems.

When choosing which problems have the highest priority for changes, high importance problems are addressed first, while lower importance problems receive later attention, resources permitting. Ideal, of course, are high importance/low cost problems (e.g., confusing error messages). This approach gives much more controllability and accountability over redesign and iteration than an ad hoc approach in which evaluators and others involved in development of the user interface simply make some guesses about which identified problems to address and in which order.

An example of another problem we encountered in an evaluation session of the graphical drawing application, the second problem listed in Table 1.2, was simply an oversight on the part of the designer. The cursor icon was a black arrow in one particular mode of the application. However, when the black arrow was moved over a black background, it stayed black and therefore disappeared. Although this was annoying, users spent very little time in this problem and it did not measurably interfere with users' performance. Its importance was therefore low. Our proposed solution was obvious: to reverse the arrow to white when on a black background, and the programmer estimated this would take about one hour. Our resolution, after our full analysis, was to do it. The basis for the decision was really more related to fixing a simple, but silly, oversight on the part of a designer, rather than modifying a problem that had a big impact on usability.

Once all columns except the Resolution column have been completed for all observed problems, we can perform a couple of different kinds of analyses that help determine a resolution for each problem, focusing on which changes will have the greatest impact on usability. These analyses include:

- Cost/importance analysis, and
- Impact analysis.

In a *cost/importance analysis*, we consider the relative costs and importances of the problems as listed in a table like the one in Table 1.2. We must first determine the resources (in particular, time and people) we have available to allocate for making modifications. In our evaluation of the graphical drawing application, we had 60 hours (across two programmers) allocated for modifications in our first cycle of formative evaluation. We totalled the Cost column to find we had more than 140 hours of suggested changes, even after selecting the lowest-cost suggestions to change for those problems for which we had multiple suggestions. We had some difficult decisions to make about which problems were going to get addressed, and which were going to remain unchanged, at least for the next cycle of evaluation.

As already mentioned, another kind of analysis, called *impact analysis* (e.g., [GSWG86]), can be used to determine what problems most affect achievement of the usability specifications we have previously defined. This analysis is based on the time a user spends in various problems, recorded in the Effect on User Performance column; this time is often the biggest contributor to not achieving the desired usability specifications. Comparing usability specification levels, observed values, and values from the Effect on User Performance column directly indicates which problems have the largest effect on meeting the usability specifications. Because the effect on user performance time is deducted from user performance times when the associated problem is solved, this will have the most impact on meeting the usability specifications. Because of this direct effect, a high importance rating is generally assigned to problems with the greatest impact on performance. In the wandering windows example, a quick scan of the videotaped sessions showed that one user spent 35 minutes attempting to perform several benchmark tasks, of which about 10 of those 35 minutes were wasted with window placement (see second column of Table 1.2). This kind of data provides a good predictor of the effect of an interface problem on achieving a usability specification. For this situation, absence of the problem would have reduced user performance time to 25 minutes across tasks.

To compare the various kinds of data collection and analysis techniques we have discussed, we can classify them into the simple taxonomy shown in Figure 1.4.

|  | *Quantitative (numeric)* | *Qualitative (non-numeric)* |
|---|---|---|
| *Objective (measures performance)* | •Impact analysis<br>•User performance metric (benchmarking) |  |
| *Subjective (involves opinion)* | •Cost/importance analysis<br>•User satisfaction metric (user preference) | •Critical incident analysis<br>•Protocol taking/analysis<br>•Structured interviews |

**Figure 1.4**   A simple taxonomy of data collection and analysis techniques

A summary of the ways in which the various kinds of data - quantitative and qualitative - are primarily used in formative evaluation is shown in Table 1.3. However, there is considerable overlap among these categories. For example, participants themselves can often suggest solutions for usability problems encountered during evaluation. Also, quantitative data from satisfaction questionnaires may reveal not only that something is wrong, but give a strong indication of what is wrong.

**Table 1.3**   Comparison of uses for quantitative data vs. qualitative data in formative evaluation

| USE THESE: | TO DECIDE THESE: |
|---|---|
| **Quantitative data** | **Something is wrong** |
| **Qualitative data** | **What is wrong** |
| **Designers** | **How to fix what is wrong** |

We can finally now complete the Resolution column of Table 1.2. If the list is ordered by importance (descending, high to low) and, within that, cost (ascending, low to high), with high importance/low cost at the top of the list followed by high importance and moderate/high cost and so on, we can determine how many problems can be addressed given the time and other resources allotted for modifications. Problems at the top of the list get first priority, unless, for example, some of the high importance/high cost problems are so critical that they must be fixed despite their high cost.

For our graphical drawing application, there were 24 different problems with high importance and low/moderate/high cost. Some of the high importance/high cost problems had to be included to make parts of the interface robust or to modify a particularly troublesome aspect of the design. We got to a few moderate importance problems, and even a couple of low importance ones (e.g., the black cursor on black background). In all, we made changes associated with 39 of the problems on our list of 54, until the 60 hours of implementer time available for changes were allocated.

### 1.4.6 Redesigning and Implementing the Revised Interface

Much of the work for this final phase of formative evaluation was done when design solutions were proposed for each observed problem. At this point, we need only to update the appropriate design documentation to reflect our decisions, and resolve any conflicts or inconsistencies in the interaction design that might have resulted from our decisions. This is the time, of course, when we realize the full benefits of empirical formative evaluation, moving out of the current cycle of evaluation and into the subsequent cycle of (re)design and (re)evaluation.

## 1.5 Conclusions

What we have been talking about here, of course, is the very heart of the user interface development process. This involves the management of very difficult decision-making as to which problems are most important in terms of interface usability. But the point is that we are, in fact, engineering the interface, striving for achievement of our usability goals, rather than perfection. This approach recognizes diminishing economic returns in attempting to achieve perfection by trying to solve all known usability problems in a user interaction design. Therefore, usability management includes quantitative techniques for making decisions about which changes to make to a design as a result of a cycle of formative evaluation.

Compared to the top-down waterfall process often used in software engineering, where management can sign off on each phase, the iterative process of interface development and formative evaluation we have described is potentially a cycle that never ends. A development process that does not have a well-defined ending point is unacceptable to most managers. A control mechanism is required, one that will help managers (and developers) know what design changes are most cost effective in meeting usability goals, whether the iterative process is converging toward a usable interface, and when to stop iterating. Without such a control mechanism, interaction developers and evaluators can be caught in an infinite loop, thrashing about without any guidance and actually producing a worse interface (in terms of its usability) through this cyclic procedure. The control mechanism is the combination of a set of techniques including usability specifications, empirical formative evaluation, and cost/importance and impact analyses. Usability specifications set quantitative target expectations for user performance and satisfaction, and formative evaluation with representative users provides data to compare actual usability of the interaction design with these specifications. Cost/importance analysis and impact analysis are used to determine which interface problems observed during evaluation to address to get the greatest improvement in usability. Finally, of course, when usability specifications are met, the development team can be confident that the desired usability for the system has been achieved, and iteration can cease.

Some developers might hesitate to add these empirical formative techniques to an already over-burdened system and interface development process with limited financial and temporal resources. However, we know of no other approach that provides empirically-based, quantitative data for managing the iterative refinement process, effectively evaluating an interface, and thereby ensuring usability in the final product.

## 1.6   Future Trends in User Interface Evaluation

We have, thus far in this paper, described state-of-the-art techniques used in formatively evaluating a user interface. Numerous avenues of exploration are open to the human-computer interaction world, to establish new techniques and trends in interface evaluation. We close by briefly discussing some of those we perceive as most important for continued advancement.

### Strengthen analytic techniques with empirical observation.

In Section 1.3.3 we critiqued analytic evaluation techniques. We do not conclude, however, that the basic concept behind analytic techniques (inspecting and manipulating a representation of the interface design to identify usability flaws) should be discarded. Instead, the drawbacks of existing analytical techniques can be addressed in new approaches. For example, many of the purely analytical approaches to modeling for interface design evaluation suffer from lack of accurate task descriptions. Empirical observation of users is especially effective at capturing descriptions of the methods by which users actually perform tasks. A trend toward inclusion of empirical approaches in analytic methods will help overcome some of the weaknesses of these analytic methods.

### Adapt global analysis techniques to situational analysis.

Complete, global modeling of an interaction design is costly, and requires persons skilled in the particular modeling technique being used. Finding variations of analysis techniques that support a focus on situations involving known usability problems can make analysis more cost effective. With such approaches, not all tasks must be described. Rather, situational analysis is used to address only tasks that are observed during formative evaluation to be problematic, those a user had difficulty with or failed to accomplish. Then, for example, tasks for which user performance met established usability goals do not have to be described (modelled). This trend will result in a savings of development time and cost.

### Extend evaluation techniques to identify specific usability problems and suggest appropriate solutions.

In Section 1.2.4, we briefly discussed Scriven's concepts of intrinsic and payoff evaluation. Carroll, Singley, and Rosson [CSR92] describe the drawback Scriven observed for pay-off evaluation: while this kind of evaluation can reveal that something is wrong (in the current context, with the user interaction design), it cannot suggest what might be the cause or how it might be corrected. This leaves no structured way to deal with the result of evaluation. However, this drawback applies mainly to quantitative data. In Section 1.4, we showed that qualitative data collected during empirical formative evaluation can, indeed, lead to attribution of a usability problem - at least to its general cause, if not specific location - in a design. Nonetheless, the iterative refinement cycle has a missing link in that there are no techniques to suggest solutions to usability problems that are identified through formative evaluation. At this point designers are usually asked to synthesize a design change to fix the problem. The development process needs a way to close the iteration loop by providing designers with a principle- or theory-based approach to attacking redesign. There is a need for techniques that can assign credit and blame, pinpointing why user performance does not meet usability goals in terms of specific interface design flaws and shortcomings.

In answer to this need, we are seeing the beginnings of a trend that makes use of a combined approach to evaluation. To call on the strengths of both intrinsic and pay-off approaches, Scriven proposes a combined approach that he calls mediated evaluation [CSR92], (p. 5). The task-artifact framework of Carroll and Rosson, discussed in Section 1.3.2, is an example of mediated evaluation in the user interface context.

**Develop more efficient, high impact usability evaluation techniques, to increase the likelihood of their use within real development projects.**

We do not yet know enough about what makes good formative evaluation work and bad formative evaluation not work. At this point in time, formative evaluation is still more an art than a science. Many developers who are hesitant to perform formative evaluations often claim that it is largely because the process is too time-consuming. Thus, there is a pressing need for new, more precise, techniques that assist in assessing user performance and usability as quickly and effectively as possible. We need ways to formalize and codify evaluation processes so they can be brought into an evaluation methodology applicable across a broad spectrum of situations. Methods are also needed to manage the problem of prioritizing, for optimum allocation of finite future redesign effort, design problems discovered in evaluation. We must develop techniques for more efficient extraction of the most relevant usability data during empirical formative evaluation. Nielsen's discount usability engineering [Nie89] and cognitive "jogthroughs" [RR92] are examples of some developments in improving the efficiency and impact of formative evaluation. Such trends will make the formative evaluation process more effective, thereby increasing the use in real world development environments.

**Expand the formative evaluation venue, from the usability lab into a real world setting.**

Empirical formative evaluation must escape the confines of the usability laboratory. Thomas and Kellogg [TK89] warn that laboratory testing, while a very productive step toward addressing usability concerns, is not enough. In particular, laboratory testing does not lead to the kind of "ecological validity" that comes from rich, qualitative observations in real work contexts with real users doing real tasks. We see a trend toward developing new techniques for capturing and analyzing data captured *in situ*, in order to evaluate a design in the most realistic setting.

### Develop better methods for setting the most effective usability specifications.

Less ad hoc, more scientific approaches to establishing quantitative usability goals are needed. Currently, a drawback of usability specifications is the subjectivity of setting levels (worst, planned, best) for each attribute. In order to improve the process of creating and applying usability specifications in the development process, we need a better understanding of the true nature of usability itself. This trend could lead to improved ways of formulating usability specifications that more directly address the usability problem in the practical arena of product development. Perhaps as the field matures, we will accumulate a knowledge base of situations and applications, and feasible usability specifications that apply, along with rationale and guidelines for setting these specifications.

Most usability specifications are centered on measurable user task performance such as timing and error rates, reflecting that user performance is a big economic factor. But in the consumer marketplace it is hard to escape the conclusion, based on how vendors allocate their resources, that user preferences and opinions are considered more important. Yet we do not seem to know how to specify and obtain reliable and useful measures of user preferences early enough to drive the design process, short of spending enormous amounts of money on market surveys. It does not appear that any other consumer industry (such as the automobile industry) really knows this, either, but in those industries the problem is simpler because the products (e.g., automobiles or cameras) are much easier to identify and are in more constrained domains. This appears to be an area that could benefit from user acceptance prediction methods such as those we mentioned in Section 1.2.3.

### Improve tools for rapid prototyping of designs.

To ensure usability of an interface, data obtained from evaluation with representative users is needed before much time and effort are invested in design and hopefully almost none invested in implementation. In order to have something to evaluate early in the development process, a prototype often must be used in place of the real system. Although we have not mentioned rapid prototyping very much in this paper, it is a well-recognized key activity in the iterative star life cycle and often a necessity for early empirical formative evaluation of the product. Rapid prototyping allows users to take a new design "for a spin," allows early observation of user behavior and performance, and encourages user participation and involvement, providing a concrete baseline for communication between developers and users.

However, developers ready to jump on the prototyping bandwagon should be aware of its limitations. For example, using a prototype leads to an evaluation of only the prototype. The higher the fidelity of a prototype to the appearance and behavior of the real system, the more effective its contribution to the real evaluation effort that it supports. Also, unfortunately, current prototyping tools are often limited in the range of applications for which they can be used to produce a prototype. Tools are typically built around a specific look and feel (e.g., Motif, Macintosh), making it difficult to deviate from those established interaction styles. And there is the very real problem of non-availability of good rapid prototyping tools on large workstations, a platform on which much interactive system development is occurring.

Many of the pitfalls associated with prototyping, especially rapid prototyping, originate from misconceptions of, misunderstandings of, and lack of agreement about the role of a prototype within a development project. Lack of understanding and failure to obtain agreement about the role of a prototype can lead to overpromising (including a feature in the prototype that will not be in the real system), loss of discipline ("it's only a toy system, who needs a methodology?"), or overworking the prototype (falling in love with the prototype and polishing it after it has served its usefulness for usability evaluation). In addition, management can view prototyping activity as wasteful or, conversely, can view the prototype as the final product and want to rush it to market.

Because of such shortcomings, there is a significant need for advancement of state-of-the-art prototyping approaches and tools. An important trend is to eliminate the distinction between tools for rapid prototyping and tools for development of the real system. The goal is graceful evolution from early prototypes to a version of the real system without the discontinuity of a throw-away prototype. Also, if the same tool is used for both prototyping and development, a better match for look and feel and functionality results between prototype and real system - higher fidelity in the prototype and therefore more realistic results from formative evaluation.

### Develop and evaluate tools for supporting the formative evaluation process.

We strongly believe it is unlikely that we will ever come close to automating all evaluation of interface designs; purely analytic approaches that replace empirical observations of real users performing real tasks do not seem feasible. There are, however, some analytic approaches that provide unusual approaches to analyzing user session data. One such technique is called maximal repeating patterns, or MRPs [SE91], in which repeating user action patterns of maximum length are extracted from a user session transcript, based on the hypothesis that repeated patterns of usage (e.g., sequences of repeated commands) contain interesting information about an interface's usability. Like other methods of instrumenting interfaces to collect user keystrokes, mouse clicks, and so on, the MRP technique produces voluminous data; only a prototype tool for automated extraction and evaluation of MRPs exists. Still, while the MRP technique does help pinpoint specific problems, it does not indicate how an interaction design should be modified to fix those problems.

Currently there are few tools available to support the formative empirical evaluation process we described in Section 1.4. Such tools are needed to assist evaluators in collection and analysis of observed qualitative and quantitative user data during evaluation sessions. The Interface Design Environment and Analysis Lattice, or IDEAL [AH92], is an interactive tool to support the process of interaction design and formative evaluation. Components of IDEAL are based on user task descriptions that comprise the design. IDEAL allows a developer to attach specific benchmark task instances to general user task descriptions. The developer can also create usability specifications, which are then stored and displayed in conjunction with the appropriate benchmark and other tasks. During formative evaluation, a developer/evaluator can record and associate observed quantitative (e.g., benchmark performance) and qualitative (e.g., critical incidents) data directly with user task descriptions. IDEAL allows direct comparison between observed data and usability specifications. It also allows comparisons of current measured usability with previously measured usability, aiding developers and managers in seeing and understanding convergence and other issues, in the usability of a design. These various components are connected via hypermedia links, based on task names. Early evaluation of a prototype of IDEAL has shown that it is useful in assisting and managing the inherently complex process of formative evaluation, helping confirm that supporting tools are also a key trend for formative evaluation.

### Encourage technology transfer/exchange, and sharing of "success stories."

User interface development, like interactive system development of which it is part, is an in-the-large process. Advances in this area will necessarily involve study of in-the-large activities. Very few such large scale project-oriented empirical studies have been done, largely because of the resources required and because of the scarcity of opportunities within real projects. It is not just a question of money and other resources. In the real world, timing is critical in project management, and researchers do not find enthusiasm for any study that might interfere with an already stressful and too-tight development schedule. There is great economic pressure not to meddle with any established real world process, however inefficient and ineffective it may be.

For university researchers, at least, these requirements mean a kind of university/industry cooperation rarely possible these days. And even industry researchers have trouble transferring their new technologies into their own environments. But such exchange is critical to advancing not just user evaluation techniques, but many other areas of computer science research as well. Such avenues of exchange are needed to generate credible success stories from which others can learn.

The area of user interface evaluation is a challenging one. It is, however, one that is critical to continued and future acceptance of interactive systems by an ever-expanding population of computer users. These trends in effective and efficient evaluation techniques will help ensure usability in future interactive systems.

**Acknowledgements**
Some of the material in Section 1.4 was drawn from [HH93]. Our Human-Computer Interaction research at Virginia Tech is funded in part by the National Science Foundation, Dr. John Hestenes, former grant monitor, Dr. Oscar Garcia, current grant monitor. We would also like to thank all the "guinea pigs" who've survived our usability test sessions over the years; their experiences have helped us formulate a more effective approach to empirical formative evaluation. Finally, two anonymous reviewers made excellent, incisive comments that helped us improve this manuscript.

# References

[AH92]      S. Ashlund and D. Hix. Ideal: A tool to enable user-centered design. In *Proceedings of CHI Conference on Human Factors in Computing Systems*, pages 119–120, New York, 1992. ACM.

[Boe88]     B. W. Boehm. A spiral model of software development and enhancement. *IEEE Computer*, 21(3):61–72, 1988.

[Car90]     J. M. Carroll. Infinite detail and emulation in an ontologically minimized hci. In *Proceedings of CHI Conference on Human Factors in Computing Systems*, pages 321–327, New York, 1990. ACM.

[CDN88]     J. P. Chin, V. A. Diehl, and K. L. Norman. Development of an instrument measuring user satisfaction of the human-computer interface. In *Proceedings of CHI Conference on Human Factors in Computing Systems*, pages 213–218, New York, 1988. ACM.

[CKR91]     J. M. Carroll, W. A. Kellogg, and M. B. Rosson. The task-artifact cycle. In J. M. Carroll, editor, *Designing Interaction: Psychology at the Human-Computer Interface*, pages 74–102. Cambridge University Press, New York, 1991.

[CM80]      S. K. Card and T. P. Moran. The keystroke-level model for user performance time with interactive systems. *Communications of the ACM*, 23:396–410, 1980.

[CMN83]  S. K. Card, T. P. Moran, and A. Newell. *The Psychology of Human-Computer Interaction.* Lawrence Erlbaum Associates, Hillsdale, New Jersey, 1983.

[CR85]  J. M. Carroll and M. B. Rosson. Usability specifications as a tool in iterative development. In H. R. Hartson, editor, *Advances in Human-Computer Interaction*, pages 1–28. Ablex, Norwood, NJ, 1985.

[CSR92]  J. M. Carroll, M. K. Singley, and M. B. Rosson. Integrating theory development with design evaluation. *Journal of Behaviour and Information Technology*, 1992.

[Dav89]  F. D. Davis. Perceived usefulness, perceived ease of use. *MIS Quarterly*, 13(3):319–340, 1989.

[DC78]  W. Dick and L. Carey. *The Systematic Design of Instruction.* Scott, Foresman, Glenview, 1978.

[GE90]  R. Gong and J. Elkerton. Designing minimal documentation using a goms model: A usability evaluation of an engineering approach. In *Proceedings of CHI Conference on Human Factors in Computing Systems*, pages 99–106, New York, 1990. ACM.

[Gil]  T. Gilb. Design by objectives. Unpublished.

[GJA92]  W. D. Gray, B. E. John, and M. Atwood. The precis of project ernestine or an overview of a validation of goms. In *Proceedings of CHI Conference on Human Factors in Computing Systems*, pages 307–312, New York, 1992. ACM.

[GJS+90]  W. D. Gray, B. E. John, R. Stuart, D. Lawrence, and M. Atwood. Goms meets the phone company: Analytic modeling applied to real-world problems. In *Proceedings of INTERACT '90 Third IFIP Conference on Human-Computer Interaction*, Amsterdam: North-Holland, 1990. Elsevier Science Publishers.

[GSWG86]  M. Good, T. Spine, J. Whiteside, and P. George. User derived impact analysis as a tool for usability engineering. In *Proceedings of CHI Conference on Human Factors in Computing Systems*, pages 241–246, New York, 1986. ACM.

[HH89]  H. R. Hartson and D. Hix. Toward empirically derived methodologies and tools for human-computer interface development. *International Journal of Man-Machine Studies*, 31:477–494, 1989.

[HH93]  D. Hix and H. R. Hartson. *Developing User Interfaces: Ensuring Usability Through Product and Process.* John Wiley & Sons, Inc., New York, 1993.

[JD92]  R. Jeffries and H. Desurvire. Usability testing vs. heuristic evaluation: Was there a contest? *ACM SIGCHI Bulletin*, 24(4):39–41, 1992.

[Joh90]  B. E. John. Extensions of goms analyses to expert performance requiring perception of dynamic visual and auditory information. In *Proceedings of CHI Conference on Human Factors in Computing Systems*, pages 107–115, New York, 1990. ACM.

[JV92]  B. E. John and A. H Vera. A goms analysis of a graphic, machine-paced, highly interactive task. In *Proceedings of CHI Conference on Human Factors in Computing Systems*, pages 251–258, New York, 1992. ACM.

[KCF92]  C.-M. Karat, R. Campbell, and T. Fiegel. Comparison of empirical testing and walkthrough methods in user interface evaluation. In *Proceedings of CHI Conference on Human Factors in Computing Systems*, pages 397–404, New York, 1992. ACM.

[Kie88]  D. E. Kieras. Towards a practical goms model methodology for user interface design. In M. Helander, editor, *Handbook of Human-Computer Interaction.* Elsevier Science Publishers B. V, 1988.

[KP83]  D. Kieras and P. G. Polson. A generalized transition network representation for interactive systems. In *Proceedings of CHI Conference on Human Factors in Computing Systems*, New York, 1983. ACM.

[KP85]  D. Kieras and P. G. Polson. An approach to the formal analysis of user complexity. *International Journal of Man-Machine Studies*, 22:365–394, 1985.

[LPWR90]  C. Lewis, P. Polson, C. Wharton, and J. Rieman. Testing a walkthrough methodology for theory-based design of walk-up-and-use interfaces. In *Proceedings of CHI Conference on Human Factors in Computing Systems*, pages 235–242, New York, 1990. ACM.

[MD89]  W. E. Mackay and G. Davenport. Virtual video editing in interactive multimedia applications. *Communications of the ACM*, 32(7):802–810, 1989.

[Mor80]  T. P. Moran. A framework for studying human-computer interaction. In e. a. Guedj, editor, *Methodology of Interaction*, pages 293–301. North-Holland Publishing Co., 1980.

[Mor81]     T. P. Moran. The command language grammar: A representation for the user interface of interactive computer systems. *International Journal of Man-Machine Studies*, 15:3–51, 1981.

[Nie87]     J. Nielsen. Using scenarios to develop user friendly videotex systems. In *Proceedings of NordData87*. Joint Scandanavian Computer Conference, 1987.

[Nie88]     J. Nielsen. Evaluating the thinking aloud technique for use by computer scientists. In *Proceedings of IFIP W. G. 8.1 International Workshop on Human Factors of Information Systems Analysis and Design*, 1988.

[Nie89]     J. Nielsen. Usability engineering at a discount. In G. Salvendy and M. J. Smith, editors, *Designing and Using Human-Computer Interfaces and Knowledge-Based Systems*, pages 394–401. Elsevier Science Publishers, Amsterdam, 1989.

[Nie92]     J. Nielsen. Finding usability problems through heuristic evaluation. In *Proceedings of CHI Conference on Human Factors in Computing Systems*, pages 373–380, New York, 1992. ACM.

[NM90]      J. Nielsen and R. Molich. Heuristic evaluation of user interfaces. In *Proceedings of CHI Conference on Human Factors in Computing Systems*, pages 249–256, New York, 1990. ACM.

[Nor84]     D.A. Norman. Managing to meet usability requirements: Establishing and meeting software development goals. In J. Bennett, D. Case, J. Sandelin, and M. Smith, editors, *Visual Display Terminals*, pages 161–184. Prentice-Hall, Englewood Cliffs, NJ, 1984.

[OO90]      J. R. Olson and G. M. Olson. The growth of cognitive modeling in human-computer interaction since goms. *Human-Computer Interaction*, 5:221–265, 1990.

[PG86]      S. J. Payne and T. R. G. Green. Task-action grammars: A model of the mental representation of task languages. *Human-Computer Interaction*, 2:93–133, 1986.

[PJ92]      V. A. Peck and B. E. John. Browser-soar: A computational model of a highly interactive task. In *Proceedings of CHI Conference on Human Factors in Computing Systems*, pages 165–172, New York, 1992. ACM.

[Rei81]     P. Reisner. Formal grammar and human factors design of an interactive graphics system. *IEEE Transactions on Software Engineering*, SE-7:229–240, 1981.

[Rei83]     P. Reisner. Analytic tools for human factors of software. Technical report, IBM Research Laboratory, San Jose, CA, 1983.

[RR92]      D. E. Rowley and D. G. Rhoades. The cognitive jogthrough: A fast-paced user interface evaluation procedure. In *Proceedings of CHI Conference on Human Factors in Computing Systems*, pages 389–395, New York, 1992. ACM.

[Scr67]     M. Scriven. The methodology of evaluation. In R. Tyler, R. Gagne, and M. Scriven, editors, *Perspectives of Curriculum Evaluation*, pages 39–83. Rand McNally, Chicago, 1967.

[SE91]      A. C. Siochi and R. W. Ehrich. Computer analysis of user interfaces based on repetition in transcripts of user sessions. *Transactions on Information Systems*, 1991.

[TK89]      J. C. Thomas and W. A. Kellogg. Minimizing ecological gaps in interface design. *IEEE Software*, 6(1):78–86, 1989.

[Vir92]     Robert A. Virzi Refining the Test Phase of Usability Evaluation: How Many Subjects is Enough? *Human Factors Journal*, 34(4):457-468, 1992

[WBGM88]    M. D. Wilson, P. J. Barnard, T. R. G. Green, and A. Maclean. Knowledge-based task analysis for human-computer systems. In G. C. v. d. Veer, T. R. G. Green, J.-M. Hoc, and D. M. Murray, editors, *Working with Computers: Theory Versus Outcome*, pages 47–87. Academic Press, London, 1988.

[WBH88]     J. Whiteside, J. Bennett, and K. Holtzblatt. Usability engineering: Our experience and evolution. In M. Helander, editor, *Handbook of Human-Computer Interaction*, pages 791–817. Elsevier North-Holland, Amsterdam, 1988.

[WBJF92]    C. Wharton, J. Bradford, R. Jeffries, and M. Franzke. Applying cognitive walkthroughs to more complex user interfaces: Experiences, issues, and recommendations. In *Proceedings of CHI Conference on Human Factors in Computing Systems*, pages 381–388, New York, 1992. ACM.

[Wil84]     R. C. Williges. Evaluating human-computer software interfaces. In *Proceedings of International Conference on Occupational Ergonomics*, 1984.

# 2

# Architectures for Interactive Software Systems: Rationale and Design

**Len Bass**

*Software Engineering Institute[1]*
*Carnegie Mellon University*

## ABSTRACT

Developing software to implement the user interface requires making choices (or using tools that have already made those choices) of which software engineering non-functional qualities are most important. These choices depend on a variety of influences and are manifested both in software architectures for user interfaces and in tools that are used to construct and execute the user interface.

In this paper, we categorize and explain the impact of the software engineering influences.  We use those influences to motivate a particular user interface software architecture and the functionalities associated with various aspects of that architecture.

## 2.1   Introduction

The user interface of a system has become one of the primary determinants of user satisfaction with that system. At the same time, production and maintenance of high quality user interfaces remains expensive. Several reports put the cost of the user interface at over half of the total cost of a system. [MR92, SS78] To enable a system developer to afford to produce a high quality user interface, techniques must be available to reduce the cost of producing and maintaining it. One of these techniques is to use a software architecture oriented toward the user interface

---

[1] This work supported by the U.S. Department of Defense

as the basis for system design. This paper discusses the issues associated with the portion of the software architecture implementing the user interface.

We first discuss the considerations during the development process that impact the production and maintenance of the user interface. These considerations can be satisfied by an appropriate software architecture. Next, we discuss various classes of functionality that the user interface software must implement. Finally, we describe a particular software architecture in terms of these functionalities and show how this architecture satisfies the requirements on the development process. At each stage in the paper, we are giving more power to the software designer by providing more information about desirable solutions, but we are also restricting the tools and techniques that can be used. Thus, there are multiple software architectures that might satisfy the process considerations and achieve the desired functionality and we only present a single one. The virtue of this paper lies in the fact that it identifies the considerations for production and maintenance of interactive systems, that it enumerates the types of functionalities required by any architecture, and that it provides a framework for discussing, and hence comparing, software architectures.

One difficulty in discussing user interface architecture is that many of the factors that impact the user interface portion of the system are, in reality, factors that impact the development of systems in general. The impact of these factors on the user interface is primarily a result of the user interface being a portion of the system being developed. On the other hand, designing a system is a process of making tradeoffs between different priorities and considerations and discussing the user interface without discussing it in a system context eliminates many of the important considerations. Consequently, we first discuss requirements of the whole system that affect the user interface. When we begin the discussion of software architecture, we then focus on the user interface software and how it relates to the system requirements.

## 2.2   Requirements on the Software Development Process

The developer of an interactive system must be concerned with both "life cycle" and usability issues. These two concerns give two different time perspectives to the developer. Usability is a run time issue; that is, usability is important when the end user is actually executing the system. Life cycle concerns, on the other hand, begin with system conception and do not end until the system is no longer used. An execution of the system is viewed as one instant on a much longer time scale. From the perspective of the developer, then, usability is one of several run time issues (along with performance, reliability, and functionality, for example) that must be juggled with the life cycle issues of cost and schedule. It is the pressure of developing a system with high usability over the longest possible lifetime while staying within reasonable cost and schedule constraints that is the root cause of the difficulty of developing interactive systems. In order to develop this theme, we first discuss the factors that influence the lifetime of a system. A system has ended its useful lifetime either when it is no longer needed or when the cost of modifications is sufficiently high to require the system to be scrapped and replaced by a new one. A system during its lifetime moves from conception to design to implementation and fielding to modification and upgrading. Decisions made in the design stage influence strongly the cost of both implementation and modification and upgrading. These decisions also influence how drastically the system can be upgraded without requiring replacement. By design, some systems have very short lifetimes; others have long lifetimes. Deciding on the intended lifetime of a system is one of the decisions that must be made early in the process.

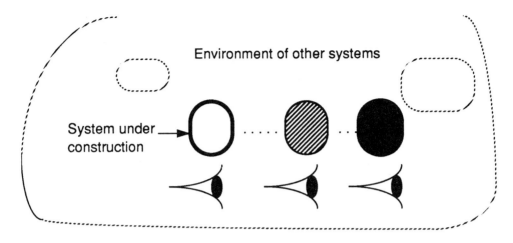

**Figure 2.1**   Influences on evolution of a system

Other factors also enter into decisions about a system. A particular system is but one of a collection of systems. The influence of these other systems provides an external environment within which design is done and within which operation is envisioned. Any single system needs to be considered in its relationships to other systems in its environment.

Figure 2.1 gives a view of the world we have sketched. There is an external environment that contains systems available for use and a collection of users of those systems. The user interface characteristics of this environment change over time as a reflection of changing technology and changing understanding of the role of computer systems in that environment. Within this environment, a particular system has a lifetime that is somewhat under the control of the designer of that system. Also, a particular system has a collection of users. Usability is an instaneous property of a particular system for a particular user. The problem, from the point of view of the system designer, is how to design a system that is usable by the intended class of users, that maintains that usability across the modifications that occur during the lifetime of the system, that conforms to and takes advantage of other systems in its world, and that has a lifetime appropriate for the investment being made in its development.

## 2.2.1   External requirements

Four elements of the external world affect user interfaces and interactive system development. First, end users have experience with using interactive systems. A single system needs to be concerned with how its use relates to the experience of the end users. Secondly, portions of existing systems can be reused in the current system. Such reuse should reduce the cost of building any particular system. Next, because of the existence of a class of similar systems, there are tools available to assist in the construction of the user interface; the use of these tools has developmental implications. Finally, for various reasons, the use of particular hardware and software platforms may be dictated.

We now discuss these four influences:

### 2.2.1.1   User Expectations

Users are conditioned by the systems with which they have experience. Currently, they expect direct manipulation systems with many user support features. In the future, these expectations will only get more stringent. Thus, in addition to the functional requirements for a particular system, requirements caused by the users expectations must be added.

### 2.2.1.2   Existing Code

Certain classes of user interface code are now considered a portion of the operating system and are routinely distributed by vendors. Thus, a system designer is influenced by the existence of this code. Two of these user interface classes are input/output resource managers such as window or graphics systems, and user interface toolkits:

An input/output resource manager manages the input/output devices for the multiple processes that may wish to simultaneously access them. The resource manager provides a collection of services and mechanisms that are required in order for a system to be interactive. In turn, these services and mechanisms require that information be presented and received from the input/output devices in a certain formalism. This formalism is specific to the domain of the devices that are being managed and, most likely, is different from the formalism used in the remainder of the interactive system. Thus, one of the effects of using a resource manager is that there must be functionalities within the interactive system that convert from other formalisms into the resource manager formalisms.

User interface toolkits are also generally available and widely used. An element of a toolkit implements a single interactive function for the end user and each instance of the element is used by a single process within the interactive system. Toolkits assume the existence of a resource manager since each instance is, typically, used by a single process.

The particular toolkit used in an interactive system influences the design of the user interface since it provides the building blocks from which the user interface is constructed. An alternative view of this process is that the designed user interface influences the elements of the toolkit that are used. In either case, there is clearly a close relationship between the designed user interface and the user interface toolkit.

User interface toolkits also use a particular formalism. The comments about formalism conversion with respect to resource managers also apply to user interface toolkits.

### 2.2.1.3   Tools

Because of the existence of a collection of similar systems, tools exist to assist in the construction of the user interface. These tools, typically, are dependent upon the existence of a user interface toolkit. Some of the tools provide simple layout ability. These tools (interface builders) have no structural implications beyond those associated with having a user interface toolkit. Other tools provide support for the dynamic behavior of the user interface. These tools (user interface management systems) make some structural assumptions about the system and, consequently, impose some structure on the system. Exactly what structure is imposed depends on the details of the tool. Interviews, an object oriented tool [Lin93], is discussed elsewhere in this volume.

### 2.2.1.4   Hardware and software platform

Often, the particular system that is being designed is constrained to run on a particular hardware platform. This can be caused by interoperability reasons, that is, the ability to easily communicate with existing systems; by historical reasons, that is, the equipment is available; or for political or marketing reasons, that is, other systems (or potential customers) in the domain have this particular equipment.

Similar considerations apply to software. There may be a mandate to use a particular language, software system or support environment. For example, a software designer may be told to use both the Motif toolkit and Ada. This severely restricts the options available. Thus, these requirements will impact the design of the portion of the system that deals with the user interface.

We have discussed the considerations that derive from external influences. These are user expectations, the existence of a resource manager, the existence of a user interface toolkit, the existence of tools to assist in the implementation of the user interface, and the mandate to use particular hardware or languages. In the next section, we will discuss the influences on the design from the life cycle of the system.

## 2.2.2   Influences from the life cycle of an interactive system

Another set of influences on the design of an interactive system come from a consideration of the life cycle of that system. The life cycle of a system begins when the system is conceived, and continues through requirements definition, design, implementation, and modification. A system also has a life time and, from the point of view of structural influences, that life time extends from system conception until the completion of the last modification.

These considerations lead to four sources of influence on the structure of an interactive system:

1. User interface design process
2. Uncertainty in the requirements for the user interface.
3. Desire to maximize the duration of the system life time
4. Desire for implementation efficiency.

### 2.2.2.1   User Interface Design Process

A reasonable process for the designer of the user interface is to hypothesize and refine the user interface in conjunction with user responses prior to the actual construction of a system. One technique for doing some of this work is to build non-functional or semi-functional prototypes that present the user interface of the system under construction. The construction of such prototypes tends to result in higher customer satisfaction with the final interface. The problem is that the construction of such prototypes represents an important investment, and there is a desire to utilize the prototype as is, rather than re-implementing the user interface in the context of a total system design.

Thus, one influence on the structure of an interactive system is the extent to which prototypical versions of the user interface are incorporated into the final system. Since the prototypes tend to consist primarily of code to execute the user interface, incorporating the prototype into the final system leads to a structure in which the user interface is generally distinct from the non user interface portion of the system. The depth to which the user interface is prototyped (the amount of functionality included in the prototype) also will influence the extent to which there is a degree of separation of the user interface.

As we will see later, separation of portions of the user interface results in a structure that is responsive to change in the user interface. In any case, using a prototype to evaluate proposed user interfaces and then attempting to incorporate portions of the prototype into the final system has a definite influence on the structure of the final system. The final system must accommodate a user interface constructed without knowledge of internal system structure and data.

This type of separation is an essential portion of all User Interface Management Systems (UIMSs). The separation within a UIMS not only supports the software engineering influences that are enumerated in this paper but also provides mechanisms for end user modifications to the user interface.

### 2.2.2.2   Uncertainty in requirements

The requirements for an interactive system evolve during the requirements phase. Uncertainty in the user interface is reduced by constructing user interface prototypes, but the user interface is not the only area of uncertainty. Other requirements also have a degree of uncertainty, and changes in these requirements usually require changes in the user interface. This suggests a structure that allows evolution of the user interface and the underlying functionality. After the system is fielded and end users gain experience with the system, they require new functionality and different methods for interacting with existing functionality. These types of changes are usually incremental; that is, the technological basis of the interactive system does not change as a result of these changes.

The influence of the uncertainty in requirements on the structure of an interactive system is that some software architectures are more amenable to change in functionality than other software architectures. In particular, the fewer components that are affected by a single modification to the system, the shorter time and the lesser expense it takes to make that modification. Thus, designing for change requires isolating the components within which the changes are likely to occur. It also requires distinguishing between major and minor changes in the user interface.

### 2.2.2.3   Maximizing system lifetime

Technological changes in the user interface have occurred quite frequently in the past (such as punched cards, teletypes, glass teletypes, and bit mapped graphics) and more changes are foreseeable (see, for example, the article by Stevens in this volume [Ste93]). As we mentioned in the prior section, changes are implemented with minimal cost and in minimal time when the impact of those changes are localized. The structural implications of allowing for user interface technological changes are that all components that depend on a particular technology are separated from technology independent components. This technique has also been called "media independence".

Maximizing system lifetime has deeper implications than allowing changes in the user interface. That is, there are some aspects of the user interface that are surface, others that are technology dependent, and still others that are independent of any particular technology. This is discussed in more detail in Section 2.3.

### 2.2.2.4 Efficiency of implementation

The time and cost of a correct implementation of the required system functionality will vary widely for different structures. The conceptual simplicity of a design impacts the difficulty of detecting and correcting errors. The time that an implementation takes depends on the number of individuals involved in implementation and the number and type of components. The cost of an implementation depends on the number of individuals and the time involved.

The influence that these problems have on the structure of an interactive design is that efficiently using multiple people on a single system depends on separating the system into independent (or mostly independent) portions. Thus, conceptual simplicity is difficult to maintain but separation is inherent in the process.

One approach to efficient implementation is the use of object oriented specification techniques. These techniques are designed to reduce the cost associated with implementation but they also have a profound effect on system structure. One portion of an object oriented technique is the use of encapsulation. Encapsulating all actions associated with a particular entity within the system means that the remainder of the system must communicate in a particular fashion with the encapsulated object. This has the effect of separating actions associated with each object. This is separation, potentially, along a different axis than the separation associated with maximizing system lifetime or allowing changes in the user interface.

## 2.2.3 Influences from an execution of an interactive system

The desired behavior of the system at a particular instance of its execution also affects the structure of the system. The behavior, in this case, means desired performance, robustness and user customizability.

Performance of a system depends on the type of functionality desired, the algorithms used to implement that functionality, and the number and type of formalism conversions implicit in that functionality. Particular algorithms may have structural implications, and the number of formalism conversions certainly has structural implications.

Robustness includes protection against user errors, which, in turn, suggests that some amount of redundancy or authentication of input must exist within a structure. It also includes the ability to undo or redo particular actions. Undo and redo require a history mechanism for user actions and, consequently, some structure to maintain and retrieve this history.

User customization requires some mechanism for retrieving and promulgating user specifications at run time, and this, in turn, requires separation, or at least exposure, of customizable attributes.

Table 2.1 summarizes the influences that we have discussed in this section. For each influence, the second column gives the structural impact that would occur if that influence were the only important influence. Notice that separation of concerns is a recurring theme in responding to the concerns.

## 2.3 A Categorization of User Tasks

We now present a categorization for discussing the tasks and end user performs using an interactive system. Tasks are categorized into abstract, metaphoric and concrete levels corresponding to the different levels of abstraction the end user must bring to accomplish the tasks

**Table 2.1**  Influences on software structure

| Influence | Influence on Design |
|---|---|
| Look and feel | encourages certain style of interface, suggests reuse of toolkit |
| Reusable code | modularity in areas that reusable code exist |
| Tools for construction of user interface | enforces certain structures |
| Hardware/Software mandates | may inhibit reuse, may contort user interface design, may encourage separation |
| Design process | encourages separation of user interface portion |
| Uncertainty in requirements | encourages separation of user interface details |
| Maximizing system lifetime | encourages separation of technology dependent code from technology independent code |
| Implementation efficiency | large systems must have separation of concerns, conceptual simplicity difficult with large systems |
| Execution efficiency | encourages coherence of design |
| Robustness when user errors occur | encourages redundancy |
| User customizability | requires exposure of customizable attributes and encourages separation of the implementation of these attributes |

[BKL93]. Once these tasks are established, we will present a particular structure in terms of these tasks and discuss how the structure satisfies the concerns enumerated in Table 2.1.

### 2.3.1   Abstract LeveL Tasks

Abstract level tasks are the high-level user tasks needed to execute some computation without reference to a model of I/O or a presentation form. This level describes the user's interactions with the system, the functions that must be performed to realize those user interactions, and the data structures that the functions manipulate. These interactions and functions are a characterization of the user's problem domain, not of the implementation of the artifact which addresses this problem domain. This is similar to Norman's "intention" [Nor86].

The user's interactions at the abstract task level are intended to achieve high-level goals within the user's mental model of the system. These goals are described in terms of the domain-specific functionality of the system. For example, in a file system interface, the user's interactions are navigating around the file system, directly modifying elements of the system (e.g., files, directories, links), and invoking applications that modify the file system for the user. In a simple electronic mail system, some of the user's interactions are to create, send, receive, and file messages. The user's interactions are high-level, and thus belong in the abstract task level only if they refer to the accomplishment of a goal which does not reference any aspect of the system's presentation. For example, in a file system, "delete a file" is a description of an abstract task level user interaction, but dragging an icon representing *file*1 to some target target1 (such as a trash can icon), typing the command "rm *file*1", or uttering the command "remove *file*1" are descriptions of low-level interactions with particular presentations: desktop, command line, and natural language.

A user's interactions at the abstract task level, being high-level, may not be representative of the processes involved in the underlying application. To illustrate this distinction, consider the process of starting a car. When one wishes to start a car, the user interaction is "insert the key into the ignition and turn it", but the underlying application (the car) must translate this interaction into a series of coordinated actions between the battery, ignition system, fuel system, starter, valves, pistons, etc. The user often has no knowledge of these underlying application actions and, as such, they cannot be considered to be user interactions. Furthermore, if the underlying technology were changed - to a diesel or electric engine for example - the user's interactions could very well be identical in each case.

### 2.3.2   Metaphor Level Tasks

A metaphor is a way of taking concepts that humans are familiar with and imbuing them with new but related meanings in the context of user interfaces. Desktop, ledger, document composition, and drawing metaphors are common examples of metaphors used regularly in user interfaces [CMK88]. The advantage of metaphors is that they allow a designer to exploit a user's vast knowledge of the real world in order to simplify the learning of a new interface. If the interface makes use of a metaphor, then the user brings a large number of expectations to that interface, such as expectations that the interface instantiations of the metaphor will respond in the same way as the real-world activity upon which the metaphor is based [Gen83]. This increases a user's initial familiarity with the concepts and activities of the system and significantly reduces learning time [FSGA87].

A metaphor is made visible to the end user through an evocative collection of presentation mechanisms. A metaphor level task is a task performed on one of the elements of the metaphor. Classes of commonly used metaphors in HCI are given by Carroll, Mack and Kellogg [CMK88]. These enumerations are not closed; new metaphors may be invented at any time. However, inclusion on one of these lists provides a reasonable criterion for determining if a task in a system being designed belongs at the metaphor level or at some other level.

### 2.3.3   The Concrete Task LeVEL

The concrete task level is the level at which the user's input events are interpreted, tokenized, and passed to the metaphor level with which these events are associated. The purpose of the concrete task level is to group the input primitives provided by the device-level software into meaningful tokens. This tokenization may be 1:1; - that is, for each hardware event such as a key press or mouse motion, one token may be sent to the associated metaphor level process - or it may be 1:n, where a number of device-level events are bundled together to produce a single output token. For example, if a move operation in a graphical drawing system provides graphical feedback, each device-level event (such as mouse motion tracking) will need to be processed so that the graphical object can be dynamically repositioned. If, on the other hand, the move operation merely requires selecting a source and a destination point, then no intermediate motion tracking needs to be captured.

The user interactions of the concrete task level are simple, device-level actions: keystrokes, mouse movements, etc. In this way, the concrete task level is identical to other descriptions of low-level user behavior, such as the keystroke model [Blu90]. As stated above, one purpose of the concrete task level might be to group these interactions into meaningful larger units (tokens). This notion is of no concern to the user. The user merely enters data; whether each input token is separately processed by the levels above it (as with semantic feedback or eager recognition [Pfa85]), or whether a composite token is returned only after a specified event (carriage return, mouse-button up, etc.) should be transparent to the user.

Similarly, the user does not need to know if the visible output tokens are device-level primitives or whether they are composite tokens. For example, when users perceive a box on the screen, they should be ignorant of whether it is an output primitive provided by the graphics server or whether it is explicitly composed from four lines.

### 2.3.4   An Example of the Classification

As an example, consider the familiar desktop metaphor used to represent an operating system's file system. The abstract level tasks are those tasks related to the file system: move, delete, create, open, etc. These tasks are independent of a particular model of input/output and could be realized by many different metaphors or user interfaces.

The desktop consists of windows, folders and a trash can. The metaphor level tasks are those tasks related to the management of the desk top: move file to trash, close window, open folder, move icon to a different location, etc. These tasks are independent of the particular choice of icons and style for the desktop but do assume a bitmapped graphics device with some pointing device.

The concrete level determines the specifics of the presentation (the icons chosen, the window decoration, etc.). A concrete level task is "push left button on mouse, drag mouse".

Thus, the end user pushes a button on the mouse and drags the mouse to the trash can icon. These operations at the concrete level are mapped to the metaphor level "move to trash" which, in turn, are mapped to the abstract level operation of "delete".

The concrete level tasks are those that the end user physically performs, the metaphor level tasks are those that are performed by the end user in terms of the representations of the metaphor, and the abstract level tasks are those performed by the system in order to achieve high level goal of the end user.

### 2.4   An Implementation Model

Given this context, we present an architecture that is designed for long life, for modifications to the user interface, and for reuse of user interface toolkits. We are also interested in providing an architecture for a system that provides a basis for allocating the various levels of tasks to software components. The architecture that follows was designed in response to these criteria.

### 2.4.1   The task based decomposition

The architecture that we present has five major components adapted from [Wor92]:

1. Base - performs functions that are independent of the existence of a user.
2. Dialogue - performs functions that support metaphoric tasks. Also includes functions that map between data from the base adaptor and presentation components.
3. Base Adaptor -performs functions that support abstract tasks. Includes functions that access data in the base component. The abstract tasks may be many to many with respect to the base functions.
4. Interaction Toolkit - performs functions that support concrete tasks.
5. Presentation - a mediation, or buffer, component between the Dialogue and the Interaction Toolkit Components that provides a set of toolkit-independent, metaphor dependent functions. These functions map from data in the dialogue component to data in the interaction toolkit component

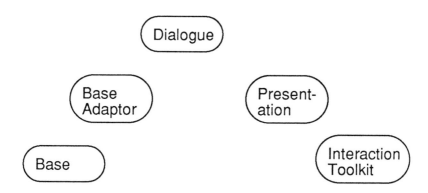

**Figure 2.2**   Task based decomposition

This decomposition of function is shown in Figure 2.2.

This decomposition supports both change and reuse. Reuse is supported by having a specific component that encompasses user interface toolkits. All of the elements of this component are assumed to have an existence in other systems beyond the one currently being constructed. User interface change in both major and minor fashions is supported by localizing the components in which that change is likely to occur into the presentation and dialogue components. Decisions about which metaphor is to be used to perform the interaction are accomplished within the dialogue component, and the Base and Base Adaptor components are thus isolated from the impact of changes in the metaphor. The elements that are changed during minor modifications are located within the presentation component and these changes can usually be effected by modification to the functions that map to the interaction toolkit.

## 2.4.2   Discussion of Components

The decomposition above is based on the desires to allow for modifications in both concrete and metaphoric tasks, to utilize a user interface toolkit, and to minimize implementation size by combining similar functionalities into components. With that type of decomposition, however, there is still a necessity to transfer data among the components, to compute the various types of functionality, and to combine concrete tasks into metaphor tasks and metaphor tasks into base functionality tasks. We now discuss those three requirements.

### 2.4.2.1   Moving between concrete, metaphor and base functionality tasks

The dialogue component is the component where the metaphors used to guide the interaction are decided. This component, then, is the location where base functionality tasks are decomposed (or composed on input) into metaphor level tasks. Thus, for example, in most desktops, there are tasks performed through the desktop and other tasks performed through a menu. These operations are combined in the dialogue component into a single base functional level task.

Metaphor tasks, on the other hand, are decomposed (or composed) into concrete tasks in both the presentation component and the interaction toolkit component. The rationale for splitting this responsibility comes from the desire to re-use existing toolkits. Some metaphors are fully realized directly in the toolkit and for these metaphors, the tasks are decomposed (or composed) in the interaction toolkit component. Other metaphors are not fully realized in the toolkit and must be constructed from the components furnished by the toolkit; this construction is done in the presentation component.

### 2.4.2.2   Nature of data exchanged

We now discuss how the data space is partitioned by these components and how data is exchanged between the various components.

The base component performs those tasks that are the reason for the existence of the system. These tasks are independent of the existence of an operator and, consequently, there is no allowance for human frailties and characteristics in the base functionality component. This allowance, at a metaphor independent level, is the responsibility of the base functionality adaptor component. This component communicates to the dialogue component in terms of conceptual objects. A conceptual object is a portion of the data space that captures base domain concepts that the system designer wishes to be externally perceivable. It captures them in a fashion that allows for differences in timing, cut-copy-paste, error detection, and recovery, and is metaphor independent. A discussion of some of the characteristics of conceptual objects can be found in [DGHL91].

The user interface toolkit component implements the physical interaction with the user via hardware and software. At run time, it contains interaction objects that actually perform the physical interaction. Each interaction object is an instance of an element of the toolkit. Although the interaction objects themselves are contained in the interaction toolkit component, the specification of these objects is shared between the interaction toolkit and the presentation components. That is, the presentation component provides the data that controls interaction objects and retrieves the input from the end user.

The presentation component contains a collection of presentation objects that are interaction objects that have no physical representation but are, instead, based on an abstract metaphor machine. Thus, presentation objects contain the data interchanged between the dialogue component and the presentation component.

### 2.4.2.3   Functionalities

In this section we will discuss some of the issues with respect to the computation of the various functionalities. Most of this discussion will focus on the dialogue component:

1.  The dialogue controller has responsibility for composing metaphor level tasks into base functionality level tasks. Each task or goal of the user corresponds to a thread of dialogue and a user may simultaneously be pursuing multiple tasks. Thus, the dialogue component must allow for multiple threads of control.
2.  The base component and the presentation component use different formalisms. One is driven by the computational considerations of the base functionality, the other is dependent on a particular metaphor dependent abstract machine. In order to match the two formalisms, data must be transformed inside the dialogue component.

3. State changes in the base functionality must be reflected in the presentation (and vice versa). Therefore links must be maintained between conceptual objects and presentation objects. A conceptual object may be rendered with multiple metaphors. Therefore, consistency must be maintained between the multiple views of the conceptual object. Such management is yet another task of the dialogue component.

The functions of managing multiple threads of control, formalism conversion and maintaining data links are well handled by using recursively specified multiple agents such as PAC [BC91, Cou91].

A PAC agent has three components: Presentation, Control, and Abstraction. The control component is decomposed in multiple other PAC agents. By having an agent for each thread of control, an agent to control multiple views, and an agent to maintain the metaphor, PAC becomes a mechanism for implementation of the dialogue component.

Each refinement reflects the operations of concretizing. Abstracting works from the low level to combine and transform events coming at the metaphoric level into base functional level events. Conversely, concretizing decomposes and transforms base functional level events into low level information. The lowest level of abstraction of the dialogue controller agents is in contact with specific presentation objects and conceptual objects. Each portion of the agent with different functions is called a facet:

- the base facet defines the functionality of the agent in the chain of abstracting and concretizing. It is related to some conceptual objects.
- the translation facet performs formalism translation between the base facet and the dialogue controller facet of the agent.
- the dialogue controller facet controls event sequencing inside the agent, maintains a mapping between the translation facet and the presentation facet of the agent.
- the presentation facet is related to some presentation object in the presentation component.

The dialogue component consists of a recursive sequence of agents where each agent has the facets listed above.

## 2.5 Summary

In this paper, we have discussed system influences that impinge on the user interface. We also have presented a framework for discussing interactive systems: the taxonomy of tasks into abstract, metaphoric, and concrete. Within that framework we presented an implementation architecture that was responsive to the system level influence. Tools, discussed elsewhere in this volume [Lin93], are mechanisms for implementing such architectures.

Although the system influences on the user interface are diverse and prevalent, the cost of developing an interactive system that is responsive to those influences important for the user interface can be reduced by an appropriate casting of the functionality associated with the user interface and by appropriate structuring of the interactive system.

## References

[BC91]     Len Bass and Joelle Coutaz. *Developing Software for the User Interface*. Addison-Wesley, Reading, Massachusetts, 1991.

[BKL93]     L. Bass, R. Kazman, and R. Little. Toward a software engineering model of human-computer interaction. In *Proceedings of Engineering for Human-Computer Interaction*, Amsterdam, North-Holland, 1993.

[Blu90]     B. Blumenthal. Strategies for automatically incorporating metaphoric attributes in interface designs. In *Proceedings of the ACM SIGGRAPH Symposium on User Interface Software and Technology*, pages 66–75, New York, 1990. ACM Press.

[CMK88]     J. M. Carroll, R. L. Mack, and W. A. Kellogg. Interface metaphors and user interface design. In W. Helander, editor, *Handbook of Human-Computer Interaction*, pages 389–394. North-Holland, Amsterdam, 1988.

[Cou91]     Joelle Coutaz. Architectural design for user interfaces. In *European Conference on Software Engineering*, 1991.

[DGHL91]   Duce, Gomes, Hopgood, and Lee, editors. *User Interface Management and Design*. Springer-Verlag, Berlin, 1991.

[FSGA87]    M. Frese, H. Schulte-Gocking, and A. Altmann. Lernprozesse in abhangigkeit von der trainingsmethode, von personenmerkmalen und von der benutzeroberflache (direkte manipulation vs. konventionelle interaktion). In W. Schonpflu and M. Wittstock, editors, *Software-Egonomie'87*. Teubnerpf, Berlin, 1987.

[Gen83]     D. Gentner. Structure mapping: A theoretical framework for analogy. *Cognitive Science*, pages 155–170, July 1983.

[Lin93]     M. Linton. Making user interfaces easy-to-build. In Bass and Dewan, editors, *User Interface Software*, Trends in Software Series. Wiley, 1993.

[MR92]      B. Myers and M. Rossner. Survey on user interface programming. In *Human Factors in Computing Systems: CHI '92 Conference Proceedings*, pages 195–202, Reading, Ma, 1992. Addison-Wesley.

[Nor86]     D.A. Norman. Cognitive engineering. In Draper Norman, editor, *User Centered System Design*. Lawrence Erlbaum Associates, Hillsdale, NJ, 1986.

[Pfa85]     G. E. (ed) Pfaff. *User Interface Management Systems*. Springer-Verlag, New York, 1985.

[SS78]      J. Sutton and R. Sprague. A study of display generation and management in interactive business applications. Technical Report Tech Report RJ2392, IBM Research Report, November 1978.

[Ste93]     S. Stevens. Multimedia computing: Applications, designs, and human factors. In Bass and Dewan, editors, *User Interface Software*, Trends in Software Series. Wiley, 1993.

[Wor92]     UIMS Tool Developers Workshop. A metamodel for the runtime architecture of an interactive system. *SIGCHI Bulletin*, January 1992.

# 3

# Making User Interfaces Easy-to-Build

**Mark A. Linton**
*Silicon Graphics Computer Systems*

### ABSTRACT

Building high-quality user interfaces often requires substantial effort. The InterViews system provides a collection of tools that simplify the construction of interactive applications. We have designed and implemented a uniform, general-purpose model for graphical and user interface objects, an interface builder with a simple yet powerful user interface, and a framework for building graphical editing applications. We have used the InterViews tools to build several substantial applications and have found the implementations of these applications to be relatively simple, highly functional, and acceptable in terms of performance.

## 3.1  Introduction

The growth of the personal computer and workstation markets during the 1980s catapulted "easy-to-use" to be one of the most important characteristics of a computer product. In competitive situations, perception that a software product is difficult to use is often worse than slow performance or a higher price. A customer could improve a product that is too slow with faster hardware, and could justify an expensive, easy-to-use product by lower training costs and higher productivity. However, a customer cannot easily improve or justify a product that is difficult to use.

For application developers, building an easy-to-use interface can be a significant hurdle in bringing a product to market in a timely manner. Systems known for being user-friendly do not necessarily provide good development tools. For example, the Apple Macintosh's user interface defines a standard of excellence against which others are compared, but the MacToolbox [Com85] provides only mediocre support for developing a Mac user interface.

The effort a developer must put into building a user interface takes away from other

*User Interface Software*, Edited by Bass and Dewan
© 1993 John Wiley & Sons Ltd

aspects of the application, such as new features, improved performance, or availability on new platforms. The consequence of this situation is that users have fewer, less powerful, and more expensive applications to choose from. If better user interface tools were available to developers, users would be able to choose from a wider variety of applications with greater power.

The InterViews research project has been exploring how to make user interfaces "easy-to-build" since late 1985. Our goal has been to reduce the difficulty and cost of developing applications that are easy-to-use. We do not presume to know what makes a good user interface; we simply try to support the construction of user interfaces that human factors experts and users have found to be easy-to-use.

Our approach in this project has been to implement both an experimental system and build several significant applications on top of it. Doing an implementation allows us to explore the precise specification of system primitives; building applications gives us a way to evaluate the power of the primitives in realistic situations. We also have made the implementation publicly available, which has provided broader feedback on the effectiveness of our ideas.

In this article, we discuss the features of InterViews that simplify the implementation of a user interface, and we describe our experience developing and using the system. We begin with some background terminology and relate our work to contemporary user interface tools. We then discuss the different levels of InterViews as it is used, and conclude with a view of the problems that we are currently exploring and how they may affect future tools.

## 3.2   Background

Just as an operating system historically has provided convenient support for terminal and file I/O, today programmers assume the system software supports the graphical user interface portion of an application. Figure 3.1 shows the different system components in a modern user environment.

In the same way that an operating system allows multiple applications to share processor, memory, and I/O devices, a *window system* allows multiple applications to share the display and input devices. The *window manager* provides a specific user interface for creating, moving, iconifying and otherwise manipulating windows on the screen. Because the window system and window manager do not directly affect the developer, we will not discuss them further here.

A toolkit represents an application programming interface (API) and run-time library. The toolkit provides the basic abstractions that are necessary to organize the graphical input and output of an application. These abstractions are often referred to as the toolkit *intrinsics*. The toolkit also provides a set of concrete components, such as buttons, menus, and scrollbars. These components are often referred to as *widgets*. An *interface builder* is a user interface for specifying the placement of toolkit widgets in a window.

In contrast to the loosely-structured, general-purpose functionality of a toolkit, a *framework* suggests a specific application organization. Frameworks provide high-level functionality that is particular to a domain or class of application. For example, Unidraw [VL90] is a framework we have built as part of the InterViews project. Unidraw supports graphical editing with features such as undo/redo, multiple graphical views, and direct-manipulation abstractions.

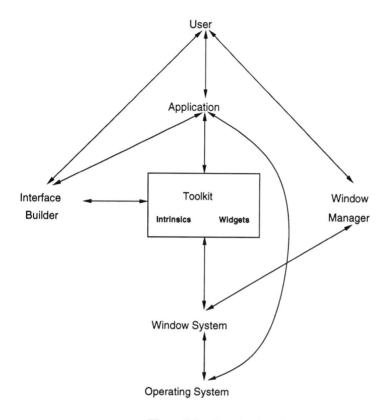

**Figure 3.1**   Organization of user environment

### 3.2.1   Separating interface and application

Most user interfaces tools support the separation of user interface and application code. This distinction is important in many aspects of design, allowing programmers to present different, independently customizable interfaces to the same data. It also permits different representations of the same data to be displayed simultaneously such that changes to the data made through one representation are immediately reflected in any others. For example, spreadsheet data might be viewable as either a table or a pie chart. One might even wish to view both the table and pie chart simultaneously, seeing changes to the table reflected immediately in the pie chart and vice versa.

Though the term User Interface Management System (UIMS) is not precisely defined, the focus of UIMSs has been on a complete separation of interface and application by specifying the user interface in a special-purpose language or other formalism such as a state transition diagram. A UI-specific language has the advantage that it can support higher levels of abstraction compared to general-purpose programming languages. A special-purpose language therefore may be better-suited for use by UI designers; however, experience [Mye88] has been that this approach limits the range of interfaces that can be built. A specification language also can be difficult to debug, optimize, and upgrade as user interface techniques evolve.

Toolkits enable separation of interface and application code at the level of individual components, but do not enforce the use of separation uniformly. One of the earliest toolkits to support separation is Smalltalk MVC [KP88], which divides components into a model (semantics), a view (presentation), and a controller (input handling). More recent toolkits, including InterViews and the Andrew Toolkit (ATK) [P⁺88], combine the view and controller into a single object that handles input and output. This consolidation reflects the tight coupling between input and output in direct-manipulation interfaces and reduces the communication overhead among components.

### 3.2.2   Using an object-oriented language

Modern toolkits, interface builders, and frameworks are all object-oriented. There are three reasons for the strong connection between user interfaces and objects:

- Users think naturally in terms of objects as the elements of a user interface.
- Objects provide a good abstraction mechanism, encapsulating state and operations, and inheritance makes extension easy.
- Polymorphism, the ability of different objects to provide distinct implementations for a common operation, matches the characteristics of a direct manipulation interface. Whether drawing, rotating, resizing, or relating objects, the user has a sense of performing a single operation for which specific objects may need to provide alternative implementations.

It is possible to implement an object-oriented toolkit using a language without direct support for objects. In this case, the toolkit provides an object model of its own. For example, the X Toolkit (Xt) [MA88], which provides the intrinsics for the Motif [Ope89] widgets, defines its own object representation in the C programming language. The disadvantage of this approach is that an embedded object model can be cumbersome to use. For example, subclassing in Xt requires writing a substantial amount of code to declare and initialize method dispatch tables. In contrast, C++, an object-oriented extension to C, provides this table management automatically.

On the other hand, GARNET [MZD89] uses a custom object system on top of Common Lisp and as a result is able to optimize performance and experiment with constraint mechanisms for user interfaces. Ultimately, the ability to embed an object model successfully depends on the extensibility of the host language (for example, GARNET would be much harder to build using C) and the level of expertise of the programmers who use the toolkit.

We wrote the initial version of InterViews in Modula-2, though we switched to C++ early in the project. Our experience has been that, compared to procedural implementation, user interfaces are significantly easier to develop and maintain when they are written in an object-oriented language. A major drawback of C++ is the lack of a simple interpreter that can be part of the run-time environment. This capability would allow greater flexibility in customizing and configuring the user interface of an application while it is running.

### 3.3   Toolkit features

The central goal of the InterViews toolkit is to simplify *composition*; that is, provide easy ways to construct new objects from existing ones. The key to being able to compose objects is to define common protocols by which different kinds of objects can communicate. To this end, we have produced a uniform model for user interface objects that supports lightweight as well as more complex objects, printing as well as screen output, and screen update for animation as well as user interaction. At the heart of this uniform model are two basic kinds of objects: a *glyph*, which is an object that can be drawn, and a *canvas*, which is a graphics state for drawing. Included as part of the graphics state is the output destination, which could be a window on the screen or a device for printing.

In the remainder of this section, we present an overview of features of the InterViews toolkit. We begin by discussing the philosophy behind glyphs, particularly as they compare to traditional, heavier-weight toolkit objects. We show how glyphs support dynamic extensibility through the use of several glyph instances in contrast to the static approach of defining a subclass. We then describe how InterViews supports printing and screen update. We next look at layout with InterViews and consider a document editor as an example. Finally, we discuss the issue of defining traditional applications, such as text or drawing editors, as objects within the toolkit.

### 3.3.1 Lightweight objects

Most user interface toolkits provide objects such as buttons and menus that let programmers build interfaces to application *commands*, but do not provide objects for building interfaces to application *data*. As a consequence, toolkits have tended to focus on the relatively small number (hundreds) of command-oriented widgets that an application creates. Supporting a user interface to application data, which may consist of many thousands of objects, requires a simpler, less expensive kind of object.

The InterViews base class for user interface objects, Glyph, is lightweight enough to represent text and graphics data and yet general enough to be the basis for more complex user interface objects. Examples of glyphs include characters, white space, rectangles, spheres, borders,buttons, menu items, scrollbars, and text editors. Though some of these objects provide additional operations beyond the Glyph base class, they all conform to the base class behavior.

#### 3.3.1.1 Glyph operations

```
class Glyph {
public:
  virtual void request(Requisition*);
  virtual void draw(Canvas*, Allocation*);
  virtual void pick(Canvas*, Allocation*, long depth, Hit*);
};
```

**Figure 3.2** Partial definition of the Glyph interface

The Glyph class operations define the geometry, appearance, and structure of a graphical object. Figure 3.2 shows the C++ definition of the three fundamental operations. The request operation returns a glyph's preference for screen space, called a *requisition*. Glyphs request enough space to display themselves in a preferred size, and they specify their willingness to stretch or shrink if the preferred size cannot be allocated. Composite glyphs calculate their own request from the requests of their components.

The draw operation tells a glyph to display itself at a given position, specified by an *allocation*. Composite glyphs apportion their allocation among their components according to the components' requests. The pick operation queries whether an object's output intersects a point or region. The Hit parameter is used to record the list of intersected objects.

### 3.3.1.2   Examples of glyphs

To illustrate the versatility of glyphs, we consider three simple examples in more detail: a text label, a solid background, and a push button. A label glyph would define its requisition to be a fixed size based on the text font and characters. The label's draw operation would render the text at the given allocation, and the pick operation would add the label to the hit list if the pick region intersected the label's bounding box.

A background is a glyph that draws a solid filled rectangle behind another glyph, called the background's *body*. Background's request operation would simply call request on its body, as the background itself has no predefined shape. The Background draw operation would render a filled rectangle first and then call draw on the body. The pick operation would call pick on the body and add the background object if the rectangle area intersected the pick region.

A push button glyph would define some flexibility in the X dimension of its requisition. By default, the button would contain some white space around the button's label (which in general would be another glyph). If the button needed to be smaller, the white space could be eliminated or reduced. If the button needed to be larger, the white space could grow equally on both sides of the label. The button's draw operation would call draw on its label, adding an offset to the allocation to account for the white space, and then draw the button's frame. The pick operation would call pick on the label and also add the button if the white space or frame intersected the pick region.

### 3.3.1.3   Passing versus storing state

The key to making glyphs lightweight is passing state through parameters instead of requiring the objects to store the state. In particular, unlike systems where objects are told to redraw themselves, a glyph's draw operation is passed the appropriate graphics context and position information. Perhaps the most important consequence of this state-less approach is that a glyph may appear in more than one place on the screen at the same time and thus be shared instead of being replicated.

For an application, lightweight objects offer the power of objects at a very fine granularity. For example, the InterViews document editor, Doc [CL92], uses a glyph to represent each character visible on a formatted page. Doing so simplifies the formatting and redisplay portions of the editor, especially in the presence of embedded figures. Because of the ability to share glyphs and the general performance characteristics of C++, Doc's memory usage and interactive performance are more than adequate.

Doc also relies on the transparency of glyphs; that is, that several glyphs can share the same screen area. The character glyphs do not redraw the background nor are they involved in highlighting a selection. Instead, Doc uses a single white background glyph behind the characters. To denote a selection, Doc draws a solid gray area between the background and the text (or uses xor in front of the text in the case of a single plane display).

The ability of glyphs to be lightweight is not a requirement; glyphs may be heavyweight. The glyph interface does not preclude, for example, a more complex document object that references explicit blocks of text instead of using the glyph-per-character approach of Doc. The uniform applicability of glyphs lets programmers choose the appropriate level of granularity for an implementation and evolve that level over time.

### 3.3.2   Dynamic extensibility

In addition to allowing the use of objects at a fine level of granularity, the fact that glyphs are cheap makes it possible to use a collection of instances instead of defining a new class. For example, InterViews defines the appearance and input behavior of a button as two distinct glyphs. Thus, a programmer can create a button with a new look, such as a raster image, without creating a new subclass (because classes already exist for image output and button input). Toolkits based on heavyweight objects, such as Motif, effectively restrict the programmer to subclassing because the cost of using a group of objects is prohibitive.

The general InterViews mechanism for instancing is a Glyph subclass called MonoGlyph, which is a glyph that contains a single glyph. A monoglyph normally is *structurally invisible*, meaning that operations that affect composite glyphs, such as append and remove, are passed on directly to the interior glyph. For example, a shadow is a monoglyph that draws a drop shadow under another glyph. A programmer can put a shadow around a composite glyph without affecting operations on the composite. Adding a child to the shadow will actually add it to the composite.

We use monoglyphs for many purposes: to perform input handling or filtering, to decorate with shadows, borders, or bevels, to perform layout alignment such as centering, and to adjust a glyph's desired size (making a stretchable glyph become rigid, for example). We also use a special monoglyph for debugging that displays parameter values for request and draw operations as they occur.

Monoglyph provides a general way to alter the behavior of a glyph without the complexity of subclassing. The behavior adjustments can also be dynamic–a monoglyph can be added or removed around another glyph at runtime. The key to making the use of monoglyphs affordable is the lightweight nature of glyphs.

### 3.3.3   Printing

Despite the ideal of a "paper-less" office, most modern applications require the ability to generate hardcopy output. Furthermore, applications want to generate the same output to a printer as to the screen without writing additional code. This requirement is actually a special case of *resolution-independence,* which also lets an application look the same on two screens with different numbers of dots-per-inch.

InterViews supports resolution-independence in two ways. First, we define coordinates as floating-point values in units of printer's points. We originally used scalable integer coordinates, but found floating point to be much more intuitive. Floating point operations are also now fast enough on current hardware.

The second way InterViews supports resolution-independence is through the Canvas class, which defines a single rendering interface with drawing operations that resemble the PostScript stencil-paint operations. The base class implements the drawing operations on top of the X Window System rendering primitives and a subclass emits PostScript text to a file. Some of the issues involved in implementing resolution- independence are described in more detail in [Lin92].

### 3.3.4   Screen update

InterViews performs screen update based on *damage* to a portion of a window. An object does not update a window directly, instead it damages the region of the window where it was drawn. To refresh the screen, all the objects associated with the window are drawn with clipping set to the damage area. An object may check to see if its output might intersect with the clip region; if not then the object need not draw itself or its children. Screen refresh occurs either if a window has been damaged and no further input events are pending or when explicitly requested by the application.

Damaged-based update has three desirable effects. First, it allows objects to share the same area of a window. For example, a label can appear on top of an image. A direct update approach could not share window area unless every object knew what objects were on top of it. In the example with the label on top of the image, the image could not be updated without also redrawing the label.

The second effect is that output may be double-buffered to give the user a smoother, less flashy appearance. Although traditionally associated with animation, double-buffering also can improve the appearance of common interactive techniques such as scrolling, text selection, and drag-and-drop.

The third effect of damage-based update is the ability of objects to determine what granularity of update is most efficient. Objects that are cheap to draw usually do not check damage; objects that are expensive to draw usually do. For example, Doc updates a document interactively as the user enters keystrokes. Doc redraws the entire line where a character is entered because it is faster to draw the characters in the line than to compute precisely which characters need to be drawn in the line (complicated by the continual reformatting of the entire paragraph). Doc does not redraw the entire page, however, as that would affect performance significantly.

Our experience with damage-based update has been very positive. The approach is simple, straightforward to implement, flexible enough to handle the needs of different kinds of objects, and performs well.

### 3.3.5   Document-quality layout

A major emphasis of InterViews has been on simplifying the specification and implementation of the physical layout of a user interface. Although an interactive builder gives immediate feedback on layout, the feedback does not by itself ease the specification of a flexible layout. Our approach has been to use ideas from document processing, particularly the TeX model of "boxes and glue."[[Knu84], [KP80]] Document processing systems such as TeX have a relatively simple, powerful, and efficient model that is straightforward to implement.

A box tiles its components in one dimension and aligns their origins in the other dimension. For example, a horizontal box arranges its components left-to-right, aligning their vertical origins. If a box's allocation is smaller than the natural sizes of its components, then the box will shrink the components to fit. Similarly, if the box's allocation is larger than expected, it will stretch its components.

Typically, the visible components in a box are rigid. Glue objects represent flexible white space that separates the other objects in the box. For example, a line of text would be represented as a horizontal box of characters, with glue between the words.

InterViews provides a class called LayoutKit for creating different kinds of box and glue

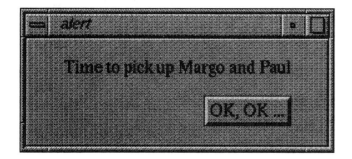

```
Glyph* vspace = layout.vglue(18.0, fil, 16.0);    // natural, stretch, shrink
Glyph* hspace = layout.hglue(36.0, fil, 34.0);
Glyph* dialog = layout.vbox(
  vspace,
  layout.hbox(
    hspace,
    layout.vbox(
      make_message(layout.vbox(), widgets, layout),
      vspace,
      layout.lmaring(widgets.push_button("OK, OK ...",widgets.quit())), 0.0, fil´
    ),
    hspace
  ),
  vspace
);
```

**Figure 3.3**   Example dialog box and code to create it

glyphs. Figure 3.3 shows a simple dialog box and a portion of the code to construct it. The variable "layout" refers to the LayoutKit object, and the variable "widgets" refers to the kit object that creates widgets such as buttons, scrollbars, and menus. The "make_message" function reads lines from a file and puts them in a vertical box.

The InterViews document editor, Doc, uses the layout objects in conjunction with higher-level *composition* glyphs provided by the library. Compositions encapsulate much of the complexity of formatting and ensuring that changes to the items are correctly reflected on the display. As in the TeX model, Doc uses *discretionary* objects to represent possible places for formatting breaks.

Doc uses a left-to-right composition to break text into lines. The composition creates horizontal boxes that contain the glyphs in each line; then it inserts the boxes into a vertical composition that determines the column breaks. Doc passes a compositor object to the composition to specify the computation of breaks. A compositor is not a glyph; it simply decides how to perform breaks based on sizes and penalties. The InterViews library provides a simple compositor that does filling as well as a compositor that implements the TeX line-breaking algorithm.

At roughly 12,000 lines of code, Doc demonstrates how the power of the InterViews composition mechanisms can be applied to a realistic application. Doc supports character styling, macro expansion, floating figures, automatic numbering, cross-referencing, embedded graphics, and simple tables. Doc does not currently support undo, outline mode, table of contents, or index generation. Figure 3.4 shows a screen dump of Doc in use.

### 3.3.6   Application embedding

Glyphs define the mechanism for *physical* composition, but do not directly support the problems of *logical* composition. Whereas the issues of physical composition involve rendering, geometry management, and screen update, the issues of logical composition include managing keyboard focus, propagating attributes such as color and font, and transcribing objects to and from an external format. The composition of logical components is often referred to as "object embedding" because the components are typically large, like miniature applications, and can be nested within one another without prior knowledge about the kind of object that is nested. For example, consider a text object and a drawing object that both support embedding. Text may appear inside the drawing and a drawing may appear inside the text, but neither the text nor the drawing implementation are aware of each other's existence.

InterViews does not currently provide direct support for object embedding, though applications such as Doc implement a limited form of embedding on top of the toolkit. We are currently adding support for embedding based on the mechanisms provided by the Andrew Toolkit.

We will extend InterViews by providing a Glyph subclass that supports embedding. We cannot add embedding support directly to the base Glyph class; that would interfere with the needs of physical composition. To see why the mechanisms should be distinct, consider the management of style attributes in Doc. The effect of a user selecting a sequence of characters and changing the font is independent of whether the characters appear on the same line or not. Thus, the organization of attributes must be separate from the physical organization of the glyphs.

Given that embedding should be handled separately, one might consider an instance rather than subclass relationship with glyphs. That is, the embedded object base class would not be a subclass of Glyph, but could contain a reference to a glyph to perform output. The problem with this approach is that logical components also must be embedded physically, must draw when refreshing the screen, and should be printable. Separating the two classes would result in two ways to organize rendering and geometry management, which would be confusing and inefficient to use. We conclude that the best approach is to define a Glyph subclass to support embedding.

**Figure 3.4**  Doc screen dump

## 3.4  Builder issues

Regardless of the simplicity and power provided by a toolkit, an interface builder always offers a more productive method to specify certain aspects of a user interface. Builders do not completely eliminate the need to write code, but they can generate the code associated with constructing and connecting user interface objects. NextStep [Web89] is an example of how a builder can significantly improve productivity.

### 3.4.1   Ibuild features

The InterViews interface builder, Ibuild [VT91] provides a direct manipulation user interface similar to what one would expect from a WYSIWYG drawing editor. The advantage of the drawing editor metaphor is a simple, familiar interface that is very flexible for editing. Ibuild's basic features allow one to create, delete, copy, and move objects as in a drawing editor, though the primitives are objects such as buttons and menus instead of rectangles and polygons.

The mechanism for creating a composite is the same as grouping in a drawing editor, except the user selects a kind of group that controls the type of composite that is created. As in a drawing editor, selection order determines the order of objects in the composite. The user can also zoom and pan the objects.

Ibuild provides three features specific to the builder domain. The first is a "relate" tool that allows the user to connect two objects interactively. The semantics of a connection depend on the objects participating, but Ibuild often can eliminate the need to specify callback functions for operations such as scrolling. An interesting characteristic of user interface objects, at least common widgets such as buttons, menus, and scrollbars, is that they normally export only a single kind of connection. Thus, there is no need to label explicit input and output "ports"; the user can simply click on the first object and then the second.

The second builder-specific feature is the "narrow" tool that allows the user to manipulate objects in a group without ungrouping them. The user selects the narrow tool, then clicks on an object. Ibuild displays a popup menu showing all the types in the hierarchy from the selected leaf up to the root. After the user picks the desired level in the hierarchy, Ibuild restricts the current view to that level. This feature, for example, allows one to modify the components of a horizontal box nested inside a vertical box without affecting the organization of the vertical box. In a typical drawing editor, one would need to ungroup both boxes to modify the contents of the inner one and then re-combine them.

The third build-specific feature is the "examine" tool that allows the user to query and update the attributes of an object. The examine user interface is the same as for narrowing; the user can choose any object in the hierarchy. The available attributes depend on the type of object, but typically include precise parameters (such as size) and naming (for customization and callbacks).

### 3.4.2   Ibuild implementation

We implemented Ibuild at the same time as the development of glyphs. Consequently, Ibuild supports an earlier, more heavyweight InterViews base class called Interactor [LVC89]. Because the implementation of Interactor requires an X subwindow, we considered an implementation of Ibuild using "live" interactors to be too difficult to undertake. For example, we could not easily zoom the interactors. Ibuild therefore *simulates* a collection of InterViews objects, constructing imitation objects instead of interactors.

Simulation has a number of disadvantages; the most important being that to let the user run an interface Ibuild must compile and link an application instead of simply directing input to live objects. The major advantage is that we were not constrained by the toolkit in the design of the builder user interface.

This lack of constraints is important. Our experience using Ibuild has convinced us that flexibility is very important and that a drawing editor interface is a good interface upon which to build. It is unlikely we would have designed such a user interface starting only from the

InterViews toolkit abstractions. We conclude that, like any other application, the design of a builder should be guided more by principles of good user interfaces than by specific features of the underlying toolkit. In the future, using glyphs will enable Ibuild to preserve the current user interface while supporting live objects.

## 3.5 Graphical-editing frameworks

Unidraw is a class library for building graphical editors in domains such as technical and artistic drawing, music composition, and circuit design. Unidraw reduces the time required to produce an editor by providing functionality characteristic of graphical editors. Unidraw does not offer toolkit-level features, but is a level above a toolkit.

Unidraw defines four kinds of objects: *components* encapsulate the appearance and semantics of a domain, *tools* support direct manipulation of components, *commands* define operations on components and other objects, and *external representations* define the mapping between components and the file format generated by the editor. Unidraw provides base classes for component, command, tool, and external representation objects. Unidraw also supports multiple views, graphical connectivity, dataflow between components, and undo/redo.

### 3.5.1 Components

A component defines the appearance and behavior of a domain-specific object. A component's behavior has three aspects: (1) how it responds to commands and tools, (2) its connectivity, and (3) how it communicates with other components. Unidraw partitions every component into two distinct objects, called the *subject* and the *view*. The component subject maintains information that characterizes the components. In the case of a logic gate, for example, the subject would contain information about what is connected to the gate and its current input values. The component view presents the information that is in a component subject. More than one view may be attached to the same subject.

### 3.5.2 Commands

Commands define operations on components and other objects. Commands are similar to messages in traditional object-oriented systems, except they are stateful and can be executed as well as interpreted by objects. Commands also can be reverse-executed, allowing rollback to a previous state. Some commands may be directly accessible to the user as menu operations, while others are only used by the editor internally. In general, any undoable operation should be carried out by a command.

### 3.5.3 Tools

Unidraw-based editors use tool objects to allow the user to manipulate components directly. Tools use animation and other visual effects for immediate feedback to reinforce the perception of dealing with real objects. Examples include tools for selecting components for subsequent editing, for applying coordinate transformations such as translation and rotation, and for connecting components.

### 3.5.4    External representations

Each component can define one or more external representations of itself. For example, a transistor component can define a netlist representation for circuit simulation. An external representation is simply a non-graphical view of the component subject.

### 3.5.5    Experience with Unidraw

We have built three graphical editors with Unidraw: a drawing editor, the InterViews interface builder, and a simple schematic capture system. Of these, the drawing editor is the most interesting because we also had implemented a drawing editor directly on top of the InterViews toolkit. Whereas this original version of the drawing editor was about 17,000 lines of C++, the Unidraw version is about 6,000 lines, has comparable performance, and offers more functionality (particularly, the support for multiple views).

## 3.6    Conclusions

The InterViews project has investigated a number of the problems associated with building easy-to-use software. We have designed and implemented an experimental system that includes a general-purpose toolkit, a builder, and a graphical editing framework. The toolkit provides a uniform graphical object model that supports lightweight objects, printing, damage-based screen update, dynamic behavior modification, and sophisticated layout.

The InterViews builder adopts the flexibility of a drawing editor, letting the user create and manipulate user interface objects in the same manner as arbitrary geometric objects. The graphical editing framework offers drawing editor functionality to any application in the form of a class library.

The InterViews drawing and document editors, two substantial applications, demonstrate the practical power of the underlying library and framework. Both applications are moderate in size, yet offer a significant amount of functionality with acceptable performance.

In the future, we plan to pursue additional aspects of building user interface software. Multimedia is becoming an increasingly important part of user interfaces; we would like to apply layout techniques from document processing to simplify the construction of time-based documents containing audio, video, and animation. Of more general concern is support for implicit and explicit concurrency in a user interface. Implicit concurrency occurs when the user expects asynchronous events such as screen refresh to be handled even if an application is performing a computation. Explicit concurrency is part of the application, such as monitoring system load on several machines at once.

## 3.7    Acknowledgements

Paul Calder designed and implemented much of the basic glyph architecture and the document editor. John Vlissides designed and implemented Unidraw and the drawing editor. Steve Tang implemented Ibuild. The work at Stanford was supported in part by Fujitsu America, Inc., by a gift from Digital Equipment Corporation, and by a grant from the Charles Lee Powell Foundation. My thanks to the referees for their help improving this article.

# References

[CL92]     P. Calder and M. Linton. The object–oriented implementation of a document editor. In *OOPSLA '92*, Vancouver, British Columbia, October 1992.

[Com85]    Apple Computer. *Inside Macintosh, Volume I*. Addison-Wesley, Reading, Massachusetts, 1985.

[Knu84]    D. Knuth. *The TeX Book*. Addison-Wesley, Reading, Massachusetts, 1984.

[KP80]     D. Knuth and M. Plass. Breaking paragraphs into lines. Technical Report Technical Report STAN–CS–80–828, Stanford University, November 1980.

[KP88]     G. Krasner and S. Pope. A cookbook for using the model-view-controller user interface paradigm in smalltalk-80. *Journal of Object-Oriented Programming*, 1(3):26–49, August/September 1988.

[Lin92]    M. Linton. Implementing resolution independence on top of the x window system. In *Proceedings of the Sixth X Technical Conference*, Boston, Massachusetts, January 1992.

[LVC89]    M. Linton, J. Vlissides, and P. Calder. Composing user interfaces with interviews. *Computer*, 22(2):8–22, February 1989.

[MA88]     J. McCormack and P. Asente. An overview of the x toolkit. In *Proceedings of the ACM SIGGRAPH Symposium on User Interface Software*, pages 45–55, Banff, Canada, October 1988.

[Mye88]    B. Myers. Tools for creating user interfaces: An introduction and survey. Technical Report Technical Report CMU–CS–88–107, Carnegie Mellon University, January 1988.

[MZD89]    B. Myers, B. Vander Zanden, and R. Dannenberg. Creating graphical interactive application objects by demonstration. In *Proceedings of the ACM SIGGRAPH Symposium on User Interface Software and Technology*, pages 95–104, Williamsburg, Virginia, November 1989.

[Ope89]    Open Software Foundation, 11 Cambridge Center, Cambridge, Massachusetts. *OSF/Motif Programmer's Reference, Revison 1.0*, 1989.

[P⁺88]     A. Palay et al. The andrew toolkit: An overview. In *Proceedings of the 1988 Winter USENIX Technical Conference*, pages 9–12, Dallas, Texas, February 1988.

[VL90]     J. Vlissides and M. Linton. Unidraw: A framework for building domain-specific graphical editors. *ACM Transactions of Information Systems*, 8(3):237–268, July 1990.

[VT91]     J. Vlissides and S. Tang. Ibuild: A unidraw-based user interface builder. In *Proceedings ACM SIGGRAPH Symposium on User Interface Software and Technology*, Hilton Head, South Carolina, November 1991.

[Web89]    B. Webster. *The NeXT Book*. Addison-Wesley, Reading, Massachusetts, 1989.

# 4

# A Multi-threaded Higher-order User Interface Toolkit

EMDEN R. GANSNER and JOHN H. REPPY

*AT&T Bell Laboratories*

## ABSTRACT

This article describes eXene, a user interface toolkit implemented in a concurrent extension of Standard ML. The design and use of eXene is inextricably woven with the presence of multiple threads and a high-level language. These features replace the object-oriented design of most toolkits, and provide a better basis for dealing with the complexities of user interfaces, especially concerning such aspects as type safety, extensibility, component reuse and the balance between the user interface and other parts of the program.

## 4.1 INTRODUCTION

In two previous papers [Rep86, Gan92], we have advocated an approach to the design of a foundation for graphical user interfaces and interactive applications. In our view, such a foundation includes support for concurrency, strong static typing, higher-order programming (i.e., functions as values), support for modular program construction, and automatic memory management. This article describes a multi-threaded X window system toolkit, called eXene, built on such a foundation.

The base for eXene is Concurrent ML (CML) [Rep91a], a concurrent extension of Standard ML (SML) [Mil90]. We employ CML as more than just the implementation language for eXene: it provides the semantic framework for the toolkit and permeates its design and use. This is particularly true concerning three aspects of eXene: concurrency, higher-level programming and memory management. Taken together, these aspects induce greater simplicity and a high degree of modularity in applications constructed using eXene.

The most significant characteristic of eXene is the fundamental role that concurrency plays in its design and implementation. Concurrency is critical in allowing the programmer to cleanly

*User Interface Software*, Edited by Bass and Dewan
© 1993 John Wiley & Sons Ltd

structure an application and its interface to handle the asynchrony and multiple contexts of interactive use. One need only consider a sample of common programming scenarios:

- A computationally intensive program that provides periodical updates to a graphical display of its status. In addition to displaying new information, the user interface must also handle external asynchronous events such as being resized by the user.
- A program for editing and analyzing multiple views of graphs, which must allow editing on one view while applying a potentially expensive layout algorithm to another.
- A language-based editor that uses incremental attribute evaluation to give the user immediate feedback about static semantic errors [Reps84]. Since a user's editing operation can result in an arbitrarily large number of attribute re-evaluations, we must structure the evaluator so that those attributes affecting the user's view will be evaluated first and those remaining will be evaluated in the background.

The majority of user interface toolkits are based on sequential languages and must emulate concurrency using event loops. While this allows features such as multiple views to be supported, it also biases the architecture of the application towards the user interface. Because the application is driven by the user interface, the event loop must be built to manage system events as well as graphics events, and computationally intensive code must be written in such a way as to divide up the work into small pieces that can be interleaved between the handling of external events. In effect, the event loop is a poor man's concurrency.

In eXene, the system architecture is not hobbled by this user interface bias. Graphical components are implemented as independent threads, separate from each other and the application code. This increases the modularity of the components and allows them and the application to be implemented more naturally, not as finite state machines. Obviously, the interleaving of computation happens automatically. This makes it simple to import code without worrying whether its execution will cripple the user interface.

The high-level language features of CML provide many of the mechanisms for creating and tailoring graphical components in eXene. Higher-order functions, parametric polymorphism, abstract event values and parameterized modules are powerful tools for building reusable, modular components. EXene promotes an applicative style programming. This increases the clarity and reliability of the code, and is especially important in a concurrent system where the possibility of interference arises. We also note that programming using eXene is type safe. Because of the complexity of building user interfaces, the safety afforded by strong static typing is too valuable to be thrown away. Most of the advantages touted for weakly or dynamically typed languages in building user interfaces are provided by the features such as polymorphism and higher-order functions mentioned above.

In a typical user interface, graphical components and system resources are heavily distributed and shared, making it difficult to determine when memory should be freed and resources released. EXene provides garbage collection and object finalization[1] to free the programmer from these decisions. As components can freely refer to other components without worrying about them disappearing, components become simpler and more modular.

It is possible to address the problems solved by eXene, or provide similar features, using conventional languages, libraries and toolkits. This, however, typically involves making the application code more complex, bending or breaking the type system, relying on programmer

---

[1] In *object finalization*, a value can be associated with a finalization function to be called on the value before the value's memory is freed. With this mechanism, we can extend the model of automatic storage collection to system objects such as bitmaps, fonts, etc.

discipline, or ignoring the problem. The thrust of the work on eXene is that, by building a user interface toolkit on top of a concurrent, high-level foundation, one achieves a system that is simpler, safer, more uniform, and more modular.

### 4.1.1 Related Work

CML and eXene are actually second generation systems emerging from these ideas. They follow from our earlier work with the Pegasus system [Rep86, Nor87, Rep88, Gan92], which used the PML language for its foundation. The work most closely related to Pegasus and eXene in spirit is Newsqueak [Pik89b, Pik89a] and Montage [Haa90]. EXene differs in being a more fully developed system, with a higher-level model of concurrency (CML events values), a richer graphics model, more support for programming at the component level, and, in comparison with Newsqueak, a richer base language. The NeWS window system [Gos89] also relies on concurrency in its design. NeWS requires that the user interface code be split between the client (typically C code), and the display server (PostScript code). The PostScript code running on the server can be multi-threaded. While this allows concurrency in interactive applications, exploiting it increases the complexity of the client-server interaction.

User interface design seems to be one area where an "object-oriented" approach has a clear utility. As a result, most graphics toolkits use an object-oriented approach. Examples include InterViews [Lin89], Xt [Nye90b], NeWS, Iris [Gan88], Trestle [Man91] and Garnet [Mye90]. EXene eschews an explicit object-oriented approach for several reasons. Structural polymorphism, first-class function values and a sophisticated module system provide similar interface inheritance. Most importantly, our experience, and that of others [Pik89a, Haa90], suggests that concurrency and delegation provide many of the same advantages as object-oriented programming.[2] Threads provide localization of state and clean well-defined interfaces. Delegation and wrapper functions provide implementation inheritance.

In general, some form of concurrency is available or could be added to any of these toolkits. Treating concurrency as an afterthought, however, prevents possibilities for simplification and component sharing.[3] We feel that concurrency should be a design principle, and be exploited at all levels of an interactive system.

### 4.1.2 Summary of the Paper

In the next section, we briefly describe the important features of CML. This is followed by Sections 4.3–4.5, which respectively describe drawing, user interaction and widgets in eXene. Section 4.6 presents some examples of eXene applications. We conclude with some future directions. Throughout the article, we assume that the reader has some familiarity with the X window system and its terminology as can be found, for example, in [Sch92]. Although we use a small amount of SML and CML notation, knowledge of these languages is not necessary in understanding the important concepts in the paper.

---

[2] This should not come as a surprise, since *delegation* was originally a concept of concurrent *actor* systems.

[3] This is also true for garbage collection.

## 4.2   AN OVERVIEW OF CML

Both the implementation and the user's view of eXene rely heavily on the concurrency model provided by CML.[4] CML is based on the sequential language SML [Mil90] and inherits the useful features of SML: functions as first-class values, strong static typing, polymorphism, datatypes and pattern matching, lexical scoping, exception handling and a state-of-the-art module facility. An introduction to SML can be found in [Pau91] or [Har86]. The sequential performance of CML benefits from the quality of the SML/NJ compiler [App87]. In addition CML has the following properties:

- CML provides a high-level model of concurrency with dynamic creation of threads and typed channels, and *rendezvous* communication. This distributed-memory model fits well with the mostly applicative style of SML.
- CML is a higher-order concurrent language. Just as SML supports functions as first-class values, CML supports synchronous operations as first-class values [Rep88, Rep91a, Rep92]. These values, called *events*, provide the tools for building new synchronization abstractions. This is the most significant characteristic of CML.
- CML provides integrated I/O support. Potentially blocking I/O operations, such as reading from an input stream, are full-fledged synchronous operations. Low-level support is also provided, from which distributed communication abstractions can be constructed.
- CML provides automatic reclamation of threads and channels, once they become inaccessible. This permits a technique of speculative communication, which is not possible in other threads packages.
- CML uses preemptive scheduling. To guarantee interactive responsiveness, a single thread cannot be allowed to monopolize the processor. Preemption insures that a context switch will occur at regular intervals, which allows "off-the-shelf" code to be incorporated in a concurrent thread without destroying interactive responsiveness.
- CML is efficient. Thread creation, thread switching and message passing are very efficient (benchmarks results are reported in [Rep92]). Experience with eXene has shown that CML is a viable language for implementing interactive systems.
- CML is portable. It is written in SML and runs on essentially every system supported by SML/NJ (currently seven different architectures and many different operating systems).
- CML has a formal foundation. Following the tradition of SML [Mil90, Mil91], a formal semantics has been developed for the concurrency primitives of CML (see [Rep91b] or [Rep92]).

## 4.3   BASIC EXENE FEATURES

Before we describe the more radical features of eXene, a discussion of some of the basic features is in order. These features for the most part follow the Xlib model, but we have attempted to provide an interface that is both cleaner, and more in keeping with the SML programming style. For example, we use immutable objects where possible (such as immutable *tiles* for specifying textures, instead of pixmaps), and we perform more client-side error checking, instead of relying on the X server for error checking.

---

[4] Conversely, the development of CML was strongly motivated by the desire to be able to support user interface systems comparable to eXene.

Following the X model, eXene supports the notions of a *display* (a connection to a server), a *screen* (a monitor driven by the server), and a *window* on a screen. An application might have multiple displays (e.g., a multi-player game), multiple screens for a given display, and multiple windows per screen. In Xlib, programmers must specify the display as an argument to most operations; in eXene, we avoid this by incorporating the display in the representation of most graphical objects (e.g., screens and windows).

Internally, eXene uses a small collection of threads to implement each display connection. These threads manage buffering and sequencing of communications with the X server. The interface to these threads is a collection of CML channels that are bundled into an abstract display value. A similar scheme is used for screens. Since these abstract values encapsulate both the state and thread of control, supporting multiple displays and screens in an application is trivial.[5]

EXene uses a cleaner, and slightly stripped-down, version of the X graphics model [Sch92]. In X, drawing operations are performed with respect to a *graphics context*, which is a server-side object that specifies the color, font, texture, etc., of the drawing operation. There are a number of drawbacks to the way that graphics contexts are supported: they are fairly heavy-weight, requiring communication with the server to create and update; the number of contexts supported by the server may be limited (e.g., if the server is an X terminal); and they are created with respect to a particular visual, and can only be used with that visual. Furthermore, the Xlib interface to graphics contexts is not uniform: the clipping mask is part of the context, but is specified independently of the other attributes.[6] Another wart is that fonts are specified both as part of the graphics context, and as an argument to the `XDrawText` operation. Not only does `XDrawText` take fonts in its argument list, it actually updates the graphics context that it uses, which makes sharing of graphics contexts more difficult. In addition to these problems, multi-threaded toolkits face the additional problem that graphics contexts are shared mutable objects, thus some form of concurrency control is required.

In eXene, we address these problems by providing a higher-level, but lighter-weight, client-side value, called a *pen*, for specifying drawing attributes. Pens provide a cleaner, more uniform interface to specifying the attributes of a drawing operation: they are immutable, they are independent of any visual, and they collect together all the drawing attributes uniformly. Pens include the clipping region, but not fonts, which are specified as an argument to the text drawing operations. Internally, concurrency control is provided by graphics-context servers (one per visual), which map pens to server-side graphics contexts. Since pens are lightweight, immutable and independent of any visual, the user is freed from having to manage graphics contexts to reduce server memory usage: the toolkit does it for her. The use of a behind-the-scenes manager allows better modularity in the application code. While Xt also provides management of graphics contexts to promote sharing, its mechanism is weaker: it only supports the read-only use of shared graphics contexts, and does not provide security against interference.

To further improve modularity, eXene supports automatic reclamation of server objects such as fonts, colors, and pixmaps. This is implemented by a finalization scheme built on top of SML/NJ's *weak pointer* mechanism. When the client-side version of the object becomes

---

[5] This encapsulation property appears elsewhere in eXene (cf., Section 4.5), and can be exploited to easily support multiple views in an application.

[6] This is because the arguments to the graphics context operations are integers, while a clipping region is represented as a list of rectangles.

garbage, a finalization procedure is invoked, which sends a request to deallocate the server-side object. This frees the user from explicit management of these resources.

The use of internal servers to multiplex server-side resources is exploited repeatedly in eXene. Another example arises in the handling of fonts. There is a per-display font server that maintains a table of open fonts, and checks requests for new fonts against the table. This reduces the amount of client-server traffic (e.g., if ten independent button widgets all attempt to open the same font). Although not part of Xlib, a similar optimization is frequently used in toolkits built on the library.

Another place in which eXene provides a higher-level model is in the support for color.[7] Colors are specified abstractly using color names or RGB values (we plan to extend this to the X11R5 device independent color spaces [Sch92]). Color specifications are mapped to abstract colors by a color server (one per screen), again reducing client-server traffic and improving modularity. Although inappropriate for color-intensive applications,[8] this model, used with finalization, is adequate for most uses of color.

EXene provides an abstract *drawable* type that gives a common interface to windows and off-screen pixmaps. Internally, a drawable is represented as a connection to a *draw-master* server that buffers drawing operations and handles the interaction with the graphics-context server. This representation allows filters to be interposed that modify the drawable's behavior (e.g., coordinate translations).

The client-server communication in X is asynchronous, and this often shows in the programming model. Ideally, drawing operations should not require exposing the asynchrony of the protocol, but there are a few places where this breaks down. In eXene, we have attempted to hide this asynchrony wherever possible, and provide a higher-level interface in those cases where, for performance reasons, the asynchrony must be exposed.

Because it requires a system call to send a message to the X server, Xlib buffers client requests so that the system call overhead is reduced. One of the most common mistakes made by the neophyte Xlib programmer is failing to flush the buffer after a sequence of drawing operations; without this, the graphics never appear on the screen. In a program structured around a central event loop (or one using the built-in event loop provided by many toolkits), this is not as big of a problem, since the output buffer is flushed prior to reading the next X event. As we noted in Section 4.1, however, structuring programs around a central event loop is not always desirable. Our approach in eXene is to have the output-buffer thread periodically flush itself out to the wire. This removes the need for the user to explicitly flush the buffer, which leads to better modularity. Unfortunately, this periodic buffer flushing does not provide fast enough turn around when real-time feedback is required (e.g., when using the mouse to adjust a scrollbar). To handle this problem, we provide a function for creating a *feedback* drawable from a drawable. The feedback drawable uses the same drawing surface, but is unbuffered for immediate visual feedback. A better solution may be to tie the mouse stream and drawable together in these situations, such that the output buffer is flushed whenever the client requests input.[9]

Another feature of the X protocol that often bites users is a race condition between the client's first drawing operation and when the server actually maps the window [Gaj90]. To

---

[7] We currently only provide access to the default read-only colormap of a screen.

[8] Since we do not expose the notion of *pixels*, applications are prevented from exploiting color-plane tricks, which may not be a bad thing.

[9] This was suggested by one of the referees.

avoid this race, an application must wait for the first exposure event[10] on the window before attempting to draw graphics. In eXene, we hide this required synchronization internally.

A third place in which the user is exposed to the asynchrony of the protocol in graphics operations is the interface to the `CopyArea` operation. When `CopyArea` is used to copy a rectangle of pixels from an on-screen window to some destination (e.g., when scrolling), it is possible that a portion of the source rectangle will be unavailable (i.e., because it is obscured by another window). In this case, the corresponding portion of the destination rectangle will have to be repainted. Conceptually, this can be viewed as a client request followed by a server reply, but if implemented this way, the round-trip delays cause noticeable screen flicker. What is needed is an asynchronous remote procedure call (RPC), sometimes called a *promise* [Lis88]. Providing an asynchronous RPC interface to the `CopyArea` operation is not possible in a language like C, so this is implemented by using X events to deliver the reply. The client receives either a `GraphicsExposure` event or a `NoExpose` event as an acknowledgment of a `CopyArea` operation. In eXene, we exploit the first-class synchronous operations provided by CML to provide a true asynchronous RPC interface to the `CopyArea` operation. When a client executes a `CopyArea` operation, it receives a CML event value that is the promise of a list of exposure rectangles (the empty list signifies `NoExpose`). The client can proceed with drawing, and later synchronize on the event to check for any needed repairs (see [Gan91] or [Rep92] for more details).

## 4.4   USER INTERACTION

The most significant departure in eXene from traditional user interface toolkits is in our approach to handling user input. As we argued in [Gan92], the multiplexing required by graphical applications maps naturally onto a concurrent programming model. Instead of a centralized event loop for processing user input, eXene uses a distributed hierarchy of threads to route user input to the appropriate place. The hierarchy basically mirrors the window hierarchy of the application. Each component in the hierarchy has an *environment*, consisting of three streams of input from the component's parent (mouse, keyboard and control),[11] and one output stream for requesting services from the component's parent. For each child of the component, there are corresponding output streams and an input stream. A component is responsible for routing messages to its children, but this can almost always be done using a generic router function provided by eXene. This event-handling model, with its top-down decentralized routing, is similar to those of [Pik89a] and [Haa90]. It is substantially different from the bottom-up approach used by most toolkits. In particular, it allows parents to interpose filters on the event streams of their children, which is an important mechanism in the composition of widgets in eXene (cf., Section 4.5.3).

To illustrate this approach, consider the implementation of a simple drawing application in eXene. The application presents the user with a window for drawing and a reset button (see Figure 4.1). When the user depresses a mouse button in the drawing window, a triangle is drawn at the cursor location, and when the user clicks on the reset button, the drawing window is cleared. This application's implementation consists of three components: a top-level component with two subcomponents (one for the button, and one for the drawing window). Each component has an associated X window. Figure 4.2 gives the thread network

---

[10] An exposure event notifies the application that a region of its windows has been damaged and requires repainting.

[11] Note that we translate X events into the appropriate types of eXene messages.

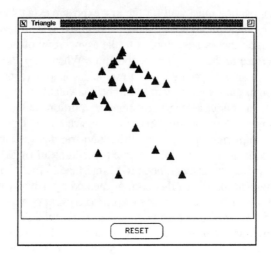

**Figure 4.1**   A simple drawing application

for these components; to simplify the picture we have omitted the output streams for requesting services, since they are not used by the application. The small unlabeled squares in this picture represent message sinks (threads that just consume input forever). For example, the top-level component ignores mouse and keyboard messages and has no graphics to redraw, so it has sinks for all three of its input streams. In addition to the sinks, the top-level component has a *router* thread associated with it. The router thread looks at the addresses of incoming messages and forwards them to the appropriate destination.

The drawing component has three threads: a sink for keyboard messages, a mouse-stream thread, and a command-stream thread that also maintains the drawing state. The mouse-stream thread looks for button-press messages, discarding all others. When a button-press message is received, it sends a drawing command to the command-stream thread. The command-stream thread is responsible for drawing the triangles on the drawing window, and for redrawing the window if it is damaged; the code for this thread is given in Figure 4.3. The thread is implemented as a tail recursive function. It receives messages from three sources: command messages from the top-level component's router (`cmdEvt`); draw messages from the mouse thread (`drawEvt`); and reset messages from the button component (`resetEvt`). For each source there is a corresponding handler function (`handleCmd`, `draw`, and `reset`). The thread also maintains a state, consisting of a list of the points on the display where triangles have been drawn. The function `drawTriangle` (not shown) draws a triangle at the specified point; it is used both to draw new triangles (in `draw`), and to redraw the screen to repair damage (in `handleCmd`).

The button component also consists of three threads: a sink for keyboard messages, a mouse-stream thread, and a command-stream thread. The mouse-stream thread looks for button-press messages; when it receives one, it sends a reset message to the drawing component's command-stream thread. The button's command-stream thread is responsible for redrawing the button when it is damaged.

When the user clicks the mouse on the button, the X server sends an X event to the application; the eXene library code routes this to the top-level component's mouse stream as

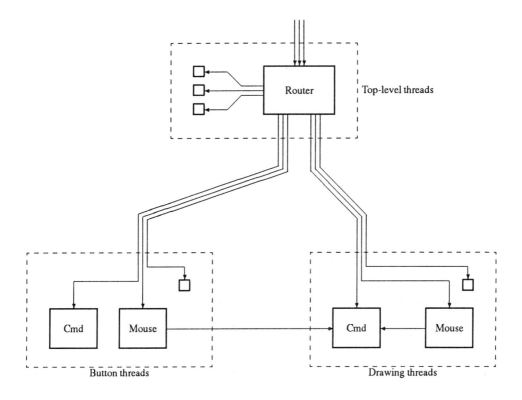

**Figure 4.2**   The application's communication network

a mouse message addressed to the button component. The router in the top-level component then passes the message on to the button component, which then sends a reset message to the drawing component.

The use of several threads per component, typically one for each input stream as well as one or more threads for managing state and coordinating the other threads, is standard in eXene applications. By breaking the code up this way, each individual thread is quite simple. This heavy use of threads is made possible by the lightweight nature of threads in CML. A thread typically incurs less than 100 bytes of space overhead [Rep91a], which makes them comparable in size to Smalltalk objects [Ung84].

## 4.5   EXENE INTRINSICS

The basic eXene features described above do not provide a general framework in which pieces of an interface can be built by various people at various times and then modified and integrated into a single user interface. Support for this is provided by the widget[12] layer in eXene. Widgets are the basic building blocks for constructing interfaces. The widget layer

---

[12] For want of a better term, we borrow the X term for a graphical object composed of a drawing area and its interaction semantics.

```
fun drawCmdLoop state = let
    fun handleCmd (CI_Redraw _) = (
            clearDrawable drawable;
            app drawTriangle state;
            drawCmdLoop state)
      | handleCmd CI_OwnDeath = ()
      | handleCmd _ = (drawCmdLoop state)
    fun draw pt = (drawTriangle pt; drawCmdLoop(pt::state))
    fun reset () = (clearDrawable drawable; drawCmdLoop[])
    in
      select [
            wrap (cmdEvt, handleCmd),
            wrap (drawEvt, draw),
            wrap (resetEvt, reset)
        ]
    end
```

**Figure 4.3**   The drawing command thread code

also provides the additional protocols necessary for cooperation among widgets, as well as
their reuse and extension.

The widget level reifies the underlying eXene approach to building graphical interfaces.

• The inherent concurrency in the user interface is made explicit. The user interface is just
  a part of an application: it does not dictate the architecture or control structure. Interfaces
  are built as networks of simple components connected by streams and event values. Each
  widget has its own threads, which separate it from other widgets and from the application
  code. A programmer can also use concurrency to simplify the internal structure of widgets,
  as described in the previous section.
• Few things are as full of state as graphical objects. With threads, the function call structure
  naturally encodes much state information, without the programmer having to maintain state
  explicitly. Additional state is encapsulated in channels.
• Input is distributed hierarchically. Events are passed from the root widget down the hierarchy to the appropriate widget. This allows the programmer to interpose widgets at any
  level to modify widget characteristics or alter the distribution of events.
• Higher-order functions, parametric polymorphism and parametric modules powerfully expand the programmer's tools for tailoring and combining interface components safely and
  simply.

As with most interface toolkits, a program using eXene creates at runtime a variety of
widgets, which are combined into one or more hierarchical structures. At some point in the
program, these structures are made visible and active. With most toolkits, after the widget
hierarchies have been instantiated, the program gives up control to an event loop supplied by
the toolkit. Alternatively, an application must be willing to provide its own event distribution
mechanism. In eXene, however, the program can continue to go about its business, whether
performing computations, reading input or interacting with the widgets. As an example,
Figure 4.4 contains the code for a simple program that uses widgets. This example creates
a button labeled "Goodbye, Cruel World!". If the user clicks on the button with any
mouse button, then the function quit is called, terminating the program. The program will

```
fun goodbye display = let
      val root = mkRoot display
      fun quit () = (delRoot root; RunCML.shutdown())
      val quitButton = mkCmdButton root {
                        label="Goodbye, Cruel World!",
                        action=quit
                      }
      val shell = mkShell root (
                     quitButton,
                     NONE,
                     {win_name = NONE, icon_name = NONE}
                  )
      fun loop () =
            if input_line std_in = "quit\n"
               then quit ()
               else loop ()
   in
      init shell;      (* make button visible *)
      loop ()
   end
```

**Figure 4.4**  Goodbye

also quit if the user enters "quit" on standard input. This is similar to the xgoodbye example in Chapter 2 of [Nye90b], but differs in one major way. In the xgoodbye example, control is passed off to the Xt event loop; in our version, the application retains control.

## 4.5.1  Widgets in EXene

As in most toolkits, a widget is a graphical object that corresponds to some control or feedback element of the user interface. But in eXene, widgets have a very "thin" interface. In addition, information is mostly distributed, with little that is global or centralized. This gives eXene widgets a very distinctive flavor. A widget only knows about the window it was handed and how it divided the window among its children. The parent widget[13] controls the external view of a child. The parent provides the child's window; it positions the window; it changes its size; it deletes it. If the child needs any of these actions performed, it asks the parent to perform the action. A child does not directly alter the external configuration of its window; it should only deal with what is inside its window.

A widget in eXene has three important attributes: a root, a boundsOf function, and a realize function. The root value corresponds to the screen on which a widget lives. A widget uses the boundsOf function to specify its size constraints. This function is usually used by the widget's parent when determining how much display space to allocate for the widget. The bounds_t type provides a fairly general mechanism for specifying geometry requirements in terms of natural size, increments and upper and lower bounds.

At the time of instantiation, a widget is passed, through its realize function, a window

---

[13] A *parent* widget is just the widget that provides the child's window and event streams. The parent widget need not correspond to a parent window of the child widget's window. In particular, a parent and child widget may share the same window.

on which to draw, the size of the window, and an input environment. This environment was described in Section 4.4. It is the widget's only built-in connection to the outside world. In addition to providing streams for the widget's mouse and keyboard events, it also supplies control channels for service requests and status events between parent and child. From its parent, a child receives notification that its window size has changed, that its window has been damaged and needs repair, and that its window has been deleted, among others messages. In turn, the child can use a control channel to request that its parent delete its window or reallocate space for it.

When its `realize` function is called, the widget configures itself corresponding to the given size and arranges to service events on its input environment. If the widget has any children, it must also layout its children, provide their windows, and call their `realize` functions. A parent widget is responsible for distributing the user events it receives to the appropriate child widget, if any, and monitoring requests from its children.

In addition to specifying how widgets interact and communicate, the widget layer provides mechanisms for writing and tailoring widgets. In eXene, we have taken the approach that one should construct small, lightweight components, with well-defined functions, and use a collection of powerful techniques to combine them to create a widget with the desired properties. These techniques can be roughly divided into two categories, as discussed in the following two sections.

### 4.5.2  Parameterization

The principal mechanism for specializing values in any library is parameterization. The library designer provides various hooks by which the programmer or user can tailor the library components to a particular use or appearance. In this regard, eXene is no different, though its design provides some atypical approaches to parameterization.

When created, a widget accesses a style database to determine various values affecting its display or its actions. These values typically involve fonts, background and foreground colors, layout parameters, and event actions, and are set to reflect the needs of the application or the preference of the user. EXene use a naming scheme for widgets and widget resources based on a logical hierarchy. As noted by Gettys [Get91] and others, there are problems with the standard naming system based on the physical widget hierarchy because it exposes too much of the underlying structure. To protect against changes to the widget structure, users would end up relying on loose bindings in resource specifications almost to the exclusion of strict bindings. Logical naming is more robust, supporting major changes to the widget hierarchy with no effect on resource naming, and more flexible, allowing resource names to diverge from the physical hierarchy. The logical naming scheme is also necessary in eXene as the widget hierarchy is created bottom up. When necessary, the application program can arrange that its choices override any user settings.

Function values form one of the most important classes of parameters used to tailor widgets. They are typically used by the programmer to specify action or callback functions that are invoked by the widget in response to some event or condition. Frequently, the application requires these functions to be executed in the context of certain values outside the purview of the widget. In addition, different widgets invoke callback functions with different types of arguments. With first-class function values available, the eXene programmer can use callback functions without subverting the type system or introducing an onerous multiplicity of types whose sole purpose is to mimic function closures.

There are other problems typically associated with callback functions as they occur in standard libraries. A client must explicitly register callback functions with widgets; it must explicitly unregister the functions when it no longer wishes the services performed. The code for managing a collection of callback functions is built into the widget. From the client's standpoint, its callback functions are invoked asynchronously. The client code must be able to accept the effects of a callback at any time. In addition, the callback function cannot involve time-consuming operations, lest it block the widget from handling other clients and potentially lock up the entire application.

In eXene, we use CML events to provide the means of communication between widgets[14]. A widget's interface can contain an abstract event value. There is no registering or unregistering of callback functions; the client just synchronizes on the event value. When the appropriate conditions occur, the widget synchronizes on the event value. The client then has the opportunity of continuing other activities until it reaches a state at which an action associated with the event is appropriate. The action executes in the context of the client's data and, thanks to the ability to spawn threads, can involve extensive computation. These semantics scale nicely to multiple clients by the interposition of a multicast channel between the widget and its clients. No change to the widget is necessary.

Widgets in eXene are often built out of even lighter weight components, offering another opportunity for parameterization. A common form of decomposition reflects a separation of the view and control aspects of a widget, somewhat in analogy to the *Model-View-Controller* idea [Kra88]. As an example, the eXene widget library supplies a mkLabelView function that, given a font, a string and an alignment, returns the size required to display the string plus a draw function. The draw function takes a drawable, a rectangle and a pen, and draws the text with the specified alignment within the rectangle in the drawable. This higher-order function is employed many places where the display of a text string is required. Another place where this technique arises is in the construction of button-like objects. The library defines a protocol for button views, corresponding to various possible button states, such as being active and set. There is a collection of button views following this protocol, such as check boxes, text buttons, and rocker switches. EXene also supplies various controller functions that implement some form of user interaction and, given a button view, use the view for visual feedback of the control state. A programmer creates a button-like object in eXene by composing a button behavior with a button view. For example, Figure 4.5 shows functions providing two of the standard button behaviors, one delivering a continuous stream of events while the button is "pressed" (mkButton) and one maintaining an on/off state for the button (mkToggle). The figure also shows functions implementing two of the standard button views, along with examples of the views. The lines indicate the four possible ways of composing the functions to get four different types of buttons. Views and controllers can either be supplied by the programmer, or taken from the eXene library.

Certain widgets are most generally parameterized over multiple types and values, more than can be easily accommodated by using SML's parametric polymorphism and function values. In these cases, the eXene programmer can use SML's parameterized modules, called *functors*. In the SML module system, functors are written as functions that create new modules when applied to a collection of modules compatible with certain specified signatures. This is precisely what is needed to factor out the dependencies of a widget over a complex structure of interrelated types and values. For example, the eXene text widget is written as a functor taking

---

[14] With the availability of threads and synchronization primitives, the concurrency problems with callbacks disappear. One simply writes a callback function to spawn a new thread or to synchronize on a CML event.

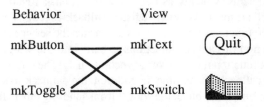

**Figure 4.5**   Composing buttons

a text buffer module as an argument. Such a module provides an abstraction for creating a two-dimensional layout of text. This abstraction includes a submodule that defines a typeball type, which is used to specify how (font face and size, color, spacing) a text string should be drawn. The role of the text widget is to provide controlled access to creating and modifying a text buffer while maintaining a projection of the buffer layout on the screen.

EXene also uses functors to parameterize viewport widgets, which allow the programmer to create a changeable "window" on a (potentially) much larger drawing area. The functor parameters are used to specify the constraints on the viewport window, how the drawing area coordinates project onto the viewport window, and how a view is implemented. For a pixel-based drawing canvas, a viewport may be an unconstrained projection of the drawing. For a text-based widget, the viewport is probably constrained by line or character boundaries. A simple view can be created by having the drawing area implemented as a subwindow of the viewport window. The programmer can construct more efficient views by using direct calls to the canvas drawing routines, circumventing the window system, and by maintaining drawing caches such as backing store, text buffers, or display lists.

### 4.5.3   Widget Wrappers

The hierarchical routing of events in eXene allows the programmer to wrap one widget within another, thereby allowing the wrapping widget to interpose its behavior between the wrapped widget and a prospective parent, essentially producing a derived widget. The wrapping widget subverts the wrapped widget's interface, providing a new `boundsOf` or `realize` function or intercepting the event stream. In a simple case, the wrapping function might do nothing more than translate keystrokes. This technique is also used to fix the size of a widget, widgets typically being written to adjust to whatever size they are given. The programmer wraps a widget in another widget, whose `boundsOf` function returns a fixed size, with equal lower and upper bounds. The text widget described above is an output-only widget: it does not respond to any mouse or keyboard events, but it handles redisplay correctly. To make a text editor or a virtual terminal, a programmer would wrap the text widget with code to handle user input, using the text widget as a simple output device. As another example of this approach, reconsider the application described in Section 4.4. If the programmer decides to attach a pop-up menu to program, she can wrap the top-level component with a function that responds to mouse button presses by putting up the menu but forwards all other events down the hierarchy.

Graphical composition occurs when a widget's window is a subwindow of that of its parent widget. This technique, standard in all interface toolkits, is also handled by widget wrapping. Thus, in eXene, a single mechanism is used to support subwindowing and derived widgets.

Because of the desire that basic components should be as simple as possible, eXene, like
InterViews, relies on composition for features that might ordinarily be built into a widget. For
example, to get a border for a widget, one inserts a widget into a frame widget, whose role is
to create a border about its child widget.

The design of eXene induces an elegance in the use of composition. For example, one can
create a new widget giving textual feedback on a slider widget[15] by composing the slider with
a text label widget in a box layout widget, and spawning a thread that monitors changes to the
slider's value, as captured by a CML event, and resets the label widget's text accordingly.

## 4.6  APPLICATIONS

EXene has served as the basis for a variety of applications, several of significant size and
sophistication. We describe some of these uses below.

As a basic "proof of concept," we have ported a number of standard sample graphics
applications, such as a hand calculator (Chapter 12 of [Nye90a]) and a bitmap editor (Chapter 4
of [Nye90b]), to eXene. Typically, the eXene versions require a third to a quarter of the code
needed for the Xt versions, largely because of the expressiveness, concurrency and memory
management provided by the underlying language.

Video game-like programs make good test cases for graphics toolkits. We mention three
that show the utility and efficiency of threads in eXene. In *bounce*, the user uses the left mouse
button to send a new ball bouncing around within a window. If the user clicks the middle
mouse button on a ball, it disappears. The right mouse button brings up a pop-up menu that
allows the user to start over, or to quit. Because of the distributed user input handling, the
balls continue to move while the menu is being displayed. In the implementation, each ball
has its own thread, which calculates the next position and passes this information to a display
manager thread. Another application using animation-like graphics is an arithmetic teacher.
The game has buttons for picking the operation (addition, subtraction, etc.) and the level of
difficulty, and a window for displaying the problem and the tentative answer. Another window
displays a scene in which a small figure climbs some distance up a pole on each correct answer.
With enough correct answers, the figure makes it to the top and waves a flag; a wrong answer
sends the figure into a pool of water with a big splash. With concurrency, the figure can still
be climbing while the user is working on the next problem. We have also ported Cardelli's
*badbricks* game to eXene.[16] The notable point here is that a typical game involves on the order
of 1600 threads.

Other sample eXene applications include an implementation of a *Graphical Fisheye Viewer*
[Sar92], and an implementation of the *DeltaBlue* incremental constraint solving algorithm
[Fre90]. The latter is an interesting experiment because of the importance of incremental
constraint solving in high-level user interface management systems. This experiment suggests
that constraints may provide a high-level mechanism for specifying the interconnection of
widgets [Yan92].

EXene has been used to provide the user interfaces for two interactive theorem proving
systems. PAM [Lin91] is a general proof tool for process algebras. Its interface consists of
a main window, which is used to compile process algebra calculi and create proofs, plus a
window for each proof. At the same time, the user can work on several problems in the same

---

[15] A slider widget provides a valuator by which the user can set a scalar value in some range.
[16] Badbricks is a demo included in the Trestle distribution.

calculus, or the same problem in different calculi. Proofs complete in one proof window can be bound as a named theorem and then used in other proofs. The system developed by Griffin and Moten [Gri92] provides as a library a logic-independent implementation of tactic trees. It is designed to be incorporated into any SML-based interactive theorem prover. It provides a structure editor for tactic trees, in which the user can move the focus to any subtree, alter the view of the tree to global, local or elided views, and modify a subtree by deletion or the application of a tactic.

### 4.6.1   Graph-o-matica

In order to discuss in more detail how the various features of eXene come together in an application, we focus on a single application, called *Graph-o-matica*, in the remainder of this section. Graph-o-matica is an interactive tool for analyzing and viewing graphs, which has been implemented on top of eXene.

There are two main types of windows used in Graph-o-matica: *command windows*, which provide a terminal-style, textual interface for manipulating graphs and their views, and *view windows*, which provide a view on a 2D layout of a graph. There can be multiple command windows, a given abstract graph can have more than one layout, and a given layout can have more than one view. A layout allows the user to modify the 2D embedding of the graph, including elision of subgraphs. A view allows the user to pan and zoom (using menus and the scrollbars) on a given embedding of the graph. Dialogue boxes and other standard graphics paraphernalia are employed in the interface. Except for the graph drawing component, Graph-o-matica uses standard eXene widgets.

Figure 4.6 illustrates a sample session using Graph-o-matica. The bottom window is a command window. Future versions might include more graphically oriented mechanisms for some of the main types of operations; however, the command window will probably always be available to the user. As a general rule, a program should have an underlying text language interface, even when the principal user interactions are graphical. Lying on top of the command window is a view of the graph of modules in the SML/NJ compiler. The top two windows provide two views of a different graph but each view uses the same layout. If a graph is edited, either using a graphical view or from a command window, this information needs to be propagated to the layouts and views of the graph. The system uses a multicast channel abstraction to manage the propagation of update notifications between graphs and layouts and between layouts and views. This simplifies the implementation of the graph object, since it does not need to know anything about multiple layouts. The layout objects, if they decide a given change affects them, can query the graph object for more detailed information. Similar simplification occurs in the layout objects. The modular style supported in eXene, based particularly on explicit, abstract concurrency and high-level memory management, facilitates this type of layering and multiplication of objects.

The need for both communication abstraction and selective communication also arises in the *virtual terminal* used in the command window. At any time, the virtual terminal must be able to handle both input from the user and output from its client (the command shell). EXene provides an abstract interface to the input stream, but since it is event-valued, it can still be used in selective communication.

Because the pieces are written to operate independently, using their own threads, the user interface need not block. For example, when Graph-o-matica presents a dialogue box to the user it may continue computation, including drawing graphics and handling user input, while

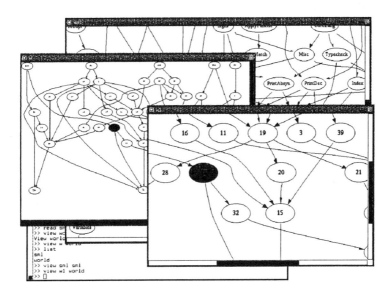

**Figure 4.6** Graph-o-matica

the dialogue box is displayed. Internally, selective communication is used by components to multiplex waiting for the result of the dialogue box with other interactions. Similarly, Graph-o-matica avoids having intensive computation, such as running the graph layout algorithm, lock up the system. These computations are run in separate threads, with completion marked by a CML event.

It should be emphasized again that similar asynchronous behavior can be achieved in many standard toolkits. Typically, an event loop plays the role of a scheduler, and the application can register and unregister functions to be called in response to user events, file system events, timer events or when no events need processing. This introduces the user interface bias discussed above. It becomes necessary to structure the application, including non-interface code, as a state machine. This approach is cumbersome and introduces distortions in the structure of the software. Imagine being required to write a potentially time-consuming algorithm that can only run in quanta of "small fraction[s] of a second" ( [Nye90b], p. 239) before returning. As a result, applications written using standard toolkits tend not to provide the level of concurrency users expect.

The approach we have taken in eXene is to make the presence of concurrency explicit, and to build the interface toolkit to take advantage of this concurrency. This allows the pieces of the application to be written in whatever style is appropriate, provides better separation of the components of the application, and makes it simple and inexpensive to use concurrency when required.

## 4.7 FUTURE WORK

Although eXene is quite usable in its current state, it is still very much a work in progress. We are already planning various changes, some at the implementation level, others providing enhancements to the user's view.

The hierarchical routing used in eXene provides the basis for the programmer's ability to wrap an old component in a function providing new behavior. Most of the time, though, events are routed through most paths unchanged. We would like to explore means of maintaining the semantics of hierarchical routing while providing more efficient direct routing when possible.

At present, eXene provides no facility by which a widget can specify interesting mouse events. It is possible that something akin to cages in Trestle [Man91] may provide an elegant solution to this problem. Essentially, a cage is a region surrounding the cursor position; the system generates an event when the cursor leaves the cage. This mechanism generalizes the X notions of mouse motion (a one pixel square cage) and window enter and leave events (a cage corresponding to a window or its screen complement).

In its current state, eXene relies heavily on X for its rendering model, and for the implementation of windows and user event routing. Using the X rendering model has the benefit that the full generality of X drawing primitives is available to the programmer. We feel this advantage is more than offset by the complexity and low-level detail of this model. In addition, having the X model visible inhibits implementing eXene on any other graphics base. Tying a widget drawing context to an X window is a mistake: it is almost a truism that X windows are too heavyweight to be used extensively. This is particularly annoying in eXene, where the flavor is that of lightweight objects, as exemplified by function closures and CML threads and channels.

We hope to overlay the present library with one that supports a higher-level rendering model and a lighter-weight window model. We also wish to explore how well a constraint system can be integrated within eXene. These goals will require that eXene provides its own window management. The library will use the underlying graphics system, such as X, solely to provide primitive graphics services and a raw stream of user input.

## ACKNOWLEDGMENTS

Some of this work was done while the second author was a graduate student at Cornell University, and was supported, in part, by the NSF and ONR under NSF grant CCR-85-14862, and by the NSF under NSF grant CCR-89-18233.

We wish to thank L. Augustsson, T. Breuel, T. Griffin, C. Krumvieda, H. Lin and T. Yan for testing the initial versions of eXene, pointing out bugs and suggesting various useful changes. We also thank the anonymous referees for their comments on the substance and style of the paper.

## REFERENCES

[App87]    A. W. Appel and D. B. MacQueen. A Standard ML compiler. In Gilles Kahn, editor, *Functional Programming Languages and Computer Architecture*, vol. 274 of Lecture Notes in Computer Science, pages 301–324. Springer-Verlag, September 1987.

[Fre90]   B. N. Freeman-Benson, J. Maloney, and A. Borning. An incremental constraint solver. *Communications of the ACM*, 33(1):54–63, 1990.

[Gaj90]   H. Gajewska, M. S. Manasse, and J. McCormack. Why X is not our ideal window system. *Software – Practice and Experience*, 20(S2):137–171, 1990.

[Gan88]   E. R. Gansner. Iris: A class-based window library. In *Proc. USENIX C++ Conference*, pages 283–292, Denver, October 1988. USENIX Association, Berkeley, CA.

[Gan91]   E. R. Gansner and J. H. Reppy. eXene. In R. Harper, editor, *Proc. Third International Workshop on Standard ML*, Pittsburgh, September 1991. Carnegie Mellon University, Pittsburgh, Pennsylvania.

[Gan92]   E. R. Gansner, and J. H. Reppy. A foundation for user interface construction. In B. A. Myers, editor, *Languages for Developing User Interfaces*, pages 239–260. Jones & Bartlett, Boston, 1992.

[Get91]   J. Gettys. Customization - Rope for a Noose, or a Lifeline for the Drowning? In *Proc. 5th X Technical Conference*, Boston, January 1991. MIT X Consortium, Cambridge, Massachusetts.

[Gos89]   J. Gosling, D. Rosenthal, and M. Arden. *The NeWS Book*. Springer-Verlag, 1989.

[Gri92]   T. Griffin and R. Moten. Tactic trees in eXene. Included in the eXene distribution, 1992.

[Haa90]   D. Haahr. Montage: Breaking windows into small pieces. In *USENIX Summer Conference*, pages 289–297, June 1990. USENIX Association, Berkeley, CA.

[Har86]   R. Harper. Introduction to Standard ML. *Technical Report ECS-LFCS-86-14*, Laboratory for Foundations of Computer Science, Computer Science Department, Edinburgh University, August 1986.

[Kra88]   G. Krasner and S. Pope. A cookbook for using the model-view-controller user interface paradigm in Smalltalk-80. *Journal of Object-Oriented Programming*, 1(3):26–49, 1988.

[Lin89]   M. A. Linton, J. M. Vlissides, and P. R. Calder. Composing user interfaces with InterViews. *IEEE Computer*, 22(2):8–22, 1989.

[Lin91]   H. Lin. PAM: A process algebra manipulator. In *Proc. Third Workshop on Computer Aided Verification*, July 1991.

[Lis88]   B. Liskov and L. Shrira. Promises: Linguistic support for efficient asynchronous procedure calls in distributed systems. In *Proc. SIGPLAN'88 Conference on Programming Language Design and Implementation*, pages 260–267, Atlanta, June 1988. ACM, New York.

[Man91]   M. S. Manasse and G. Nelson. Trestle reference manual. *Technical Report 68*, DEC Systems Research Center, December 1991.

[Mil90]   R. Milner, M. Tofte, and R. Harper. *The Definition of Standard ML*. The MIT Press, Cambridge, Massachusetts, 1990.

[Mil91]   R. Milner and M. Tofte. *Commentary on Standard ML*. The MIT Press, Cambridge, Massachusetts, 1991.

[Mye90]   B. A. Myers, D. A. Giuse, R. B. Dannenberg, B. V. Zanden, D. S. Kosbie, E. Pervin, A. Mickish, and P. Marchal. Comprehensive support for graphical, highly interactive user interfaces. *IEEE Computer*, 23(11):71–85, 1990.

[Nor87]   S. C. North and J. H. Reppy. Concurrent garbage collection on stock hardware. In Gilles Kahn, editor, *Functional Programming Languages and Computer Architecture*, vol. 274 of Lecture Notes in Computer Science, pages 113–133. Springer-Verlag, September 1987.

[Nye90a]  A. Nye. *Xlib Programming Manual*, vol. 1. O'Reilly & Associates, Inc., 1990.

[Nye90b]  A. Nye and T. O'Reilly. *X Toolkit Intrinsics Programming Manual*, vol. 4. O'Reilly & Associates, Inc., 1990.

[Pau91]   L. C. Paulson. *ML for the Working Programmer*. Cambridge University Press, New York, 1991.

[Pik89a]  R. Pike. A concurrent window system. *Computing Systems*, 2(2): 133–153, 1989.

[Pik89b]  R. Pike. Newsqueak: A language for communicating with mice. *Technical Report 143*, AT&T Bell Laboratories, April 1989.

[Rep86]   J. H. Reppy and E. R. Gansner. A foundation for programming environments. In *Proc. ACM SIGSOFT/SIGPLAN Software Engineering Symposium on Practical Software Development Environments*, pages 218–227, Palo Alto, California, December 1986. ACM, New York.

[Rep88]   J. H. Reppy. Synchronous operations as first-class values. In *Proc. SIGPLAN'88 Conference on Programming Language Design and Implementation*, pages 250–259, Atlanta, June 1988.

ACM, New York.

[Rep91a]    J. H. Reppy. CML: A higher-order concurrent language. In *Proc. SIGPLAN'91 Conference on Programming Language Design and Implementation*, pages 293–305, Toronto, June 1991. ACM, New York.

[Rep91b]    J. H. Reppy. An operational semantics of first-class synchronous operations. *Technical Report TR 91-1232*, Department of Computer Science, Cornell University, August 1991.

[Rep92]     J. H. Reppy. *Higher-order concurrency*. PhD dissertation, Cornell University, Department of Computer Science, January 1992. Available as Technical Report TR 92-1285.

[Reps84]    T. W. Reps. *Generating Language-based Environments*. The MIT Press, Cambridge, Massachusetts, 1984.

[Sar92]     M. Sarkar and M. H. Brown. Graphical fisheye views of graphs. *Technical Report 84*, DEC Systems Research Center, March 1992.

[Sch92]     R. W. Scheifler and J. Gettys. *The X Window System*. Digital Press, 3rd edition, 1992.

[Ung84]     D. Ungar. Generation scavenging: A non-disruptive high-performance storage reclamation algorithm. In *Proc. ACM SIGSOFT/SIGPLAN Software Engineering Symposium on Practical Software Development Environments*, pages 157–167, Pittsburgh, Pennsylvania, April 1984. ACM, New York.

[Yan92]     T. Yan. An incremental constraint solver for eXene. Included in the eXene distribution, 1992.

# 5

# Animation in User Interfaces: Principles and Techniques

JOHN T. STASKO
*Georgia Institute of Technology*

## ABSTRACT

Recently, animation has become an increasingly important component of many user interfaces. Animation can be valuable because it allows designers to convey the time-varying behavior of application programs. In this paper we survey existing utilizations of animation in user interfaces, and we speculate why animation has not been applied even more widely to interface design. We also discuss the motivations for adding animation to a user interface, noting that a surprisingly broad variety of design goals can be accomplished using animation. Finally, we describe fundamental design and implementation principles of animation to help guide further development.

## 5.1  OVERVIEW

Is there a place for animation in user interfaces? Until recently, user interfaces consisted primarily of static graphical objects. The addition to interfaces of interaction objects, such as scrollbars that move, dialog boxes that pop up, and menus that pull down, has been characterized as the presence of animation in interfaces, but this does seem to be stretching the definition of animation a bit far. Which leads to an important point—What is animation exactly?

Most people think of animation in terms of cartoons and Saturday morning childrens' television shows, in which a series of hand drawn cels are transferred to film as frames. The imagery in each cel is slightly moved or adjusted from its position in the previous cel. When the frames are shown rapidly in order, often 30 frames per second, the human eye is unable to distinguish the individual frames, and an illusion of continuous motion results.

Computer animation involves a different set of materials, but the results are much the

---

*User Interface Software*, Edited by Bass and Dewan

same. Animation developers use graphics software toolkits and drawing editors to specify the placement, size, and color of objects. The underlying graphics software is responsible for drawing or rendering the objects onto the display. However, individual cels no longer are present. Graphics are drawn into logical buffers or windows that are shown on the computer's display or that can be transferred to the display. Animation developers must invoke operations that update the display and show the objects as they should appear in the next frame.

The flexibility of computers allows designers to specify interfaces that change over time in a variety of manners. Deciding precisely when an interface transitions from a static display into animation is a challenge and is somewhat subjective, however. Some people will only consider a long sequence of gradually changing scenes to be animation. Others will deem a few appropriate color changes or cursor flashes to be animation. In any case, animation at its essence involves smoothly changing positions or attributes of objects so that a viewer can observe the relationship between time $t$ and time $t + \Delta t$.

Computer animation has been an important topic of study in the computer graphics field for over 20 years. Hundreds of articles about animation have appeared in the SIGGRAPH conference proceedings. The application of animation to user interfaces, however, is just now receiving attention by researchers and developers.

Current examples of the use of animation in interfaces may be so subtle that they are taken for granted. For example, on many window-based interface systems such as the Macintosh, when a new window or application is opened, it does not instantaneously appear. Rather, a series of rectangular window outlines grow out of the chosen application to the eventual target window destination. Also, when a lengthy operation such as a file copy occurs, the interface presents a thermometer-style gauge that is filled according to the percentage of the operation completed so far. These types of percentage-done indicators [Mye85] help users understand the current state of the application or system. Animation need not only be of this start-stop variety, however. On many computers, cursors continually blink and analog clock depictions show second hands that continually move, thus providing a truly animated interface.

In [Bae90], Baecker and Small provide an excellent overview of the history of animation and the challenges it presents to developers on computers. They detail the motivation for using animation in interfaces, listing eight significant uses of animation. They describe how animation can be used for

- **Identification** – Animation can help focus attention on an item of interest or help identify what an application does.
- **Transition** – Animation can help orient users to state changes within an application or system.
- **Choice** – Animation can be used to cycle through and enumerate a set of actions or options within an application.
- **Demonstration** – Animation can help illustrate the actions and results of dynamic operations in a more direct manner than a static depiction.
- **Explanation** – Animation can be used to build dynamic tutorials that depict sequencing scenarios within user interfaces.
- **Feedback** – Animation can help convey the changing status of or activity within an application.
- **History** – Animation can be used to present the sequence of steps or operations that were carried out to arrive at the current condition.

- **Guidance** – Animation can be used to illustrate the series of actions necessary to achieve the user's goal within an interface.

The authors also explain each of these purposes by providing examples of interfaces that apply animation for that particular purpose.

To complement Baecker and Small's assessment, we focus here on the different principles and challenges for incorporating animation into user interfaces. We also describe different systems that help developers build animations for user interfaces. Finally, we survey four recent research projects that have utilized animation in a user interface or program interface. These projects provide a glimpse of how animation might be more successfully applied in the future, and they illustrate how different animation implementation techniques are appropriate for different tasks.

## 5.2   ANIMATION PRINCIPLES

Building animation scenarios and incorporating them into user interfaces can be difficult because it presents two equally important but dramatically different challenges. First, an animation must be conceptually designed to be informative and to convey the appropriate message(s) to the user. The developer must consider an animation's aesthetics: how the animation looks; what colors, if any, are used; how fast does the animation run; do the animation's actions accurately depict the operations they are modeling, and so on. This challenge tests the artistic and expressive qualities of the developer.

The second hurdle of incorporating animation into an interface is the software implementation. Once an animation has been conceptually designed, it must be implemented properly to correctly reflect the design choices. The developer must choose an implementation technique that is appropriate for the animation task and the computer graphics platform involved. Issues such as timing and duration of the animation must be considered. This challenge tests the computer graphics and system building qualities of the developer.

Of course, sufficient computer hardware must be available to support the animation too. Unfortunately, real-time animation capabilities still severely tax many of today's computers. Our subsequent discussions assume that appropriate graphics hardware is available. We focus primarily on the software aspects of animation.

Because these two challenges require such diverse capabilities, different people must often be used to perform the two operations. For the design task, a developer with a strong human factors background and an understanding of the operation being animated is ideal. For the implementation task, a developer with a strong computer science and systems building background is required.

Below, we examine both the design and implementation challenges of adding animation to user interfaces. In particular, we list and describe the key principles of each challenge that an animation developer must address.

### 5.2.1   Design Principles

In order to make an animation effectively convey the information to which it is intended, the animation must be developed with certain key design principles in mind. Of course, any interface design, be it static or dynamic, must pay close attention to layout, use of color and fonts, ease-of-use, naturalness and so forth. The dynamic nature of animation, however, introduces a new set of design issues. We have identified four design principles for animation in user interfaces: appropriateness, smoothness, duration/control, and moderation.

**Appropriateness:** When animation is introduced to an interface, it is usually done so to represent an operation or a process of the underlying application or system. End-users of the interface will have their own mental model of the application and of the operations involved. The objects involved in an animation should depict application entities, and the animation actions should appropriately represent the user's mental model.

Consider the "window-selection" animation discussed earlier. Users may think of an inactive application program as being a closed folder or box. The act of selecting the application "opens" the folder and activates the underlying application. The simple, but effective, outward-growing rectangle animation provides an appropriate representation of this process.

**Smoothness:** For an animation to be effective, viewers must be able to perceive its actions and motions in a clear manner. Animations that abruptly commence or terminate, or animations involving wildly changing imagery and scenery can be very difficult to comprehend. Smooth, continuous animation scenarios that preserve the context of the animation as its motion occurs are easiest to follow.

For example, rather than having an object move to a new position in one jump, an animation can show the object moving smoothly across the screen. Rather than having an object change color instantaneously, an animation can show the object continuously blending into the new color.

These types of animations may not be technically accurate with respect to the underlying operations they represent. For instance, variables or parameters inside a computer program change instantaneously; they do not gradually transition to a new value. But what the animation provides here is a sense of context, locality, and the relationship between before and after states. In this case, complete fidelity to the underlying application is not as important as the display of smooth, comprehensible, expressive actions.

For complex motion animations in particular, the use of acceleration, deceleration, and even motion blur can be especially effective. By accelerating into a motion and decelerating out of the motion, the motion's important endpoints are highlighted. This technique matches real world phenomena as well.

**Duration/Control:** Different animation purposes dictate the design of different animation duration and control models. Consider user interface animations that are divided into three categories: animation of instantaneous or immediate unit operations such as selection, animation of operations with real-time clock correspondences, and animations as explanatory or instructional aids.

Animation scenarios representing simple, immediate operations, such as selecting a file to examine, should be brief so that the user does not become bored. Humans make unprepared responses to stimuli within about a second [New90], reported in [Car91]. This period of time seems to be a good duration for animation actions depicting these simple types of operations. If shorter durations are used, it becomes difficult to perceive the animation's activities.

Animations of actions such as a file copy or compilation must accurately or closely reflect the state of the operation. In these animations, the viewer is using the animation to provide feedback about the progress of the computation to guide when further actions can be taken. These types of animations need to be designed to present an accurate chronological summary of the operation they are modeling.

Finally, in animations that are serving as help or instructions to the user, designing the animation so that the viewer can control its speed is critical. Different viewers may have differing levels of experience with the interface. Novice users may require deliberate animations in order to make the appropriate mental connections between the animation, its imagery, and the underlying application. Expert users may simply require a rapid, brief refresher animation. These types of interface animations work best when the viewer can set the animation's speed, can pause the animation when desired, and even can replay important sequences of the animation to reinforce the material being conveyed.

**Moderation:** The eye-catching, appealing nature of animation can tempt designers to apply it to many facets of an interface. Animation is, however, another attribute in which the oft-quoted design principle "less is more" does apply. When a user opens a folder, if we show a small person appear, grab the folder, shake it a bit, and then toss it across the screen, we are surely overdoing things. The first time a user witnesses such a scenario, it will undoubtedly be appreciated. But after watching it twenty times a day, users may spend their free time thinking of ways to "kill off" the window-opener.

Animation can make interfaces more fun to use, but the daily, continuous nature of our interactions with computers dictates that appropriate, moderate applications of animation are the best application of the technology.

## 5.2.2  Implementing Animation

A surprisingly large variety of techniques are used to implement animation scenarios in user interfaces. The techniques range from simple line drawing methods to advanced 3D methods involving complex rendering algorithms, motion models, and lighting techniques. In this article we focus on a number of different 2D techniques because the vast majority of user interfaces remain 2D. For general information on 3D animation, consult a computer graphics text such as [Fol90].

2D animation techniques can be divided into a number of different categories. Below we list some these techniques. The list is by no means exhaustive; many other techniques or small modifications of those discussed here do exist, but the list does provide an overview of the most commonly used techniques.

**Preset frame sequences:** In a preset frame sequence, a series of animation frames are predetermined and rendered. Typically, the images in the frames change slightly between the frames. To achieve animation, the frames are displayed rapidly in a sequence. This technique can be used only when the animation to be shown is preset and will be the same over and over again. Figure 5.1 shows a series of bitmaps which model a clock face and the movements of a clock hand.

When a preset animation scenario is insufficient, that is, when individual graphical objects can make independent, non-predetermined movements, then more advanced animation techniques are required. These *structured graphics* techniques support the manipulation of individual graphical elements, and hence, are much more general purpose than preset frame sequences.

**Exclusive-Or Drawing:** The exclusive-or (XOR) drawing mode supports a drawing style in which the individual bits of the source and destination pixels are combined according to the exclusive-or logical operation (0x0=0; 0x1=1; 1x0=1; 1x1=0). Objects can be made to "move" via a series of draw-redraw pairs. On a monochrome display, the first drawing operation inverts all pixels underneath it, effectively "drawing" the object, then the subsequent redraw returns all pixels to their earlier state, effectively "erasing" the object again. By rapidly repeating such an operation, e.g., by following the cursor, an animation effect results. XOR drawing

   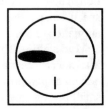

**Figure 5.1**   A sequence of bitmaps which when displayed in series illustrates a hand moving around a clock.

techniques work best on monochrome displays because the exclusive-or combination of two colors does not follow a regular, expected color pattern.

**Screen Redraw:** When color is required and a simple technique is still desirable, simple on-screen redraw is often used to provide animation effects. To simulate the motion of an object, we first "erase" the object by redrawing it in the background color or pattern, then we draw the object at its new position for the next frame. Simple screen redraw may not be desirable if multiple graphical objects change over time. Because the objects are being erased and redrawn from the same window or view in which we observe them and because the objects must be redrawn in some order (assuming object redraw as a single operation), the frame-to-frame nature of animation is lost. If enough objects are redrawn, our eyes will detect the cycling order of drawing operations on the display, and the images will seem to flicker. For both screen redraw and XOR drawing, graphical artifacts also occur if the drawing is not synchronized with the monitor's refresh cycle.

Many computers and display devices include the capability of providing two logical buffers or memory areas into which graphics can be rendered and from which the monitor's display can be generated. At any time only one of the two buffers drives the display. The other buffer is available for drawing operations, thus hiding the effects of on-screen redraw. This concept is known as *double buffering*. Below we discuss a few techniques to implement double buffering.

**Dual Display Pages:** Some machines provide two equivalent memory areas, each of which can drive the computer's display. Graphics operations on such machines can be directed to either area. The machines also provide access to a very fast hardware operation that can change which area is used to drive the display. To achieve animation with this type of double buffering, we simply redraw all the graphical objects into the hidden buffer at their positions for the next animation frame. Because the buffer is hidden, the sequential nature of the draw operations is masked. When the buffers are swapped, all the objects appear to update in unison; one complete new frame is generated.

**Color Lookup Table:** Another way to achieve simple double buffering is to logically divide the color lookup table into two regions, then use the hardware's masking capabilities to only allow one region at a time to drive the actual display presented on the monitor. This type of color table animation [Sho79] can be extended so that each plane of the table holds a logically different image, thus moving from double buffering to n-way buffering. Even simpler animation effects can be achieved with the color table by simply resetting objects colors to the background color, thus making them disappear and appear. Hence, the use of the lookup table for animation can be an effective way to present simple motion effects such as a bouncing ball.

**Blting:** The blting (<u>bl</u>ock <u>t</u>ransfer) technique for achieving animation can be quite simple and very powerful. In this technique an offscreen pixmap or canvas with size equal to the display window in use is maintained. This offscreen pixmap serves as the hidden buffer into which graphics can be rendered. To make the hidden buffer's contents appear on the display, a block of the memory area of the buffer is copied into the display memory area (frame buffer).

Blting is usually the most conceptually and programmatically "clean" and powerful technique for achieving animation, particularly when hardware double buffering support is not available. Unfortunately, the software block transfer operation is often not fast enough to provide desirable frames-per-second ratios to achieve smooth animation especially on very large windows. Recent improvements in display hardware, including hardware support for blting, are rapidly changing this fact, however.

All the preceding concepts and techniques of this section address low level animation concerns. The addition of animation to user interfaces also requires that an equally important set of higher level issues be addressed too. Integrating animation into an existing user interface system places further challenges on an already difficult software development task.

For example, general user interface software design principles stress the importance of the separation of application code from the code implementing the interface. The addition of animation to the fold places an even greater strain on this separation because animation often requires large amounts of continuous data from the application. Hence, the software architecture must provide clear access channels for communication between the two. But, focusing too much of the computation load of an interface on animation tasks can handicap the modules responsible for responding to user actions such as mouse selections or keypresses. These interaction routines are arguably the most important within a user interface application and any loss in their responsiveness will usually not be tolerated.

Another challenge in integrating animation with a user interface is synchronizing the animation with other interface activities, or simply synchronizing different animation actions. For example, during continuous animations with a lengthy duration, the interface may change state according to certain points in the animation. This requires that the animation code be written so that it can be monitored closely and can provide intermediate feedback. On distributed client-server graphics systems, coordinating the underlying computation with its accompanying graphical state may be difficult.

Issues such as the division of computation focus, synchronization, concurrency, modularity, etc., all must be addressed in the integration of animation within a user interface system. Animation simply amplifies many of the user interface software development challenges discussed in other articles within this volume.

An elaboration of these higher level software integration issues is worthy of several more articles and is beyond the scope of the discussions here. Such issues are far less "settled" than those involving low level animation implementation techniques, and we expect future research to focus on these problems.

## 5.3   MAPPING OPERATIONS TO ANIMATIONS

When animation is to be added to or utilized by a user interface, the operation which is being animated and the purpose of the animation often dictate the style of animation technique that should be used. By operation and purpose, we mean the application action, such as "window selection" or "compilation progress," that is being depicted in the animation. In particular, two aspects of the operation strongly influence how its animation should be carried out

- The level of operation-specific parametric information required to drive the animation
- The number of application entities, and consequently graphical objects, that will be manipulated in the animation.

The level of operation-specific parametric information required to drive an animation ranges from no data at all to a large quantity of data. Interface animations that convey only one state of an application, like the clock animation with the twirling hand, really require no parametric data from the underlying operation being depicted. The animation is simply started and terminated at the appropriate times. These types of operations are best animated by using preset frame sequences. The total predetermination of the task supports a preset animation scenario.

Most application tasks, however, operate on one or more application data objects or they involve attribute values that change over time. An animation of such tasks must accurately depict the objects involved or the appropriate attribute values. For example, when a user selects a folder on a desktop interface, an animation of this operation must know which folder was selected. It would be impossible to predefine an animation for every possible folder that could exist. Rather, it would be best to define a *generic* "folder selection" animation that is parameterized on the folder involved.

As another example, consider a dynamic load monitor display for a workstation, shown as a bar chart that changes over time. This animation is simply an interface onto processor load statistics. Here, work load values dictate where the chart's bars should be.

Animations such as these last two examples cannot use preset frame sequences. Rather, they require one of the structured graphics implementation techniques described earlier. This leads us to the second criteria for how to implement an interface's animation, the number of application entities manipulated in the animation.

When an application operation involves only one object at a time, it is often best to use an exclusive-or or screen redraw animation technique. These on-screen updates are fast, efficient, and usually easier to implement than the more complex buffered techniques. Because only one graphical object at a time is changing, updates on the display still preserve the frame-to-frame desired quality of an animation.

When more than one screen object is to be updated concurrently, the double buffer animation techniques are the best implementation choices. They allow many graphical objects to be changed "in step" by writing to the hidden buffer. When the hidden buffer is installed, either by a hardware swap or a blt, the frame-to-frame nature of an animation is preserved.

## 5.4   BUILDING ANIMATIONS

Once an interface developer has settled on an animation technique to use, he or she is faced with the challenge of building the planned animation scenarios. One of the most frequently cited reasons for the lack of animation in interfaces is the absence of good tools for building animations and the relative difficulty of using the few methods that do exist.

To build preset frame sequences, one typically uses a bitmap editor tool such as `bitmap(1)` under the X Window System. These types of tools show "blown-up" views of bitmaps, and they allow individual bits to be set or colored. When a bitmap's design is complete, it can be saved in a format for display on the screen. To generate an animation scenario, a developer must either use some form of player-tool for displaying the bitmaps in a repetitive sequence, or use blting operations of the support graphics environment.

Some tools exist for helping to automate this process. Animation editors, such as the commercial product MacroMind Director [Mac], contain graphics editors for building individual animation frames along with time-line style positioning tools. These tools allow a developer to draw a picture and then specify its placement at differing times (frames) in the resultant animation. The tool then interpolates intermediate positions for the picture and generates the corresponding frames. A few tools such as [Har, Cor] also support imagery changes throughout the frames, either as in picture in-betweening or shape-blending [Cat78, Sed92]. Tools for building animation changes driven off application parameter values, however, are difficult to find.

When animations using structured graphics techniques are necessary, the most common method to build animations is by hand-coding with a graphics toolkit. Unfortunately, powerful graphics toolkits such as the X Window System's Xlib library [Jon89] are large, very imposing, and usually quite time-consuming to learn.

It would, however, be naive to believe that extremely simple-to-use tools for creating complex animations, like those possible through Xlib, can be built without substantial thought and effort, simply because the generation of animation sequences is such a complex activity. But it should be possible to make animation more accessible to interface designers. One important way to achieve this goal is to move away from coding and programming and toward graphical direct manipulation [Shn83]. In the same way that graphical user interface builders now permit simplified layout of interfaces, graphical animation editors could allow designers to create animation scenarios for their interfaces in a simplified direct manipulation manner. The added dimension of time is what makes the development of these tools so challenging.

Some forms of these graphical animation builders already exist. The Dance animation designer [Sta91] supports the graphical creation of animations for the Tango algorithm animation system [Sta90b]. Algorithm animations are dynamic graphical illustrations of computer algorithms and programs, primarily for instructional purposes. An algorithm animation functions as a visual interface onto a program, giving concrete representations to the program's data and operations. In the next section we discuss the animation techniques of Tango further.

Dance allows developers to instantiate graphical objects and to specify how the objects should move and change in the animation. Developers can sketch out paths for objects to follow, and these different actions can be related to program events. When a developer has completed an animation's specification, he or she can instruct Dance to generate the corresponding Tango programming code that will carry out the animation.

The Whizz system [Cha92] also supports graphical creation of animation scenarios, and it specifically targets program interfaces such as games or debuggers. Whizz uses a musical metaphor to describe the graphical objects in an animation and their behaviors. It includes a graphical editor for building objects, specifying their motions, and testing the resulting designs.

The main drawback of graphical animation builders so far is that they are restricted to generating animations within the system paradigm in which they are implemented. That is, they do not generalize well. Dance, for example, can generate animations for the Tango system, but the code it generates can not be utilized elsewhere directly. Developing a graphical animation builder that can be used for programs in a broad context such as X Window system applications and that can use a number of different animation implementation techniques would benefit many interface developers.

Building better tools for creating the final appearance of an animation is still not good enough, however. Frequently, the main challenge of implementing an animation scenario is in acquiring the data to drive the animation, and then mapping the data to the appropriate animated images.

Consider the use of animation in percentage-done indicators to convey how far a process such as a compilation or a regular-expression search has progressed. On many computer operating systems, tools for performing these types of processes were not designed to provide intermediate feedback about the progress of their computation. Consequently, no data is available to drive the animation.

As alluded to earlier, many uses of animation in interfaces follow this pattern: An application produces a stream of parametric data, and particular values of the data map to corresponding animation states. Interpolating between the states requires scaling and the calculation of many intermediate points. Tools must be built which help users map data into animations that correspond to underlying states and conditions.

In the preceding sections we have analyzed animation from a number of different dimensions: fundamental definitions, design and implementation principles, appropriate application mappings, and the challenges of building animations. In the next section we survey four actual applications of animation to user interfaces.

## 5.5   ANIMATION IN INTERFACES: EXAMPLES

A user interface exhibiting, using, or involving animation is not a common occurrence. The absence of animation is primarily due to the lack of hardware support (speed) and the relative difficulty of implementing animation scenarios. Recently however, interface developers have begun to incorporate animation capabilities into their designs, even though these difficulties still exist. In this section we describe four projects that utilize animation in a user interface or program interface. They involve animated icons, animated help, program animations, and 3D interface animations, respectively. Each project is prototypical of a broader utilization, goal, or application of animation. In particular, these four projects involve in order

- Animation to help convey functionality
  (What is this for?)
- Animation for explanatory help information
  (How do I accomplish this?)
- Animation for understanding complex, time-varying processes
  (What is happening there?)
- Animation as a navigation and status aid
  (Where am I now?)

## 5.5.1  Animated Icons

A primary challenge of building a good user interface is conveying the available commands and their functionality. One of the best ways to convey functionality is by demonstration–explanation by example. In an interface with command choice implemented as icon selection, demonstration of functionality is difficult due to the static nature of icons. Making icons more expressive would help users, particularly novices, quickly learn how to use an application and would better convey the capabilities offered by the application.

In a project seeking to make interfaces more expressive, Baecker, Small, and Mander studied animated icons as aids for conveying functionality in user interfaces [Bae90]. Animated icons are icons that display short animation scenarios of command behaviors.

The focus of this study was the tool palette of the Hypercard program, which includes commands for drawing graphical objects, drawing text, painting, selecting groups of objects, and so on. In Hypercard, each command is chosen by selecting a static icon (22 x 20 bitmap) from the palette.

Baecker, Small, and Mander developed new animated icons for each command by creating sequences of bitmaps to be displayed in rapid succession (the preset frame sequence technique described earlier). To help with this process, the authors hired an experienced animator who was familiar with the Macintosh. Nevertheless, they reported that the animation process was arduous and that proper tools for designing and implementing the animation were lacking. Figure 5.2 shows a few examples of bitmap sequences that were developed for some of the Hypercard commands.

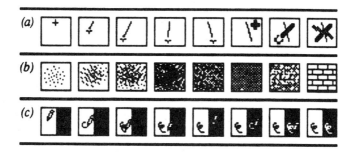

**Figure 5.2**  A series of bitmaps that were used to build the animated icons. Here (a) shows the line drawing tool, (b) shows the spray can tool, and (c) shows the pencil drawing tool. (Reprinted courtesy of ACM, ©1991.)

The authors conducted an empirical study of the icons' effectiveness for conveying command functionalities. Nine subjects, four having no experience with paint programs, four having some experience, and one paint program expert were shown the static icons, and were subsequently asked to characterize what command each icon activated. Of the 15 icons examined, the functionality of 10 of the icons was clear from their static representations for the novices, but the functionality of the other five was not clear. When the animated icons were used, all the subjects were able to identify the functionality of all the icons. The authors reported that all the subjects liked the animated icons and felt they were helpful for conveying the tool functionalities.

A number of interesting issues concerning the use of animation also were uncovered in the study. First, the authors needed to decide how and when the animations should be activated in the Hypercard palette. Having the animations play continuously was rejected as being "too busy." The final method used was to play an animation whenever the mouse cursor entered an icon. This required users to position the cursor near the border of the icon in order to not obscure the animation.

The subjects also suffered some confusion between simply watching the explanatory animated icon state and actually selecting a new command which required a mouse button selection. Sometimes a subject would move the cursor into an icon to activate the animation, but the subject would forget to actually select the icon with a mouse click.

The authors also reported that animations depicting different modes of a command sometimes confused users by fostering the thought that a particular mode could be chosen by selecting the icon at the instant the animation illustrated that mode.

This study of animated icons illustrates how animation can greatly enhance a user interface. The study also uncovers some subtle but extremely important issues in proper utilization of animation scenarios.

## 5.5.2  Animated Help

Learning how to operate a user interface of a software system can be a confusing and time-consuming task, particularly if the underlying system is complex. Undoubtedly, new users will make errors or simply not know how to invoke desired commands. These problems have emphasized the importance of including help information, or better yet, a help subsystem, with a user interface. Typically, help systems provide textual descriptions of the sequence of actions necessary to perform a given task. Textual descriptions frequently lack appropriate context, however, and they may not adequately describe the series of actions required for interface operations.

Sukaviriya has implemented a system, called Cartoonist, that provides context-sensitive animated help descriptions to assist users interacting with program interfaces [Suk90]. Her intention is to generate an intelligent help system which can demonstrate a user interface of an application. The animated help in her system displays a mouse moving on the screen demonstrating which object to select or which menu item to choose in order to complete a task. The animations also display characters flowing out from a keyboard icon to a destination text entry in order to designate character input.

Cartoonist's animated help is context-sensitive, that is, animation scenarios are dynamically constructed at runtime each time help is requested to reflect the current state of the screen and the application. For example, demonstrating how to rotate an object is shown as selecting "rotate" from its designated pulldown menu, clicking on an object, and specifying the amount of rotation desired (a few frames of this animation is shown in Figure 5.3). An existing object created by the user at its current screen position will be selected as part of the animation. Context-sensitive animation such as this is possible because the help system is tightly integrated with the user interface architecture; they share a common knowledge base of application semantics and user interface representations.

Cartoonist's animations can be started, stopped, and restarted at any time by the user clicking on the left mouse button. Sukaviriya chose to use animation to create help which resembles another human being helping out a fellow novice user by showing what needs to be done (from the stage he or she is in).

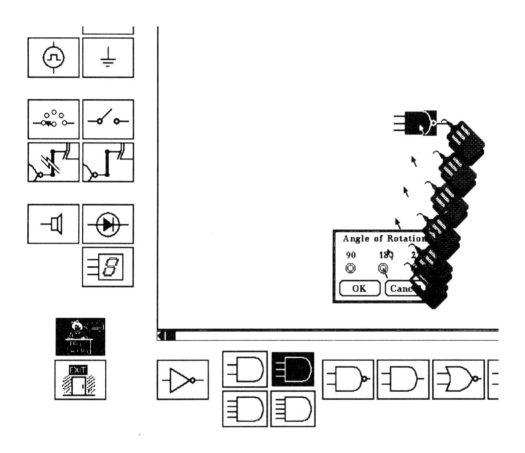

**Figure 5.3** A sample animation sequence showing an animated help scenario. (Picture courtesy of Noi Sukaviriya.)

The animation in Sukaviriya's system is one for which preset animation scenarios are far from being sufficient because the animation is determined only after checking the positions of objects to be selected or where a text entry is in a dialog box. Consequently, Cartoonist's animations are generated using XOR operations and techniques.

Sukaviriya is currently performing empirical tests to determine just how effective animated help can be. Her study is actually even broader than simple animated help: she is comparing animation to other techniques and media such as simple text, audio, video, and combinations thereof.

### 5.5.3  Animated Algorithm/Program Depictions

Quite often, a program's user interface is a depiction of the relevant entities and processes within the program. An interface can provide a high-level abstraction or view of the most important attributes of an application, and allow the user to analyze and interact with those attributes.

The field of *software visualization* and *animation* [Pri92, Sta92b] (frequently also labeled *program visualization* and *animation*) involves the use of graphics and animation to portray the execution of computer programs, processes, and algorithms. Animation provides a medium in which dynamic, time varying processes can be illustrated. Software visualization is challenging because programs are animated "on-the-fly" as execution occurs, and because many of the parameters for the animation are not available until they are determined at run-time.

When a software visualization depicts the fundamental problem and high-level abstractions of a program as they change over time, the visualization is called an *algorithm animation* [Bro88b]. The film *Sorting Out Sorting* [Bae81] shows animations of a number of different sorting algorithms in order to explain their functionalities and compare their performances. The film inspired a number of subsequent systems such as Balsa [Bro88a], Animus [Dui86], and Movie [Ben91] which all support the development of algorithm animations.

Animus' model of animation is particularly interesting. It is built on top of the constraint-based system Thinglab [Bor86], but Thinglab's constraints are automatic, that is, they include no notion of duration or sequencing. Animus adds the notion of temporal constraints, thus supporting dynamic, time-varying behaviors. The system was used to build a number of physics-related animated "simulations" such as the motion of weights on springs.

Another algorithm animation system, Tango [Sta90b], even provides an explicit animation methodology, the path-transition paradigm [Sta90a], and toolkit. This methodology was developed to make the specification and implementation of animation scenarios easier for programmers without extensive computer graphics and animation experience.

In the path-transition paradigm, graphical objects (called *images*) are created and manipulated as individual elements. Rather than making the programmer specify where each image should be in every frame, the paradigm provides *path* objects to help specify movements and changes in size. Paths are generic path-based motion descriptions [Bae69], and their attributes such as beginning or ending point, motion characteristics, offset spacing, etc., can be specified via run-time parameters.

To specify an animation action, a programmer "connects" a path to an image. The resultant logical action is encapsulated as a *transition* object. Transitions can be composed and concatenated to help specify concurrency and ordering of animation actions. When a transition is *performed*, the animation action it encapsulates is carried out. This entire process is specified at a high level to help shield programmers from the difficult pixel-level operations that must be carried out to generate animation scenarios. Figure 5.4 shows an animation of a binary search algorithm that was built using the XTango system [Sta92a], a descendant of Tango.

The conceptual path-transition animation methodology of Tango is implemented using two techniques described earlier. The first uses double buffering by dividing the eight bit planes of a color display into two logical buffers (actually only three bits are used for each buffer, leaving two bits unused). Implemented on top of the X Window System, this technique provides fast animation, but it only supports 8 colors. The second technique uses an offscreen pixmap and blting.

Software animation systems provide interfaces to computer programs in which the interface illustrates the ongoing processes of the program. As animation becomes easier to implement, these types of process description animation sequences will appear in more application user interfaces. Keeping the user updated about the state of the underlying command or computation is a key element of a user interface. The techniques that software animation systems have pioneered for illustrating dynamic processes should be applicable for helping to achieve these goals in a wide variety of user interfaces.

## 5.5.4   Animated 3D Interfaces

As user interfaces become more complex and the applications they serve become larger and more difficult to model, new methods of representing interfaces will begin to emerge. For interfaces serving large applications and/or data sets, methods for navigating through the application's data and states become extremely critical.

Card, Robertson, and Mackinlay have introduced a model for representing the user interface of information retrieval systems called the Information Visualizer [Car91]. This model uses 3D graphics and a number of specific visualization metaphors to provide users access to large information spaces.

The Information Visualizer is based on two key components: the 3D/Rooms metaphor for encapsulating virtual work areas and the Cognitive Co-processor scheduler-based user interface control agent [Rob89]. The 3D Rooms environment includes a number of "rooms" or virtual work areas (encapsulated in display windows) into which the user can enter and exit. Navigating through the rooms requires only the use of the mouse. Animation effects are used to provide a true sense of movement or walking between rooms. When the animation is smooth, users receive context to help them navigate to desired places.

One of the most interesting types of rooms displays Cone Tree information views [Rob91], which use a 3D tree structure to represent information spaces such as directory hierarchies. A Cone Tree is shown in Figure 5.5. When the user selects a node in the tree to be examined, the entire tree rotates smoothly to bring the selection to the forefront. The system's authors state that these types of animation effects are used to make typical interface retrieval tasks more of a perception task rather than a cognitive task, thus reducing the user's cognitive burden.

The Cognitive Co-processor architecture is responsible for carrying out the Information Visualizer's animation effects. The system uses hardware double-buffering on a high-end 3D graphics workstation for implementing the animations. A scheduler module is responsible for assuring that the appropriate responses to user tasks occur, and a governor module enforces that an appropriate number of frames per second are generated to provide smooth animation effects. If the system begins to fall behind, the governor reduces the amount of object rendering done per frame in order to "catch-up."

Unfortunately, 3D animation techniques such as those exhibited by the Information Vi-

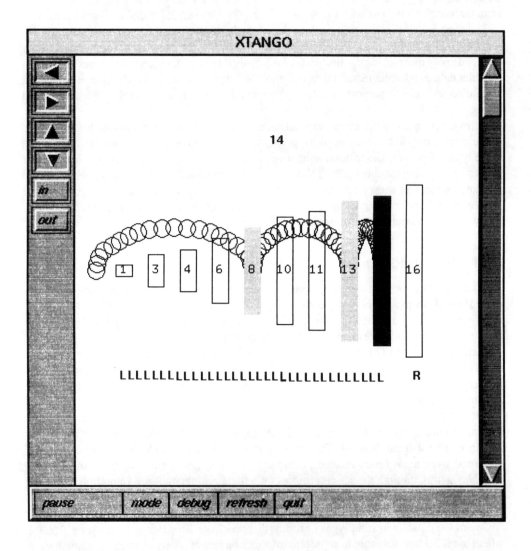

**Figure 5.4** This figures shows an animation of the binary search algorithm built with the XTango system. Here, a number of frames have been superimposed to help illustrate how the animation would appear. The "bouncing" circle traced the guesses of values in the array. The sequence of "L's" illustrated the movement of the left boundary pointer in the algorithm. Array values that were checked, unsuccessfully or successfully, are highlighted in two different colors. The XTango window contains buttons for panning and zooming (left), pausing (bottom), and a scrollbar for speed control.

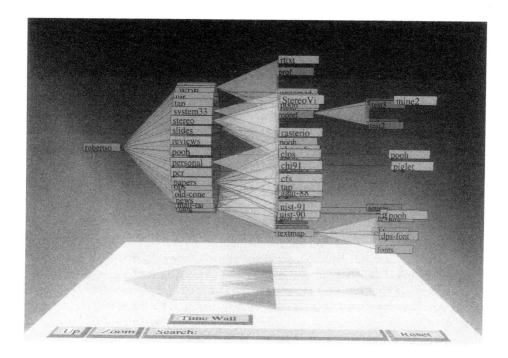

**Figure 5.5**  A view of a Cone Tree from the Information Visualizer. Each object represents a directory. When a user selects a directory into which to move, the entire structure smoothly rotates to bring that structure to the front. (Reprinted courtesy of George Robertson and ACM, ©1991.)

sualizer require extremely powerful graphics hardware that is currently out-of-reach for the vast majority of users. Nevertheless, the Information Visualizer illustrates the potential of 3D graphics and animation for user interfaces. At a time when few interfaces utilize 2D animation scenarios, the use of 3D graphics, and the knowledge required to implement such a metaphor, appears ominous. The introduction of easy-to-use tools not requiring an extensive 3D graphics background, however, can make generating 3D interfaces and animations a more practical and widely available option.

## 5.6   THE FUTURE

In the preceding sections, we have discussed motivations for adding animation to user interfaces, animation design and implementation principles, the challenges of mapping applications to animation scenarios, tools for building animations, and a few recent projects involving animation in interfaces. Regardless of these descriptions, the application of animation in user interfaces is still in its infancy. This absence is primarily due to two problems: (1) We need better tools for designing and implementing animations—tools that are easy-to-use and do not require graphics expertise. (2) We need to evaluate the effectiveness of animation in interfaces and determine where and how to best utilize animation.

Future research must address these problems for animation to become more prevalent in interfaces. The current emphasis on multimedia interface design further emphasizes the importance of good animation tools and techniques.

Care must be observed along this development path, however. The flash and appeal of animation can make its application a tempting proposition, but the scatter-shot use of animation without evaluating its effectiveness for a particular task is unwise. Relatively little research on assessing the effectiveness and appropriateness of animation in interfaces has been conducted. The study of animated icons discussed earlier is one of the few examples of this type of work. Palmiteer and Elkerton [Pal91] found that animation, when coupled with textual explanations, can initially improve both accuracy and speed of subjects following procedural instructions. These advantages were lost after a seven day time period, however, leading the authors to question the value of animation for retention of information.

Many more studies of this nature are required before we can better understand how to utilize animation properly in user interfaces. In particular, it is still unknown what types of processes, tasks, states, etc., can be well represented using animation, and exactly which styles of animation best convey the pertinent information. Our intuition, from working with animation on a number of research projects, is that animation is best applied when portraying or illustrating the state of time-varying processes. The future research agenda for animation in user interfaces challenges scientists to prove, disprove, or clarify this claim, and to create better tools for developing animated interfaces.

## ACKNOWLEDGMENTS

Thanks to Jim Foley, Noi Sukaviriya, and the paper's referees for providing helpful feedback on the improvement of this article.

## APPENDIX: IMPLEMENTING ANIMATIONS UNDER X

The X Window System has become a de facto windowing and interface standard for the UNIX workstation market. Every day, many new applications and their interfaces are developed using X as a support platform. In this appendix, a sort of "practitioner's corner," we sketch out some simple techniques for implementing animation scenarios using the X Window System's Xlib package.

X provides a number of different ways to implement animation scenarios discussed earlier in this article. To use the exclusive-or drawing technique, a programmer must create a graphics context (GC) and set its drawing function to XOR drawing mode. The simplest call to carry out this operation is

```
XSetFunction(display, gc, GXxor);
```

Subsequent drawing operations will then combine source and destination pixels according to the XOR logical mode.

X includes a number of system extensions, one being the Double Buffering extension that was developed to help animation design. Unfortunately, since extensions are not part of the standard X distribution, many installations may not have the double buffer capability. If system portability is a concern, using the double buffer extension is not recommended. Otherwise, the double buffer extension can be a good way to develop animation scenarios.

The most common way to implement animation under X is through blting. Let us assume that we have a 500x500 Window on a color display in which we want to present animation sequences. We must begin by creating an offscreen pixmap of equal size to this window.

```
pixmap = XCreatePixmap(display, drawable, width, height, win_depth);
```

For us, the `width` and `height` arguments should be `500`.

Because a pixmap's contents are undefined at creation, we must clear out the pixmap before we proceed with animation. Let us also assume that the desired background color (e.g., white) has been loaded into a GC to be the current drawing color. To clear the pixmap, we do

```
XFillRectangle(display, pixmap, gc, x, y, width, height);
```

The `x, y` pair defines the upper left corner of the pixmap at which to draw the rectangle and the `width, height` pair specifies how much of the pixmap should be drawn into. We want `x, y` to be `0, 0` and `width, height` to be `500, 500`.

Now that the offscreen pixmap is ready, we can draw the imagery for the first animation frame into it using X's drawing operations. When all the drawing is complete, we transfer the entire contents of the pixmap to the display window using the call

```
XCopyArea(display, pixmap, dest_win, gc, src_x, src_y, width, height,
          dest_x, dest_y);
```

The parameters to the call specify where the block should be taken from, transferred into, and how much of the pixmap should be transferred. For us, both the source and destination `x, y` pairs should be `0, 0`.

The simplest way to generate subsequent frames is to repeat the `XFillRectangle` call, draw the new imagery, and `XCopyArea` call sequence. We must clear the pixmap each time because the old frame's images are still there. Unfortunately, this simple process can be slow because of the number of pixel-write operations involved. The comprehensive XFillRectangle call each frame, in particular, is usually expensive (slow) under X.

One straightforward way to improve this process is to "erase" each object in the old frame by re-drawing it in the background color, rather than simply clearing out the whole buffer. Although this doubles the number of drawing operations for each frame, it will run much faster than the one XFillRectangle call, even for a fairly large number of objects. It can be slow and inefficient if a very large number of objects exist and relatively few are modified per frame, however.

An alternative, more sophisticated solution requires the acquisition of object bounding boxes or extents and the use of clipping operations. In a clipping operation, a region (usually rectangular) can be specified so that only drawing operations within that region affect the buffer's contents. Any part of of a drawing operation that occurs outside the region is not performed. In this technique as we keep track of the objects that are modified for the next frame, we can also maintain a cumulative bounding box for the region inside of which all modified objects' extensions fit. The bounding box must include both the current and next positions for all modified objects. When the final bounding box has been determined, it is used as a clipping region for the subsequent erase and redraw operations via XSetClipRectangles. Setting a clipping region to this area ensures that graphics rendering operations will not modify anywhere outside of the region. Finally, we simply erase the "damaged" region via an XFillRectangle call and proceed to redraw objects.

Every object in the buffer potentially may be inside the damaged region. But rather than automatically drawing each object and relying on the clipping to mask all but the damaged region, it may be advantageous to first check if an object intersects with the damaged region. If it does, it is redrawn. If not, the algorithm simply moves on to the next object.

One final bit of care must be taken for implementing these blt-based animation sequences. When the onscreen window is resized, we must destroy the old offscreen pixmap and create a new one of the appropriate size. Because resize-window events are often passed to onscreen windows before all their start-up initialization has occurred, the pixmap destruction and re-creation code should check that an active pixmap does already exist before it proceeds.

# REFERENCES

[Bae69]  Ronald M. Baecker. Picture-driven animation. In *Spring Joint Computer Conference*, volume 34, pages 273–288. AFIPS Press, 1969.

[Bae81]  Ronald M. Baecker and David Sherman. Sorting Out Sorting. 16mm color sound film, 1981. Shown at SIGGRAPH '81, Dallas TX.

[Bae90]  Ronald Baecker and Ian Small. Animation at the interface. In Brenda Laurel, editor, *The Art of Hunan-Computer Interface Design*, pages 251–267. Addison-Wesley, Reading, MA, 1990.

[Ben91]  Jon L. Bentley and Brian W. Kernighan. A system for algorithm animation. *Computing Systems*, 4(1), Winter 1991.

[Bor86]  Alan Borning and Robert Duisberg. Constraint-based tools for building user interfaces. *ACM Transactions on Graphics*, 5(4):345–374, October 1986.

[Bro88a]  Marc H. Brown. Exploring algorithms using Balsa-II. *Computer*, 21(5):14–36, May 1988.

[Bro88b]  Marc H. Brown. Perspectives on algorithm animation. In *Proceedings of the ACM SIGCHI '88 Conference on Human Factors in Computing Systems*, pages 33–38, Washington D.C., May 1988.

[Car91]  Stuart K. Card, George G. Robertson, and Jock Mackinlay. The Information Visualizer, an information workspace. In *Proceedings of the ACM SIGCHI '91 Conference on Human*

*Factors in Computing Systems*, pages 181–188, New Orleans, LA, May 1991.

[Cat78]     Edwin Catmull.   The problems of computer-assisted animation.   *Computer Graphics*, 12(3):348–353, 1978.

[Cha92]     Stephane Chatty. Defining the dynamic behavior of animated interfaces. In *5th IFIP Working Conference on Engineering for Human Computer Interaction*, Ellivuori, Finland, August 1992.

[Cor]       Corel-Draw! 2.0. Corel Systems Corporation, Ottawa, Canada, 1990.

[Dui86]     Robert A. Duisberg. Animated graphical interfaces using temporal constraints. In *Proceedings of the ACM SIGCHI '86 Conference on Human Factors in Computing Systems*, pages 131–136, Boston, MA, April 1986.

[Fol90]     James D. Foley, Andries Van Dam, Steven K. Feiner, and John F. Hughes. *Computer Graphics Principles and Practice*. Addison-Wesley, Reading, MA, 1990.

[Har]       Harvard Graphics 3.0. Software Publishing Corporation, Sunnyvale, CA, 1991.

[Jon89]     Oliver Jones. *Introduction to the X Window System*. Prentice Hall, Englewood Cliffs, NJ, 1989.

[Mac]       Macromind Director. MacroMind Inc., Chicago, IL, 1991.

[Mye85]     Brad A. Myers. The importance of percent-done progress indicators for computer-human interfaces. In *Proceedings of the ACM SIGCHI '85 Conference on Human Factors in Computing Systems*, pages 11–17, 1985.

[New90]     Alan Newell. *Unified Theories of Cognition*. Harvard University Press, Cambridge, MA, 1990.

[Pal91]     Susan Palmiteer and Jay Elkerton. An evaluation of animated demonstrations for learning computer-based tasks. In *Proceedings of the ACM SIGCHI '91 Conference on Human Factors in Computing Systems*, pages 257–263, New Orleans, LA, May 1991.

[Pri92]     Blaine A. Price, Ian S. Small, and Ronald M. Baecker. A taxonomy of software visualization. In *Proceedings of the 25th Hawaii International Conference on System Sciences*, volume II, pages 597–606, Kauai, HI, January 1992.

[Rob89]     George G. Robertson, Stuart K. Card, and Jock Mackinlay. The Cognitive Coprocessor architecture for intercative user interfaces. In *Proceedings of the ACM SIGGRAPH '89 Symposium on User Interface Software and Technology on Human*, pages 10–18, Williamsburg, VA, November 1989.

[Rob91]     George G. Robertson, Jock Mackinlay, and Stuart K. Card.   Cone trees: Animated 3D visualizations of hierarchical information. In *Proceedings of the ACM SIGCHI '91 Conference on Human Factors in Computing Systems*, pages 189–194, New Orleans, LA, May 1991.

[Sed92]     Thomas W. Sederberg and Eugene Greenwood. A physically based approach to 2-D shape blending. *Computer Graphics*, 26(2):25–34, July 1992.

[Shn83]     Ben Shneiderman. Direct manipulation: A step beyond programming languages. *Computer*, 16(8):57–69, 1983.

[Sho79]     R. G. Shoup.  Color table animation.  *Computer Graphics: SIGGRAPH '79*, 13(2):8–13, August 1979.

[Sta90a]    John T. Stasko. The Path-Transition Paradigm: A practical methodology for adding animation to program interfaces. *Journal of Visual Languages and Computing*, 1(3):213–236, September 1990.

[Sta90b]    John T. Stasko.  TANGO: A framework and system for algorithm animation.  *Computer*, 23(9):27–39, September 1990.

[Sta91]     John T. Stasko. Using direct manipulation to build algorithm animations by demonstration. In *Proceedings of the ACM SIGCHI '91 Conference on Human Factors in Computing Systems*, pages 307–314, New Orleans, LA, May 1991.

[Sta92a]    John T. Stasko. Animating algorithms with XTANGO. *SIGACT News*, 23(2):67–71, Spring 1992.

[Sta92b]    John T. Stasko and Charles Patterson. Understanding and characterizing software visualization systems. In *Proceedings of the IEEE 1992 Workshop on Visual Languages*, pages 3–10, Seattle, WA, September 1992.

[Suk90]     Piyawadee Sukaviriya. Coupling a UI framework with automatic generation of context-sensitive animated help. In *Proceedings of the ACM SIGGRAPH Symposium on User Interface Software and Technology*, pages 152–166, Snowbird, Utah, October 1990.

# 6

# Virtual Reality: Perspectives, Applications, and Architecture

**Chris Esposito**

*Virtual Systems Group*
*Research and Technology Division*
*Boeing Computer Services*

## ABSTRACT

From a participants perspective, a fully immersive virtual reality experience is probably unlike any other encounter with a computer they have ever had. From a human engineering point of view, VR is a next step in adapting technology to the user, rather than the other way around. From a system designers point of view, VR is an integration of some existing technologies and some that are either new or just starting to flower. This paper discusses these differing perspectives, highlights difficulties and developments in applications of VR, and deals with VR system architectures and system implementation issues.

## 6.1   Introduction to Virtual Environments

One of the difficulties with a broad term like 'virtual reality' (VR) is that so many different fields of human endeavor can plausibly lay claim to creating them or allowing people to experience them. We enter into some sort of a virtual world every time we read a work of fiction, see a play, run a simulation, or put on a head mounted display (HMD). In order to reduce the scope of this chapter to a tractable size, we will primarily be concerned with computer-generated three-dimensional environments that contain objects with geometry and behavior.

From a participants perspective, a fully immersive virtual reality experience is probably unlike any other encounter with a computer they have ever had. From a human engineering point of view, VR is a next step in adapting technology to the user, rather than the other

---

*User Interface Software*, Edited by Bass and Dewan

way around. From a system designer's point of view, VR is an integration of some existing technologies and some that are either new or just starting to flower. These differing perspectives make a definition acceptable to all difficult to come by, so what we will focus on in the first part of this chapter are the different perspectives. The next major section highlights difficulties and developments in applications of VR. The final section deals with VR system architectures and system implementation issues.

## 6.1.1   The System Designer's Perspective

One view of VR is that it is one type of highly interactive three dimensional (HITD) application. Green, Shaw, and Pausch [GSP92] define an HITD application as one that addresses a domain that naturally supports three dimensions, presents application data in a 3D form, and allows the user to interact with the data using 3D manipulation and interaction techniques. The 'highly interactive' portion of the name indicates the tight temporal coupling between user actions and system responses.

Simulation is another area with close ties to VR. The controlled exploration capability provided by computer simulations of complex physical systems has significantly increased the amount and quality of insight someone can gain into the properties of the system. Some of these simulations have been non-interactive and nongraphical. Others, such as the animations in the "Mechanical Universe" series of physics videos [Bli91] are graphical but not interactive. The systems that provide a graphical or multisensory display as well as real-time interactivity often provide the greatest potential for insight. As an example, see the 'virtual wind tunnel' work described in Levitt and Bryson [LB91].

Human engineering is an aspect of engineering design that adapts the design to take advantage of human perceptual, cognitive, and motor skills, while at the same time respecting (or even helping to overcome) human limitations in the same areas. Human engineering (also called usability engineering) is not a young discipline - the recently published notebooks of Leonardo Da Vinci repeatedly remark on its importance. Given the highly evolved skills people have for dealing with their environment, these human factors considerations are of the highest importance if the full potential of VR is to be realized.

Some of the ways that human engineering is particularly relevant to VR are in the area of specialized and somewhat exotic (at least in current terms) I/O devices. The intent of these devices is to provide a much more natural and direct high-bandwidth connection between the users body and the virtual world than is typically possible using other interface devices like keyboards and mice. Examples of these devices include HMDs that fill a wearers field of view so they feel as if they are in the scene, rather than looking though a window; digital signal processors that can spatially localize a sound source, so that it sounds as if it were coming from a particular point in space; position tracking and gesture recognition systems that allow the user to use motor skills well beyond 'pointing and clicking'; and tactile/force feedback that can simulate the perception of touch, texture, and physical constraints.

## 6.1.2   The Participant's Perspective

The most distinctive aspect of immersive VR is also the most difficult to describe in a way that matches the compelling nature of the experience. There is a strong sense that the user is much more actively involved when using an immersive VR system than when using most other software. There is often a corresponding shift in terminology to reflect this, so we will often use the term 'participant' as a way of referring to someone that is currently 'inside' a virtual world. Independent informal surveys conducted at Autodesk, VPL, HITL, NASA, and Boeing report that upon completion of a demo, over 90% of first-time subjects reported a very positive experience, one that involved a moderate to strong sense of presence [Bri90]. By presence, we mean that their subjective sense of where they were shifted temporarily from the room they were standing in to the environment displayed in the HMD. In this section, we will examine the participants perspective from two directions. First, by briefly discussing the ways in which our senses contribute to our sense of presence. Second, we will look at some criteria that have been proposed for classifying virtual worlds and the experiences they have to offer.

### 6.1.2.1   Presence and Virtualization

The words 'presence' and 'telepresence' have related but distinct meanings. The aspect they have in common is the idea of being able to affect objects in environments other than the one the participant is physically in. Telepresence has usually been used in conjunction with remote physical environments; remote control of a robot is one example of telepresence. As described in the previous section, presence is more of a psychological phenomena, and the pictured environment may not exist at all. Presence is also an end result. One of the processes that is partly responsible for producing it is virtualization. As defined in Ellis [Ell91], virtualization is "the process by which a human viewer interprets a patterned sensory impression to be an object in an environment other than that in which it physically exists." As this definition suggests, virtualization is not limited to any particular sensory modality, although the higher bandwidth of vision compared to the other senses means that it will dominate the others, so that an image of an object may be virtualized even if no other sense inputs are present. In addition, the immersive nature of some HMDs and the sense of presence they help induce means that virtualization is not just a property of objects, but also of the environment they are in.

### 6.1.2.2   Vision and Virtualization

There is a broad range of capabilities that may be present in anything that may plausibly be a VR display, although there appear to be two principal axes that serve to position VR display systems. The first axis has to do with perceived properties of the image(s) presented to the eye(s), and the second has to do with the sources of the image data and the extent to which they are real or synthetic.

The first axis has to do with levels of virtualization. As discussed in Ellis [Ell91], there are 3 levels. The first is virtual space, which is the process by which a viewer perceives a 3D layout of objects in space when viewing a flat surface. The objects displayed contain just the cues of perspective, shading, occlusion, and texture. This process is the most abstract because most of the physiological responses associated with a real 3D environment are either missing or wrong.

The second level is the virtual image. This level involves the perception of the object in which the additional cues of accommodation, convergence, and stereoscopic disparity are present. Accommodation is the focusing of the eye to sharpen the image on the retina. Convergence is the amount of inward rotation of the eyes needed to produce one apparent image. Stereoscopic disparity is the difference in the binocular parallax of a point as measured from each eye. As pointed out in Robinett and Rolland [RR92], in most current HMDs the accommodative and convergence cues are inconsistent, which can lead to viewing being more tiring than normal. Almost all HMDs have focus depth fixed at infinity, although Kaiser Electronics has announced a model which allows some variation in depth of focus. In order for a variable-focal length system to be useful, it needs to take physical display geometry into account and be closely integrated with the eye and head tracking systems so that the virtual object being focused on can be determined and the focus set appropriately.

The third level is the virtual environment. This final and most realistic form of virtualization involves the additional cues of observer-slaved motion parallax (head/eye tracking), depth of focus variation, and a wide field of view (FOV) without a significant frame. Most immersive display systems systems strive to provide as wide an FOV as possible, with the current high end at 162 degrees combined horizontal FOV in the CAE Fiber Optic HMD. The lower bound on a horizontal FOV that produces a sense of inclusion is about 60 degrees.

The second axis may be called the real/synthetic axis. At one end of this axis (the 'real' end), the HMD is see-through, so the wearer clearly sees most or all of the environment they are physically in. The design of this HMD is similar to a wearable heads-up display (HUD), in that images can be projected onto the semi-transparent display areas in front of the eyes. These HMDs often differ from existing HUDs in that the HMD wearers' head (and possibly eyes) are being tracked, with the image projection constantly adjusted so that the images appear to be in a fixed position, as if they were "painted" onto objects in the real world. The physical environment is in view, but it appears to be annotated or augmented with the additional information or objects. This is a case in which presence and virtualization are decoupled. It is possible for the displayed image to be virtualized, because it appears to be a decal on an object, but the viewers sense of presence does not shift. For a discussion of a design and potential uses for this sort of display, see Caudell and Mizell [CM92].

At the other end of this axis are the immersive displays. Some of these are HMDs, and some are external very wide screen displays that have a sufficiently wide FOV. The completely immersive HMDs are the 'goggles' part of the 'goggles and gloves' canonical definition of VR usually seen in the popular press. The images displayed are completely synthetic, as opposed to being a recreation of the surrounding physical environment. The worlds displayed may also be completely unreal, in that they don't or can't exist.

A middle point on this axis holds systems that are hybrids in one way or another. Typically, these involve an integration of some synthetic imagery (as in the immersive displays) and image data from the real world, although instead of normal human vision (as in the see-through displays) the source of the image data is ultrasonic, infrared, millimeter wave radar, amplified light, or stored images, to name some possibilities. If a common use for the immersive displays is to allow us to see new or alternative worlds, a common use for some of the hybrid systems is to allow us to see the existing world in new ways, as if we had new senses. For a description of a system that combines video with 3D scenes synthesized from 2D ultrasound images, see Bajura, Fuchs, and Ohbuchi [BFO92].

### 6.1.2.3   Three-Dimensional Audio

Many investigators have pointed out that the auditory system is an important information channel, either complementing, or in some cases, substituting for other channels [Dea72, DGEF86]. A virtual 3D sound is a sound that has been processed so that it appears to be coming from a point in a virtual world. Additional capabilities include reflections off of objects in the environment with specified material properties [FW91].

Acoustic signals have several useful characteristics. They can be detected more quickly than visual signals [Pat82]; they can be used to produce an alerting or orienting response, and the sound source can be accurately localized in 3 dimensions in real time. These characteristics suggest how spatially localized sound can complement 3D visualization. The combination of the speed of detection, extreme sensitivity to small changes over time, and the ability to localize sounds outside the field of view make 3D audio a very effective means for allowing the ears to "point the eyes" [Wen92], or direct the view towards a new or significant event in the environment.

### 6.1.2.4   Tactile/Force Feedback

The ability to reach out and touch a virtual object is often presented as one of the most compelling aspects of a VR experience. Several commercially available whole-hand input devices [VPL87, MC88] work in an open loop system, without tactile or force feedback. Studies [Hil76] have shown that completion time for some complex manual tasks is reduced by up to 50% when the loop is closed and force feedback is provided. It is important to distinguish tactile feedback from force feedback. Tactile feedback is used to produce a sense of touch, of one surface contacting another. It can also be used to provide a sense of an objects' shape, but the tactile feedback provided to a virtual hand will not prevent it from penetrating the surface of the touched virtual object. Force feedback, on the other hand, can in principle be used to prevent inter-object penetration or it can also be used to rigidly constrain motion, as in the modeling of inter-atomic forces described in Brooks, et. al. [BOYBK90].

## 6.1.3   Classifying Virtual Worlds

In this section we will briefly review some of the schemes for classifying virtual worlds and some aspects of the experiences they provide to their inhabitants. It is important to remember that virtual worlds are developed for a variety of different reasons and sometimes conflicting goals. One of these goals is that the worlds be as realistic as possible. The different forms of realism include visual, in high-performance flight simulators; behavioral, as in a very detailed and accurate model of legged motion [MZ90], and auditory, as in a simulation of the sound of an orchestra bouncing off walls made of different materials and different geometries.

### 6.1.3.1   The Quest for Realism

Currently there are often substantial tradeoffs between realism and performance, as well as tradeoffs between cost and performance. If we simply and linearly extrapolate some current research trends, the conclusion we are led to accept is that the "holy grail" of VR is a world that contains fully autonomous agents that behave as their physical counterparts do and that presents a sensory experience that is arbitrarily close to the real thing. While the social and philosophical implications of VR are just beginning to be unfolded [Rhe91, Sto91] it is already clear that some of the greatest advantages may come from the ways in which we are selectively freed from physical constraints. For example, several current projects involve the development of systems that allow a human user to remotely manipulate objects using mechanical arms or other devices that provide force feedback. If several hundred pounds of pressure were suddenly and accidentally applied to the robot arms, faithfully replicating this force and applying it to the human users' arms would be seen as a serious bug, not a feature.

### 6.1.3.2   Integration, Verity, and Interface

Several dimensions have been proposed as a way of classifying VR and related systems, such as flight simulators and some kinds of computer games. Thurman [Thu92] proposes three dimensions: integration, verity, and interface. Integration refers to the extent which multiple sensory modalities are used in coordinated fashion. verity is the dimension that describes the extent to which virtual objects "behave" as their physical counterparts do. Interface is the dimension that is labeled 'highly artificial' at one end and 'highly natural' at the other. It is tempting to simply fix some sorts of interface devices and techniques at one end (such as the use of mice and keyboards at the low end) and others at the high end (datagloves, head tracking, etc.) but it needs to be emphasized that the naturalness of an interaction technique is task-specific, and what may be natural for some tasks may not be natural for others.

### 6.1.3.3   Autonomy, Interaction, and Presence

A somewhat different set of dimensions have been proposed by Zeltzer [Zel92]: autonomy, presence, and interaction. Autonomy is a qualitative measure of a virtual object determined by the range of events and stimuli it can respond to as well as the range and complexity of the responses. At one end are passive objects that have nothing but geometry and other graphical attributes. Their only "behavior" is to display themselves. At the other end are "virtual actors", such as those described in Zeltzer and Johnson [ZJar], that are capable of much more sophisticated planning and behavior of various kinds.

Presence is a measure of the number, fidelity, and appropriateness of the sensory input and output channels. What modalities ought to be present, and the devices used to support them are a function of the task.

Interaction measures the degree of access to model and object attributes or parameters at runtime. Most VR systems and HITD systems fall on the upper end of this dimension. However, simply providing access to these attributes is not sufficient, because the usability of the system will substantially depend on the access interface provided to the user. There are many current applications outside of the VR domain that provide a great deal of power through the many features they provide. The sheer number of these features and their interactions often overwhelms the new or casual user, so usability issues become paramount. If we attempt to control interacting features in anything close to real time, then the problem can be much more difficult, because the number of degrees of freedom can be quite small (3-6) and still provide a challenge for experienced users. For example, when people were required to simultaneously control all 6 position/orientation degrees of freedom, maintaining a desired viewpoint proved to be very difficult, with many people spinning off into the virtual void [Bri90].

## 6.2   Applications

An attendee at a recent VR conference was heard to remark that many of the applications being presented were as virtual (i.e., unreal) as the realities they were to generate. There is, as of late 1992, a kernel of truth in this casual assessment. There are several hurdles in the way of wider adoption of VR, but there are also prospects for improvement and some compelling reasons to believe that, given these improvements, real and significant VR applications will be emerging in the next five years. In this section we will look at some problem areas for application developers, followed by a partial list of those application areas likely to create significant pull on VR technology.

## 6.2.1   Development Hurdles

There are several problems that VR application developers face in putting VR to work in solving real problems: immature technologies, high costs, and system integration difficulties. Some of the problems that need to be solved, such as faster graphics, are being pushed towards solutions by markets and needs far larger than VR, so it may be sufficient for VR to piggyback on these markets. Others, such as personal position tracking and HMDs, do not yet appear to have any other significant user than VR, and here there is a bit of a chicken and egg problem - the technological capabilities are not adequate, so the applications that would demonstrate the benefits of VR are not there, so the markets for the products needed to use the applications do not exist, so the potential vendors are not motivated to create products with adequate technical capabilities. It is still too early to tell how and when this situation is going to resolve itself.

### 6.2.1.1   Immature Technologies

It will be immediately apparent to anyone that tries on almost any currently available HMD that their resolution, weight, and comfort leave a lot to be desired. These difficulties make it all the more remarkable that according to several informal surveys of first-time VR users, the vast majority find it to be a very positive experience. While there is some progress in this area (see section 6.3.3.4), HMDs are not the only problem. Each of the currently available position tracking technologies (magnetic, acoustic, optical, mechanical) has its share of difficulties, although some of the technologies with future potential, such as microaccelerometers and microgyroscopes, are progressing in various research labs. Although systems for 3D localization of sound are commercially available, many of the other modalities (tactile, force feedback, texture) are still in the basic research labs, or just barely emerging.

### 6.2.1.2   High Cost

While the cost of computing in general has dropped dramatically over the last decade, the price/performance curve for VR systems is still fairly steep. The hardware for a sample standalone low-end system might consist of:

- a 386/486/68030/68040 system w/keyboard and mouse
- video display / graphics accelerator boards
- 1 or more position trackers (e.g., Logitech, Polhemus, or Ascension)
- 3D sound localization board
- 1 or more glove or other input devices (wands, joysticks, etc.)
- 1 Head Mounted Display

The software for such a system would likely include:

- CAD/3D modeling software
- device drivers for specialized input devices
- rendering software
- simulation and control software

The cost for just the hardware listed above is easily in the $15-20,000 range, with the software adding between $1-3,000, which puts the total cost of the system beyond the reach of most individuals. While many companies can afford these amounts, the performance offered by these systems limits the size and complexity of the virtual world to roughly 1000 polygons at 5-15 Hz, with simulation capabilities roughly equal to a video game. The marginal cost of additional performance rises very quickly - for example, at the upper end of the cost/performance curve, a multiprocessor SGI Reality Engine, which can produce several hundred thousand antialiased texture-mapped polygons per second can also cost several hundred thousand dollars. In addition, the old saying that a chain is only as strong as its' weakest link comes back with a vengeance here. For example, the resolution in the vast majority of the currently commercially available HMDs is sufficiently low that much of the wonderful visual realism produced by high-end graphics systems is not seen and so is not useful to the end user. More generally, the users' perceptions of how well the system performs and how much of an aid it is greatly depends on how the system performs as an integrated whole, rather than as a collection of components, so the existence of weak links can have a disproportionately large impact.

The architectural components that VR systems share with more conventional systems, such as 3D rendering hardware and software, can expect to benefit from, and possibly help drive, the continuing improvements in price / performance ratios for this equipment. There is much less evidence, either positive or negative, that suggests what the future holds for those components that are unique to VR, and the companies that make them. Both Latta [Lat92] and Wexelblatt [Wex92] have done more in depth work on the business, market development, and technology transfer issues that need to be addressed in order for there to be a viable VR industry.

### 6.2.1.3   System Integration

If VR is to succeed outside the research arena, then it must take into account the needs of the designers, artists, engineers, and educators that would be its end users. Since much of the promise of VR lies in the adaptation of technology to take much greater advantage of human perceptual and cognitive capabilities, this promise will go unrealized unless some sort of user - centered design is done that takes these capabilities and limitations as a central focus, rather than an inconvenience to be worked around. Virtual reality draws on many technology areas, and there are three broad stages of development that must be gone through to achieve a satisfactory level of system integration.

1. Demonstrate sufficient capability in each of the technology areas
2. Integrate these capabilities into research lab prototypes
3. Deal with manufacturability, reliability, and usability issues from the perspective of the end user.

Past and current researchers may be willing to put up with things like HMDs that are awkward to put on and only semi-comfortable to wear, but the partial list of end users shown above probably won't. Some observations from each of the three stages are briefly given below.

As currently conceived, VR requires advances in several technology areas. In some of these areas, such as 3D graphics, current capability growth rates indicate that the needed level of performance is very likely to be there at or near the time it is needed. For some other technologies, such as speech recognition, there are promising approaches to solve existing problems so it is likely that sufficient capabilities will be available for a prototype, although with a lower degree of certainty than above. For other requirements such as untethered extended range position tracking, none of the existing solutions are adequate, and many of the alternative solutions are barely in the research lab prototype stage.

The integration of all of the individual technologies required is likely to be a significant effort in itself. If we accept the notion that even in the field-deployed systems, users will still wear some sort of I/O devices, such as head-mounted display goggles, then a collection of ergonomic criteria emerge:

a) portable
b) lightweight
c) comfortable
d) safe
e) easy to put on/take off
f) non-intrusive
g) robust/rugged enough for normal day-to-day use

The disparate software technologies (3D interaction, voice recognition / understanding, 3D graphics, simulation etc.) also all need to work together in a responsive and coordinated fashion. Taken altogether, these requirements dictate a level of software and hardware integration and manufacturing / packaging sophistication that is well beyond what is usually seen in research prototypes used to demonstrate technical capabilities.

## 6.2.2   Real and Potential Applications

In this section we will look at some of the real and probable applications of VR. Given the early stage that most of the development systems are in, the number of applications that have been proposed is quite large. In fact, overselling the potential and the unrealistically high expectations that follow are a real problem for VR in light of all of the coverage it has recently received. The application areas we will discuss are scientific and financial visualization, entertainment and recreation, design preview and analysis, and training. Additional discussion of applications can be found in Rheingold [Rhe91], and Matrix [Ser90].

### 6.2.2.1   Visualization

*Scientific Visualization*   Many applications involve the graphical presentation of 3D (or higher dimension) data, and the data often varies as a function time. Fluid flows and volume visualization are examples of this. The ability to interactively view and change the parameters of a simulation can greatly increase the viewer's insight into the simulated phenomena. An example of this is the immersive CFD visualization (the 'virtual wind tunnel') described in Levitt and Bryson [LB91]. This system shows fluid flows over the surface of a space shuttle, and allows the viewer to change their viewpoint, and change the number and placement of tracer streams in the fluid flow.

*Financial Visualization*   While scientists have long enjoyed increasingly sophisticated dynamic visualization tools for looking at their multivariate data, they have only recently come into use in the financial community. An example system called Portsys uses mathematical models of stock behavior to simulate and visualize investment portfolio behavior [Rob91].

The models for this system have been developed by Stanley Pliska, head of the Finance department and head of Advanced Financial Research at the University of Illinois. Example variables that make up the dataset for a portfolio include the number of stocks, the number of shares in each one, and the price and trading volume data for each stock over time. Additional work on interactive visualization of financial data is being done by Citicorp and American Express. Some of this work is described in Feiner and Besher [FB90].

### 6.2.2.2   Entertainment and Recreation

The most visible examples of entertainment applications are the VR video games, such as Battletech, or Virtuality from W industries. Other companies, including MGM and Walt Disney, are reportedly working on entertainment applications but few details have been released.

### 6.2.2.3   Design Preview and Analysis

The complexity of the design and manufacturing processes for many large modern physical structures is staggering; for example it is estimated that a Boeing 747 has close to five million parts, and a brand new plane rolls off the assembly line every few days. The opportunities and potential payoffs for VR are every bit as large as the challenges. For example, some past aircraft design/build methodology calls for the construction of a series of increasingly realistic physical mockups. These are very expensive and time consuming to build. Further, once a design is sufficiently advanced that a prototype can be built, the large number of design dependencies between components make problems discovered at this stage much more difficult and expensive to fix. Since the CAD or digital representation of an assembly is much easier to modify than a physical one, there are a variety of substantial benefits to discovering and fixing these problems at the digital design stage.

While reachability and visibility checking are part of existing design practice for cockpit and flight deck design, there are other areas that would benefit from the naturally interactive capabilities VR would bring to bear. For example, consider the problem faced by a design engineer responsible for the design and layout of engine components in a car or a boat. Access to the equipment from the outside is through a hatch. Space is in very short supply, but on the other hand, dials, gauges, and other status indicators need to be clearly seen. In addition, several pieces of the equipment will need to be replaced or adjusted, each with its own tool. How does the engineer convince manufacturing (or how does the vendor convince the customer) that all of the parts are reachable? That there is room to fit and use all of the needed tools? That once the part is reached, the posture the maintainer is put in still allows for enough strength to do the required operations? These are difficult questions to answer, and they are made more difficult by that fact that it is not sufficient to answer them for a single person, because a whole group of people, with varying degrees of height, strength, and reach, need to be able to do the tasks.

### 6.2.2.4   Training and Rehearsal

VR offers a number of unique opportunities for training and rehearsal. Some of the characteristics of applications that will benefit are those which involve costly mistakes or significant danger to the participants. The current use of flight simulators is an example of a rehearsal to reduce the number of costly and dangerous mistakes. The continuing reductions in size and cost of high-end interface and simulation equipment, coupled with their increasing performance, are beginning to make it possible to bring comparable levels of realism to other areas. For example, rehearsing for surgery by performing its virtual counterpart on a digital model of the patient allows much greater opportunity to evaluate alternative treatments without any immediate risk to the real patient. Personnel responsible for the maintenance of aircraft or other physical systems can train on virtual mockups that reflect the current state of the design, so they are substantially trained when the product is delivered. Amburn [Amb92] describes a prototype VR system for mission planning and debriefing that has been used in the replay of air-to-air scenarios in the USAF Red Flag range. Future plans for this system include the development of an electronic 'sand table' for military planners.

## 6.3   System Architectures

In the first two thirds of this section we will look at some of the architectures that have been used in a representative set of current VR systems. The last third will take a more detailed look at several of the key architectural components and some significant issues that have arisen for each of them.

### 6.3.1   Architectural Requirements

6.3.1.1   Application Requirements

The goals of VR research are quite ambitious, involving the integration of work from areas that have not had a great deal to do with one another, from novel I/O devices and user interfaces, to high-performance rendering systems, to distributed object-oriented simulation. Several researchers have noted in passing that while assembling the components of a VR system is a significant challenge, each of the component technologies is a fertile research area in its own right, so it is all too easy to focus on some of the components, at the expense of the system integration needed for a more generally capable system. One approach that can provide some focus to the architectural effort is to choose a few high-payoff application areas and use the application requirements to drive the technology requirements. By extracting a common core of technical requirements from the applications, it is possible to derive a high-level specification for the kernel of a VR system, with application-specific requirements as extensions to that kernel. A complementary approach to deriving system requirements is to tap into the wide variety of models of human perceptual, cognitive, and motor performance [BYC78, How82, Bla83] as a source of data on human constraints and capabilities.

A system requirement common to all applications and systems is rapid response to viewpoint changes, such as when the participant turns their head. Although the hard constraints on what are acceptable response latencies will vary somewhat from application to application, they usually range from 10-20 msec ( 60 Hz) for flight simulation systems down to 80-100 msec ( 10-12 Hz) as a lower bound on the level of acceptable response. This is a particularly important requirement because significant mismatches between visual and vestibular data can lead to motion sickness or other difficulties.

6.3.1.2   System Functional Requirements

Table 1 lists several functional capabilities common to most VR systems, although few, if any systems have implemented all of them, and the level of implemented capability varies from system to system.

## 6.3.2   Comparison of Some Existing VR System Architectures

The goals and architectures of the three systems to be described here differ substantially. The RB2 system from VPL Research is a commercially available application development environment with a fairly closed architecture that has 2 processes at its runtime core - one for rendering and one for managing everything else [BBH+90]. The World Toolkit (WTK) from Sense8 is also a commercial product, but takes a different architectural approach. Instead of embedding your application inside a preexisting development framework as VPL does, WTK is a C-callable library of routines that can be embedded inside of the application [Sen91]. WTK permits in some ways, but offers no particular support for distributing the application over multiple processes and processors. The VUE (Veridical User Environment) system developed at the IBM T.J. Watson Research Center was designed from the start for in-house research and is a multiple process (and possibly multiple processor) system that enforces a much greater separation between the user interface portion of the system and the underlying simulation than is present in the other two systems [ALK+92]. VUE is by no means the only distributed system used for VR work; for other significant systems see VEOS [Bri90], Bolio [ZPS89], and the MR Toolkit [SLGS92]. In order to provide a common framework for comparing the three systems to be discussed here, Figure 1 is a diagram of an abstract functional architecture that supports the functional requirements previously listed. The RB2, WTK, and VUE systems differentiate themselves by the ways in which they map this functional architecture into a physical architecture consisting of communicating devices and processes attached to CPUs. Following the diagram is a brief discussion of each of the systems.

### 6.3.2.1   VPL RB2

The RB2 system consists of 3 programs, Swivel-3D, Body Electric, and Isaac. At world design time, Swivel is used as the 3D modeling system. As of 1992 Swivel and Body Electric run only on the Macintosh, with Isaac running only on Silicon Graphics (SGI) workstations. Future plans include the development of SGI versions of Swivel and Body Electric, and an accompanying dramatic increase in their capabilities. Models from other systems can be imported into Swivel once they are translated into Swivel Command script files. The modeler makes it fairly easy to create articulated figures, and allows specifying rotational or translation constraints from each object or subtree of objects. No non-graphical properties can be associated with objects inside of Swivel. In addition, several advanced rendering capabilities supported on the SGI in their GL library, such as textures, fog, antialiasing, and a variety of lighting models are not yet supported in the current system.

   Isaac is the renderer; as mentioned it currently only runs on SGIs, although this may change with the coming of OpenGL. Both monoscopic and stereoscopic viewing are supported. Configuration options include running both eyes on a single pipeline machine (a 4D/320VGX, for example), both eyes on a Skywriter (1 eye/pipeline), or 1 eye on each of 2 SGIs that are

Geometric Modeling
    creation
    modification
    importing external data
    composition (assembly / subassembly info)
    manipulation

Attribute specification and binding
    texture
    color
    other material properties
    behavior / kinematics

Rendering Subsystem
    Culling
    Drawing
    Level of Detail management
    View Control
        Filtered views (layers, object visibility control, etc.)

Interaction Techniques
    mapping physical inputs into virtual actions
    mapping virtual responses into physical outputs
    navigation
    object selection
        manipulation
        construction
        modification

Simulation
    object behavior / kinematics execution and control
    collision detection
    integration of pre-existing simulations into the VR system
    support for distributed simulations

Data Management
    support for large volumes of data
    real time storage/retrieval
    automatic object persistence
    version control / configuration management

**Table 6.1**    Desirable Capabilities in a Virtual Reality System

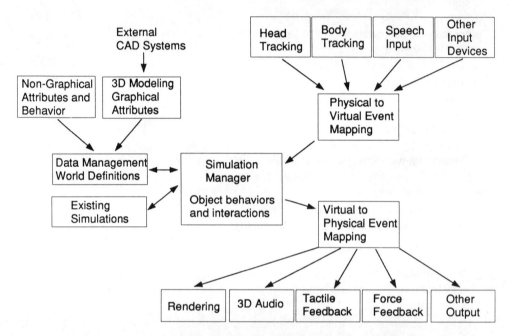

An Abstract Functional Architecture for Virtual Worlds
Arrows indicate data flow direction

**Figure 6.1**   Abstract Functional Architecture

networked together, with either hardware or software synchronization. Each SGI has its own local copy of the world(s) being rendered, and all of this data remains in memory throughout execution.

Body Electric is the software that implements or controls most of the other functional components shown in Figure 1. The list of I/O devices supported is growing but there is little support for an end-user who wishes to add a new one. At design time, Body Electric is used to construct a dataflow network (using a visual programming front end) that is the central component for specifying the mappings between physical actions and virtual actions, interactions with objects, and any other simulation activities in the system. It is possible, although not simple, to associate non-graphical attributes and external simulations with objects in the world through the use of external modules and communications with external processes. This may require a shadow copy of some of the world definition (object names and hierarchy info) as a way of linking object data inside Body Electric with data outside.

At runtime, all of the relevant Swivel files and dataflow networks are loaded into memory, where they reside throughout execution. Body Electric is responsible for polling all of the input devices, doing gesture recognition, and controlling object behavior. As the state of the objects or viewpoints change, change records in a custom protocol are shipped over a local ethernet to each running copy of Isaac, which redraws the scene appropriately.

### 6.3.2.2   Sense8 World Toolkit

The World Toolkit (WTK) has its origins on PCs, but has since expanded to run on Suns and SGIs. There are several differences between RB2 and WTK, with the biggest in flow of control and the openness of the architecture. RB2 is an application development environment in which specific worlds, objects, and behaviors are embedded. WTK is a library of C-callable routines that can either be embedded into a user application, with the application in control (using the universe_go1() function to get a single trip through the WTK simulation manager loop), or WTK in control and responsible for handling I/O devices and managing the state of the world.

The WTK has a loose object-oriented structure, and the functions it provides are grouped into the classes "universe", "object", "sensor", "viewpoint", "light source", and "animation sequence". Although no modeler is included, the system can import objects in Autocad DXF format and in a documented neutral file format. There is some support for texture mapping of objects. In addition, because object and world loading can be controlled by the application, the developer has much greater ability to easily extend the list of attributes and constraints associated with an object.

There is substantial support for adding a new sensor or input device. However, reading input devices, the rendering component, the data management needed to support it, and a part of the simulation component (object and universe action functions) are centralized in a single central control process, which effectively constrains the viewpoint to change no faster than the slowest simulation task. Objects can be dynamically added or deleted from the world at any time, and arbitrary behaviors (action functions in WTK terminology) can be dynamically attached or detached from objects at any time. Any mapping between physical input events (e.g., glove postures) and their corresponding virtual events (selection, flying, etc.) are the responsibility of the developer. The ability to attach arbitrary routines to objects means that it is in principle possible to distribute the simulation workload across several processes or machines, but the burden of providing the IPC mechanism and ensuring the consistency and validity of the resulting distributed simulation is on the developer.

### 6.3.2.3   IBM VUE

The VUE (Veridical User Environments) systems is based on a decomposition of a virtual world into a collection of processes that may run on heterogeneous systems. The types of processes supported are device servers, a dialogue manager, and application processes [ALK+92]. The device servers are responsible for managing input and output devices, such as mice, position trackers, gloves, and renderers. The only architectural constraint on the application processes is the requirement to interface with the dialogue manager. Apart from that, all other issues regarding object geometry, attributes, and behaviors, data management, and simulation functionality are left to the application developer.

The dialogue manager is the only client for all of the device servers, and one of the clients for the application processes. The primary task for the dialogue manager is to accept physical input events, map them into virtual events at various levels of abstraction, route these virtual events to the application processes, and then route output virtual events from the application processes to output device servers. The dialogue manager is composed of several dialogues, each of which is divided into subdialogues. These subdialogues span a conceptual hierarchy. Each one consists of a collection of rules, and each rule can convert a physical event into a generic event, convert a generic event into an interaction technique, or convert an interaction technique into an action [LKL91]. All communications between rules with the dialogue manager and between the dialogue manager and the device and application servers is asynchronous.

While the VUE system leaves several aspects of the functional architecture in Figure 1 unspecified, the framework that has been developed offers several advantages over the other two systems presented. First, the clean separation of device, interaction, and application processes makes the replacement or addition of any piece much easier than the more tightly integrated systems, with only a small reduction in performance due to IPC and network communications. The asynchronous nature of the communications allows each piece of the system to run at its full rate, without the delays that can be introduced by blocking or synchronization. However, distribution of a system often creates challenges of temporal or logical coordination in the simulation and the presentation of the results to the user, and none of the architectures presented here offer much support in meeting these challenges. Finally, the stratification of subdialogues, their relatively small size, and their modular rule-based nature make it easy to change the mapping between physical and virtual actions.

## 6.3.3   Architecture Component Issues

It should come as no surprise that building and managing a world, even a virtual one, can be every bit as daunting a task as it sounds. Most of the current virtual worlds publically demonstrated so far only suggest the sensory richness and behavioral complexities of the real world. To the extent that VR has succeeded so far, it has done so in spite of the cartoonlike qualities of many worlds, and because the promised capabilities are expected to be so valuable. Whether or not systems are developed that fulfill this promise depends on technology advances in several areas, the integration of these technologies in ways not often or yet done, and the ergonomic, economic, and manufacturing sophistication to turn the integrated prototypes into products that are sufficiently safe, affordable, and usable for their intended applications. In this section we will discuss some significant issues and expected future developments for some of the technology areas critical for further VR development in terms of the functional components in Figure 1.

### 6.3.3.1   World Building

An environment and the objects in it can be described by many different kinds of data - geometric, graphical, physical, behavioral, etc. In this section we will look at some of the issues regarding the geometric and graphical data; other kinds will be discussed in the next section.

Manual construction of the 3D geometry needed to specify a 3D world and its objects can be a tedious and time-consuming process. Specifying additional object attributes, such as colors, textures, and various reflectivities (specular, diffuse, etc.) can add a significant additional burden. Powerful 3D solid modelers are not yet in widespread or common use, and many other existing modelers being used have been designed for other applications than VR, such as video production or traditional keyframe animation, and so there is something of a mismatch between the features offered and the features desired. Some of the modelers that have been used successfully, such as Autocad or Swivel-3D, are limited in the scale of the virtual worlds they can handle, due to the limitations of the PC and Macintosh platforms they run on. There are three reasons to believe that world building will be less of a problem in the future than it is today, although it is not likely to ever be a simple task.

First is the development and/or adoption of better tools. These include modelers and editors specifically designed for VR work or the replacement of older and less capable systems such as CATIA with general purpose design systems that offer greater power, performance, and ease of use.

The second reason is the increasing use of 3D solids design systems in industry to support product design and manufacturing. For example, the aerospace industry has large numbers of engineers doing digital design and 3D modeling of various kinds of aircraft. If VR systems can import models from these systems (a hot topic with most VR system vendors), then this sort of design re-use will help companies leverage their often enormous CAD/CAM investment into productive use of VR for design review and manufacturability checking.

The third reason lies in the area of programmatic or generative CAD design. This is the automatic generation and layout of CAD objects according to constraints and requirements specified in geometry grammars. These systems can also be used to automate the development of design alternatives as an aid to rapid exploration of a design space - rapid prototyping (as defined in the user interface literature) as applied to CAD. For a further discussion of generative design, see Heisserman [Hei91].

### 6.3.3.2   Attribute and Behavior Specification and Binding

Where as the previous section focused on geometry creation and graphical attributes such as texture, color, and other material appearance properties, this section will focus on non-graphical properties such as mass, density, and kinematics.

Depending on the task at hand, the VR applications developer may wish to associate a broad range of data with a virtual object or a class of objects. Some of this data is of the simple attribute-value pair variety, such as volume, mass, or density. Other kinds of data are constraints on slot values, such as position or orientation limits, or relations between slots, so that, for example, when the geometry or construction material are changed volume and weight are automatically updated. Other kinds of data include relations between objects or groups of objects, such as definition/instance or assembly/subassembly.

Other kinds of "data" associated with an object or assembly may be the behaviors carried out by or invoked through this object. These range from the simple kinematics of opening an overhead luggage compartment to the more complex kinematics of deploying landing gear to a full-blown aerodynamic flight simulation that governs the flight of a virtual aircraft. Those virtual worlds intending to realistically model some slice of the physical world may also need to simulate some of the physics involved. These simulations may involve the modeling of gravitational and electromagenetic forces, as well the complex interactions of many objects and constraints, such as billiard balls colliding and re-colliding on a pool table. The ability to "plug in" existing simulations can be a significant advantage to a VR system, for much the same reasons that importing CAD is useful in world geometry creation. Several existing VR systems already support this capability and most of the other systems are moving towards it. However, at this time, most of the publicly demonstrated worlds have had fairly simple underlying simulation models, although the work of Phillips, Zhao, and Badler [PZB90], Brooks, et. al., [BOYBK90], and Appino, et al. [ALK+92] are a few notable exceptions.

Taken together, the above requirements suggest that some sort of extensible object-oriented database system would be useful. Such products, while not exactly brand-new, do not yet support the level of real-time performance that a VR system really needs, so there is clearly additional work that needs to be done in this area.

### 6.3.3.3  Data Management

Many of the existing VR systems deal with data management issues as in the following example scenario:

1. At program start-up, or at least outside of a main simulation/event loop, one or more files containing world and object information are completely read into the memory of a single computer. If more that 1 computer is used, each has its' own copy of the data. The data format used by the VR runtime system is often custom to that system and different from that used in the modeling/generation environment.
2. All of this data remains in memory throughout execution, although parts of it may be frequently updated as objects are moved or manipulated.
3. If the world or some portion of it needs to be saved, it is the responsibility of the applications developer to see that the right pieces are saved at the right time.
4. The data is rarely exported back out of the VR runtime environment and back into the CAD or design environment. If someone needs to change the world, the changes are made to a separate copy in the design environment and the new world is fed into the VR runtime system.

Of course, there are a few exceptions to this description. For example, the VEOS system from HITL supports some forms of distributed and cooperative execution through a Linda-like database mechanism [Bri90]. Some of the work going at at Boeing deals with worlds that are several hundred megabytes and up, too large to fit even into virtual memory. However as worlds grow in size and complexity, and as VR moves out of the lab and into production use, there are several issues that must be dealt with. These are still research issues, so they will just be raised here.

### Data Volume

A variety of applications, from aerospace to architecture to automotive design involve very large amounts of data, ranging from tens of megabytes to several gigabytes. How can we store and retrieve datasets of this size so that they are available when they are needed? If the worlds are largely static, then the sort of extensive preprocessing described in Funkhouser, Sequin, and Teller [FST92] which creates several levels of visibility graphs may be applicable, although it is not clear how this can be used in worlds which allow large numbers of objects to move around.

### Persistence

Imagine someone engaged in an architectural walkthrough/design review of a very large building or other physical structure with data volumes on the order just described. The participant rearranges the design (perhaps by moving a door or a window) in a room in one corner of the structure, proceeds to go to some distant portion of the structure for an extended period of time, and then returns to the rearranged room. It would be a serious violation of the users conceptual model of the world if the moved objects were not in their updated position upon the users return to the room but instead were in their original positions, as if that portion of the model was simply read in again. The large size of the world (relative to physical/virtual memory) and the extended period of time that may have elapsed between accesses to this data make it inevitable that at some point, the data for our changed room must be stored externally to the runtime system, with the updated data retrieved when needed. Since the user does not and ought not to have to know about this level of storage decision making, what is required here is some sort of persistence mechanism that can manage the data automatically.

### Configuration control

As VR systems move out of the lab and into end-user applications, it is likely to become more tightly integrated into existing business processes like design and manufacturing. Just as there are advantages in allowing VR systems to leverage off of existing design systems by importing data from these systems, it is likely that there will come a time when it is desirable to close the loop and feed the design changes discovered through the use of the VR system back into the originating design system. At this point we can expect to see much more careful configuration management and version control than currently exists (mostly none) applied to the data used in the VR system and the ways in which it feeds back into the originating design system.

### 6.3.3.4   Rendering and Display

The graphics performance and levels of realism available to the VR system developer continue to increase at rapid rates. The introduction of systems such as the Reality Engine from Silicon Graphics provide the means for greatly improving the cartoonlike quality of many of the worlds in those application areas where increasing levels of graphical realism and detail are important.

However, in an immersive VR system, the rendering system is not the final link in the chain; usually some sort of HMD is. As previously noted, the most visible difficulty with the currently available HMDs is the lack of resolution, although weight and wearability are important secondary problems. Substantial progress in improving resolution is being made. Small quantities of one inch field-sequential color CRT displays with resolution approaching 1024 x 1024 are expected to be available in 1993. The development of field - sequential color LCD displays with comparable resolution is also progressing, but LCD technology development usually lags behind CRT development [Alt92]. LCD displays offer several advantages over CRTs, including substantial reductions in size, weight, voltage, and electromagnetic fields near the head. In addition, depending on the choice of LCD technology, some displays can be either see-through or immersive, depending on the presence of a cover plate behind each of the eyepieces [Lew92]. Longer term research includes the development of low-power laser microscanners that beam the images directly onto the retina. This work is being done at the Human Interface Technology Lab.

Several other approaches to increasing resolution have been looked at, and most involve the use of two physical displays whose images are optically combined into one image, with one of the displays used to display a high resolution inset, and the other to display the lower resolution surrounding visual field. In some systems, such as the CAE Fiber Optic HMD, the location of the image in the hi-resolution inset can be slaved to gaze direction, so it moves as the eye moves. However, accurate and stable eye tracking is still fairly costly, and there is some evidence that if a stationary and centered high-resolution inset can provide a 30 degree field of view, the benefit of eye tracking is marginal [BAS75].

A problem area that has often been overlooked but is is now being addressed concerns the interactions between display geometry and placement within the HMD, the effects of the wide field of view optics on the displayed images, and the ways in which the rendering software needs to be modified in order to take the display geometry and optics into account. These problems are briefly summarized below; for a more complete discussion, see Robinett and Rolland [RR92].

- Many HMDs have optical axes that are not parallel; some also have display screens that are off-center from the optical axes. This condition creates an asymmetric viewing volume that requires an off-center perspective projection, rather than the symmetric perspective that is so much more common in 3D graphics.
- The physical placement of the display screens and the creation of virtual screen images through the optics define the physical field of view (FOV). The parameters in the call to the perspective transform that define the rendering FOV should but often do not match the physical FOV.
- Producing a wide FOV from physical screens that are 1-2 inches from the eye requires optics that will move the virtual images out from the eye to a comfortable distance as well as horizontally and vertically spreading the image to widen the FOV. A side effect of these optics is the nonlinear distortion of the image, where the amount of distortion is a function of the distance off the optical axis. A variety of solutions to this problem have been proposed or implemented, including predistorting the geometry with the inverse of the optical distortion function before it goes through the rendering pipeline, modifying the rendering pipeline itself to produce the inverse distortion [How92], and pixel-by-pixel adjustment of the scan-converted image [RR92]. No systematic comparison of the strengths and weaknesses of the various approaches has yet been done.

### 6.3.3.5   Simulation

As the behavioral fidelity and complexity of virtual worlds continue to increase, it may be desirable, for performance reasons if no other, to distribute the execution of separate object behaviors onto separate processes and/or processors. As discussed in Shaw, *et. al.* [SLGS92], decoupling head tracking, rendering, and application simulation code into separate processes allows the viewpoint to be as current as possible and updates to run as fast as the rendering will allow, instead of pegging it to run as slowly as the slowest simulation task.

Several systems support some form of distributed simulation ([Bri91] [ALK$^+$92], [SLGS92]). However, distributed object-oriented simulation carries with it its own set of challenges, including issues such as ensuring the consistency and validity of the results of the multiprocess simulation, when compared with the results of a single-process simulation of the same system. These issues do not appear to have been sufficiently addressed in the above systems. For further discussion of existing solutions to these and other issues in distributed simulation, see Sowizral and Jefferson [SJ], or Hagsand [Hag91].

### 6.3.3.6   User Interface

One of the reasons an immersive VR experience is so compelling, and one of the reasons it offers so much promise, is the enormously higher bandwidth between user and application, as compared with the more conventional WIMP (Windows, Icons, Menus, Pointers) style of interface. Instead of a keyboard, a mouse, and a bandwidth as narrow as a mouse cable, it is now possible, and will be increasingly convenient, to use a person's entire body and several senses as an input and output device.

Bandwidth isn't the only reason, though. One of the promises of VR is for a more natural interface to many interactive tasks. Instead of manipulating a set of coordinate axes to change a viewpoint, turn your head. Instead of using a mouse to select and move an object, reach out with your hand and grab it.

Even the use of the word 'interface' is somewhat problematic. In conventional non-VR applications, there are clear subjective boundaries between the user and the application/data. The user is on the *outside* of the screen and the application and its data are on the *inside*, with clearly visible interface devices and software artifacts that physically and logically come between them. In an immersive environment, the subjective impression is that the barriers that came between the user and their data have disappeared - the 'interface' is gone.

## 6.3.4   Interaction Techniques

One of the ways that the newness of VR (and 3D interaction in general) manifests itself is that 3D interaction devices, techniques, and metaphors are not as well developed as in 2D world. One of the central tasks for HITD and VR systems is to "escape the FlatLand of 2D user interface technology" [VD92]. In this section we will describe some of the interaction techniques a VR system should support, some issues that have arisen in allowing users to navigate in a 3D space, closing with the importance and role of metaphor. Bricken [Bri90] lists several general categories of interaction techniques: relocation/navigation, construction, and manipulation. A fourth category, selection, will be added and discussed.

### Selection

Selection is the way in which the participant indicates what object(s) they are interested in. There are already a large number of ways to select objects in 2D and 3D systems; this number will increase as our experience with HITD systems and I/O devices continues to grow. Three common techniques found in many current systems are described below. One way to do this, especially useful if the object is not in sight, is to call its "name", and in response the object may blink, change color, or pop into view. If the object is in view but out of reach, the participant may project a ray that intersects the desired object, or move their virtual hand to grab the object, possibly making a gesture to indicate that this hand/object intersection is to be intended as a selection.

### Manipulation

Once an object has been selected, it can be manipulated, moved or modified. Some objects may have special behaviors or functions associated with them. For example, pushing one of several buttons on the flight deck of the original Boeing VSX would start or stop the rotors or tilt the engines up or down [EBB91].

### Construction

Currently, most systems only allow object creation outside of the virtual world. However, object creation is a natural extension of the object manipulation and modification techniques currently or soon to be available. There is research underway at a variety of places to support a general facility for object creation inside the virtual world. For example, the work described in Bryson [Bry92] describes several techniques for surface creation and sculpting inside a virtual environment.

## 6.3.5   Relocation/Navigation

The ability to move freely in three dimensions in a virtual world satisfies, in some way, a desire that mankind has had for a very long time - to fly unaided. The same position sensing and viewpoint transformations that supports "flying" through a virtual world also supports movements of a more earth-bound nature: standing up, kneeling down, turning around to see what is behind you, and moving your head from side to side to get a better view of something that is partially obstructed.

Designing an effective and usable mechanism for 3D navigation (e.g., "flying") is more difficult than it might first appear. Requiring that the user simultaneously manage all 6 degrees of freedom (x, y, z, roll, pitch, and yaw) is beyond the abilities of almost everyone that tries [Bri90]. The multi-axis spinning that usually results is disorienting and unpleasant. In addition, there are several different purposes for travel.

Mackinlay, Card, and Robinson [MCR90] lists four kinds of travel: general movement, targeted movement, specified coordinate movement, and specified trajectory movement. They present an algorithm for targeted movement that uses a logarithmic velocity function based on the distance between the viewer and a point on a selected object of interest. This allows large distances to be traveled quickly, and small distances to be traveled more controllably than a constant velocity model would allow. The path of motion is completely specified given the initial viewpoint position and point of interest, so issues like staying on target and avoiding overshoot are not a problem. However, the requirement that a definite point on an existing object be selected makes this not always useful for general travel.

Other techniques that have been used for general motion include the 'point-to-fly' technique used in many VPL worlds, among others, and gaze-directed flight, in which the user flies forward or backwards along a vector determined by the direction they are looking in. Informal experiments done at Boeing support the results found elsewhere that gaze-directed flight is usually easier to control than other control mechanisms, especially for novices.

### 6.3.6  Metaphor

A metaphor is like an an analogy in that it helps someone to transfer knowledge by allowing them to use some or all of a familiar model in an unfamiliar domain. The value of metaphor in user interface design is widely acknowledged. The desktop metaphor popularized by the Apple Macintosh is a well-known example of a fairly successful user interface metaphor. The claim is that the computer screen and the objects therein are in some ways like a desktop and the objects on it. It is often not explicitly spelled out what the limits of the metaphor are.

Virtual worlds are designed with some purpose(s) in mind - entertainment, training, data visualization, etc. As pointed out in Furness [FI88] and the usability engineering literature [Kar91] it is critical to develop some metrics that will allow designers to assess how well the various aspects of the world design support the participants in accomplishing their intended tasks. These detailed measures may in turn be chosen with the guidance of some higher level metaphors in mind.

In some cases, the virtual world and objects are intended as substitutes for the physical - virtual mockups of aircraft, cars, and buildings can have significant advantages over their physical counterparts. The kinds of metrics we may be interested in for worlds like these are those that measure the extent to which the virtual resembles or functions like the real in whatever respects deemed important for the task at hand.

However, there is a bit of a balancing act here. As the previous discussion about flying pointed out, sometimes the benefits of VR lie in its unreality, or the ways in which the virtual world and participants are freed from the constraints of the physical one. For example, if one of the benefits of a VR application is the ability to walk through walls and fit in places too small for a mouse in order to examine wiring layouts, this departure from reality needs to be made clear or the benefit will not be fully realized. More generally, the limits of the "reality" metaphor should be clearly communicated if the benefits of freedom from its constraints are to be best gained.

The previous discussion assumes that for some application of VR, there is a pre-existing model of what the relevant portions of reality are or ought to be like. What do we do when no such model (or an insufficient one) exists? Some examples include the visualization and interaction with high-dimensional abstract data, such as the financial visualization work described in Feiner and Besher [FB90]. It is precisely areas like this in which good metaphors are the least available and so would be the greatest help. Finding them is one of the most challenging and important areas for VR research in the years to come.

### References

[ALK⁺92]   P. Appino, J. Lewis, L. Koved, D. Ling, Rabenhorst D., and C. Codella. An architecture for virtual worlds. *Presence*, 1(1):1–17, 1992.

[Alt92]      P. Alt. An overview of display technologies. In *Opening Address, SID '92*, Boston, MA, 1992.

[Amb92]     P. Amburn. Mission planning and debriefing using head mounted display systems. In *Proceedings of EFDPMA Conference on Virtual Reality*, Washington, D.C., 1992.

[BAS75]     A. Bahill, D. Adler, and L. Stark. Most naturally occurring human saccades have magnitudes of 15 degrees or less. *Investigative Opthalmology*, 14:468–469, 1975.

[BBH+90]    C. Blanchard, S. Burgess, Y. Harvill, J. Lanier, A. Lasko, M. Oberman, and M. Teitel. Reality built for two: A virtual reality tool. *Computer Graphics*, 24(2):35–36, 1990.

[BFO92]     M. Bajura, H. Fuchs, and R. Ohbuchi. Merging virtual reality with the real world: Seeing ultrasound imagery within the patient. Technical Report TR92-005, Computer Science Dept., University of North Carolina at Chapel Hill, 1992.

[Bla83]     J. Blauert. *Spatial Hearing*. MIT Press, 1983.

[Bli91]     J. Blinn. The making of the mechanical universe. In Ellis, Kaiser, and Grunwald, editors, *Pictorial Communications in Virtual and Real Environments*. Taylor and Francis, 1991.

[BOYBK90]   F. Brooks, M. Ouh-Young, J. Batter, and P. Kilpatrick. Project grope - haptic displays for scientific visualization. *Computer Graphics*, 24(4):177–185, 1990.

[Bri90]     W. Bricken. Veos: Preliminary functional architecture. Technical Report TR HITL-M-90-2, Human Interface Technology Laboratory, Seattle, 1990.

[Bri91]     M. Bricken. Virtual worlds: No interface to design. In M. Benedikt, editor, *Cyberspace*. MIT Press, 1991.

[Bry92]     S. Bryson. Paradigms for the shaping of surfaces in virtual environments. In *Proceeding of 25th Hawaii International Conference on Systems Sciences*, Kauii, Hawaii, 1992.

[BYC78]     J. Borah, L. Young, and R. Curry. Sensory mechanism modeling. Technical Report AFHRL TR78-83, Air Force Human Resources Laboratory, 1978.

[CM92]      T. Caudell and D. Mizell. Augmented reality: An application of heads-up display technology to manual manufacturing processes. In *Proceeding of 25th Hawaii International Conference on Systems Sciences*, Kauii, Hawaii, 1992.

[Dea72]     B. Deatherage. Auditory and other sensory forms of information presentation. In Van Cott and Kincade, editors, *Human Engineering Guide to Equipment Design*. U.S. Government Printing Office, 1972.

[DGEF86]    T. Doll, J. Gerthe, W. Engleman, and D. Folds. Development of simulated directional audio for cockpit applications. Technical Report AAMRL-TR-86-014, Wright Patterson AFB, Dayton, OH, 1986.

[EBB91]     C. Esposito, M. Bricken, and K. Butler. Building the boeing vsx: Operations with virtual aircraft in virtual space. In *Proceedings of CHI '91*, New Orleans, LA., 1991.

[Ell91]     S. R. Ellis. Nature and origins of virtual environments: A bibliographic essay. *Computing Systems in Engineering*, 2(4):321–347, 1991.

[FB90]      S. Feiner and C. Beshers. Visualizing n-dimensional worlds with n-vision. *Computer Graphics*, 24(2):37–39, 1990.

[FI88]      Thomas A. Furness III. Harnessing virtual space. In *Proceedings, SID International Symposium*, pages 4–7, 1988.

[FST92]     T.A Funkhouser, C. Sequin, and S.J. Teller. Management of large amounts of data in interactive building walkthroughs. In *Proceedings of 1992 Symposium on Interactive 3D Graphics*, Cambridge, Mass., 1992.

[FW91]      S. Foster and E. Wenzel. Virtual acoustic environments: The convolvatron, 1991. Demo System presented at the Tommorows Realities Gallery, SIGGRAPH '91, Las Vegas, NV.

[GSP92]     M. Green, C. Shaw, and R. Pausch. Virtual reality and highly interactive three dimensional applications. In *Chi '92 Tutorial Notes*, 1992.

[Hag91]     O. Hagsand. Consistency and concurrency control in distributed virtual worlds. In B. Pehrson and Y. Sundblad, editors, *Proceedings of 2nd MultiG Workshop*, pages 43–56, 1991.

[Hei91]     J. Heisserman. *Generative CAD Design in the GENESIS System*. PhD thesis, Carnegie Mellon University, Pittsburgh, PA, 1991.

[Hil76]     J. Hill. Study to design and develop remote manipulator systems. Technical report, NASA, Ames Research Center, Moffet Field, CA, 1976.

[How82]     I. Howard. *Human Visual Orientation*. Wiley, 1982.

[How92]     E. Howlett, 1992. personal communication.

[Kar91]     C. Karat. Cost/benefit and business-case analyses for usability engineering. In *CHI '91*

*Tutorial Notes*, 1991.

[Lat92] J. Latta. Virtual reality - are there real applications? In *Proceedings of EFDPMA Conference on Virtual Reality*, Washington, D.C., 1992.

[LB91] C. Levitt and S. Bryson. A virtual environment for the exploration of three dimensional steady flows. In S. Fisher, editor, *Stereoscopic Displays and Applications II*. 1991.

[Lew92] C. Lewis. Virtual reality group, inc. product literature, 1992.

[LKL91] J. Lewis, L. Koved, and D. Ling. Dialogue structures for virtual worlds. In *Proceedings of CHI '91*, pages 131–136, New Orleans, LA, 1991.

[MC88] B. Marcus and P. Churchill. Sensing human hand motions for controlling dextrous robots. In *Proceedings of Second Annual Space Operations Automation and Robotics Workshop*, 1988.

[MCR90] J. Mackinlay, S. Card, and G. Robertson. Rapid controlled movement through a virtual 3d workspace. *Computer Graphics*, 24(4):171–176, 1990.

[MZ90] M. McKenna and D. Zeltzer. Dynamic simulation of autonomous legged locomotion. In *Proceedings of ACM SIGGRAPH '90*, pages 29–38, Dallas, TX, 1990.

[Pat82] R. Patterson. Guidelines for auditory warning systems on civil aircraft. Technical Report 82017, London Civil Aviation Authority, 1982.

[PZB90] C. Phillips, J. Zhao, and N. Badler. Interactive real-time articulated figure manipulation using multiple kinematic constraints. In *Proceedings of 1990 Symp. on Interactive 3D Graphics*, pages 245–270, Snowbird, Utah, 1990.

[Rhe91] H. Rheingold. *Virtual Reality*. Summit Books, 1991.

[Rob91] P. Robertson. Financial Visualization and Virtual Reality *Computer Graphics World*, July 1991

[RR92] W. Robinett and J. P. Rolland. A computational model for the stereoscopic optics of a head mounted display. *Presence*, 1(1):45–62, 1992.

[Sen91] Sense8 Corporation, Sausalito, CA. *World Toolkit Reference Manual*, 1991.

[Ser90] Matrix Information Services. Virtual reality: The next revolution in human-computer interaction, 1990.

[SJ] H. Sowizral and D. Jefferson. Fast concurrent simulation using the time warp mechanism. Air Force Contract F-49620-77-C-0023, U.S. Air Force, ??

[SLGS92] C. Shaw, J. Liang, M. Green, and Y. Sun. The decoupled simulation model for virtual reality systems. In *Virtual Reality and Highly Interactive Three Dimensional Applications*, Monterey, CA, 1992. CHI '91 Tutorial Notes.

[Sto91] A. Stone. Will the real body please stand up?: Boundary stories about virtual cultures. In M. Benedikt, editor, *Cyberspace*. MIT Press, 1991.

[Thu92] R. Thurman. Simulator and training based technology. In *Proceedings of EFDPMA Conference on Virtual Reality*, Washington, D.C., 1992.

[VD92] A. Van Dam. Plenary address. In *Proceeding of 25th Hawaii International Conference on Systems Sciences*, Kauii, Hawaii, 1992.

[VPL87] VPL Research, Inc., Redwood City, CA. *DataGlove Model 2 Operating Manual*, 1987.

[Wen92] E. Wenzel. Localization in virtual acoustic displays. *Presence*, 1(1):80–107, 1992.

[Wex92] A. Wexelblatt. Near term commercialization of virtual reality technology - the 5 and 10 year picture. In *Proceedings of EFDPMA Conference on Virtual Reality*, Washington, D.C., 1992.

[Zel92] D. Zeltzer. Autonomy, interaction, and presence. *Presence*, 1(1), 1992.

[ZJar] D. Zeltzer and M.B. Johnson. Motor planning: An architecture for specifying and controlling the behavior of virtual actors. *The Journal of Visualization and Computer Animation*, 2(2), (to appear).

[ZPS89] D. Zeltzer, S. Pieper, and D. Sturman. An integrated graphical simulation platform. In *Proceedings of Graphics Interface '89*, pages 266–274, Ontario, Canada, 1989.

# 7

# Designing Software For A Group's Needs: A Functional Analysis of Synchronous Groupware

**GARY M. OLSON**
*University of Michigan*
**LOLA J. McGUFFIN**
*University of Michigan*

**EIJI KUWANA**
*NTT Software Laboratories*
**JUDITH S. OLSON**
*University of Michigan*

## ABSTRACT

We propose a scheme for analyzing the functionality of synchronous groupware systems as a step toward creating a more general framework within which to design usable group systems. The goal is to be explicit about the kinds of functions that systems might support, and then to analyze how individual systems support specific functions in particular situations. The goal in each situation is to find the proper blend of social practices and system supported functions so that group work can proceed smoothly and effectively. We discuss four clusters of functionality: *task, interface, session,* and *environment.* We also describe three cross-cutting concepts: *linking, awareness,* and *undo,* or the general concept, *returning to previous states.* We describe these areas in detail, and then analyze several synchronous group editors to illustrate how the proposed scheme works.

## 7.1 INTRODUCTION

Designing software systems for users should be rooted in an understanding of the kinds of tasks the users will carry out with the help of the system. The dictate "user centered design"

*User Interface Software*, Edited by Bass and Dewan
© 1993 John Wiley & Sons Ltd

prescribes that good designs flow from an understanding of the appropriate allocation of task functions to the system or social practices or methods. The first step is to conduct a detailed analysis of the work itself. Ideally, systems should be designed to provide help for those elements of tasks that are difficult or tedious for people, and people should be able to use their skills and knowledge to advantage in carrying out those aspects of tasks which fit what they know. Finally, once a task allocation has been made, there is the difficult design task of figuring out exactly how the system should provide its support.

This user-centered strategy is common to all forms of system design. However, as we have argued elsewhere, we feel that this approach is particularly critical in the case of software designed to support group tasks, called groupware [Ols91]. This kind of software is usually used in situations of considerable cognitive, social, or organizational complexity. The initial analysis of the work is more difficult, and there is a less well-established body of principles to draw upon both for the allocation of functions to system and users and for the design of systems to best support its set of functions.

The magnitude of these difficulties can best be appreciated by examining an evolutionary perspective on the field of computer-supported cooperative work (CSCW) [Ols93]. This analysis draws on a perspective first put forth by [Car91] in characterizing the development of the field of human-computer interaction (HCI). He argued that system technologies in general evolve through four schematic stages, as illustrated in Figure 7.1. According to this scheme, designers progress from:

- building illustrative **point systems**, or examples of what can be done to support work with computers,

- to evaluating, comparing, and reviewing systems so that we understand the **dimensions** (by which systems and work vary) that seem to affect the success of a system,

- to analyzing the dimensions so that we can **characterize the relationships** in more detail,

- **articulating the models and laws** that governto finally behavior with systems.

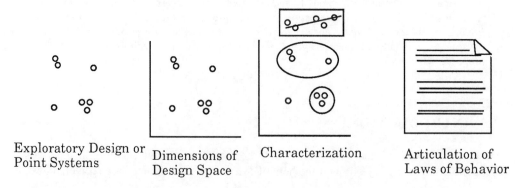

| Exploratory Design or Point Systems | Dimensions of Design Space | Characterization | Articulation of Laws of Behavior |

**Figure 7.1** The four stages of the development of the field of HCI, from building example systems to articulating laws of behavior.

[Ols93] argue that whereas in HCI we are between stages 2 and 3, in CSCW applications, or groupware, we are still mostly at the stage of building point systems. Many different systems have been built; only some have been evaluated. All show both the promise and the difficulties of computer support for group work. We are just beginning to dimensionalize the design space of such systems, and look forward to characterizing these dimensions more generally.

Here we attempt to provide just such a dimensionalization of a significant class of groupware systems, those that support synchronous work. We have extensive experience with these kinds of applications: we have built them [Mcg92]; we have used and analyzed many applications built by others [Ols90]; we have carried out laboratory investigations of the use of such systems [Ols92c]; and we have observed a number of systems being used in field settings. On the basis of this experience, we here characterize some of the dimensions of groupware functionality as an effort to help the field go beyond building point systems.

As indicated earlier, the first step in such an analysis is to understand the nature of the tasks to be done with systems. Although many investigators have proposed various taxonomies of group tasks [Ste72, Mcg84], these taxonomies tend to be at a fairly high level. McGrath [Mcg84], for example, contrasts decision-making tasks with planning tasks. While not irrelevant to system design, the function allocation process requires a more detailed analysis of function components. For example, in one such detailed analysis, Olson et al [Ols90] focused on the substages of problem solving, and analyzed the extent to which these substages could be carried out in serial or parallel by group members. This was relevant to the usefulness of a group editor that offered parallel editing as a function. A different cut at this lower level analysis of task and technology appears in [Nun91].

Our current, extended analysis of groupware functions aims at this lower level, where one can match specific system functions to details of the users' tasks. However, when trying to enumerate specific functions that might be embodied in a system, we find that the total space of possibilities is very large. Many functions are specific to the particular domain (e.g., software engineering, finance) or to a generic task (e.g., design, project planning). Some functions are familiar from single-user applications (e.g., text editing, graphics, sketching). However, new functions and new interface needs arise from the fact that a *group* of people are working together. Some functions are explicitly designed for group tasks like voting or brainstorming. Other functions arise primarily from the need to coordinate the work of the group members. The Prep Editor [Neu90], for example, collates comments of various reviewers in a side-by-side interface, while Aspects [Gro90] designates who wants to type next by a raised hand.

Just because these group-specific functions *can* be supported by a computer doesn't mean they *should* be. It is an open question as to which of these functions should be supported by technology. In a number of cases, the functions may be better supported by social protocols. We will discuss this issue in more detail later. Our goal in explicitly laying out functions specific to groupware is to make designers and researchers aware of the space of issues involved in constructing and evaluating interfaces to group systems.

In this paper we focus on *synchronous*, or real-time, group interactions because they present an interesting and rich array of coordination needs that help us illustrate the utility of our analysis. Our characterization of functions as presented here can be extended to include asynchronous systems as well, but in order to keep our discussion in this paper manageable we will not examine such systems here. The situation we have in mind is one where a shared workspace is available on two or more group member's computer screens that allows them to interact simultaneously and to be able to see the other people's actions. The actions on the shared work objects provide much of the shared context for the group. But we also assume that the group members can at least talk with each other, if not see each other as well. These systems may permit text, graphics, images, audio, video, or any other type of data objects. The participants in a session may be face-to-face, distributed with varying degrees of communication support (e.g., audio, video), or various mixed cases.

## 7.2 DIMENSIONS OF GROUPWARE FUNCTIONALITY

Definitions of dimensions of groupware functionality can take the perspective of the user or the system. We have found a blend of both to be the most fruitful. From the user perspective, we can draw on our experience with studying group behavior in the field [Ols92b] and in the laboratory [Ols92c]. We have drawn upon several discussions of groupware functionality that have already been published [Gri88, Ols90, Ell91]. From the system perspective, we have found a number of discussions of system architectures to be very useful in suggesting clusters of functions [Lai88, Lee90, Pat80, Dew92]. The clusters of activities we describe below are in large part a synthesis of these diverse perspectives, with additional detailed analysis of specific systems of the kind we illustrate later.

We first describe four areas of activity that form significant clusters of functionality. Then we describe three cross-cutting concepts, linking, awareness, and undo, or more generally, returning to previous states. Linking of two or more people's work and awareness of what others are doing are at the heart of what it means to do coordinated work. Indeed, the power of groupware over unsupported "natural" work comes from the ability, in software, to vary the degree of linking and awareness of various functions across wide ranges. Returning to previous states (extended undo) is a set of concepts that cross-cut all the specific activities we describe, and because of the nature of group work, presents a special challenge to those thinking about the design of groupware systems.

### 7.2.1 Four Activity Clusters

Four clusters of activity include: task activity, interface activity, session activity, and environment activity. These are natural foci of group work: the object of the work, how it looks, who else is involved and what else is going on, and how the work fits into the global environment. Within these activity clusters, we define concepts and map out functionality to cover different communication and collaboration considerations as well as the activity requirements. Table 7.1 shows a summary of the functions within each activity cluster. We introduce the activity clusters in this section, and describe the specific activities within each cluster in more detail in the next section.

#### 7.2.1.1 TASK ACTIVITY

Task activities consist of the set of data manipulation activities that group members perform on their shared task objects. A task object might be a proposal, a graphic of a widget, minutes from a meeting, etc. These objects contain the content of what a group is working on, the task-related, conceptual information that is being manipulated. This is similar to the "abstract objects" described for Rendezvous [Pat90].

**Table 7.1** Clusters of Activities that Reflect the Functionality of Synchronous Groupware Systems

| Task | Interface | Session | Environment |
|---|---|---|---|
| *change* | *control joint attention* | *set participation schemes* | •personal & group scheduling |
| •create | •establish | •manage session | •task assignment |
| •modify | •maintain | enrollment | •import & export data |
| •save | | •set roles | |
| •annotate | | •set access privileges | |
| •update control | *locate* | •control of turn taking | |
| | •navigate | •set awareness levels | |
| *locate* | *set policies* | *set session structure* | |
| •navigate | •update control | •serial vs. parallel | |
| •search | •filter control | •split & merge | |
| •sort | •fidelity control | sessions | |
| •compare | •format control | •form & disband subgroups | |
| | •window attributes | | |
| | | *set session support* | |
| *set policies* | | •tracking tasks | |
| •set permissions | | •manage task transitions | |
| •version control | | | |
| | | •tracking session history | |
| | | •provide communication channels | |
| | | •configure session resources | |
| | | •configure a set of applications | |

## 7.2.1.2 INTERFACE ACTIVITY

Interface activity refers to those things users do to manipulate the *display* of information presented to them on the screen. It has become quite customary in discussions of both single-user and multiple-user applications to separate the underlying information from that which is presented to the user (the same distinction between "abstract objects" and "view objects" in [Pat90]). Dewan and Choudhary [Dew92] have described and analyzed many of the benefits of this separation from the system perspective. First, an individual could have more than one interface object for a task object. Secondly, the interface objects could differ among users, allowing each to customize the interface object not only in its physical characteristics (e.g., window size) but also in the data object's representation (e.g., pie chart versus x-y coordinate graph). This flexibility in mapping task objects to interfaces is one of the significant features that give groupware systems their potential power.

## 7.2.1.3 SESSION ACTIVITY

We define a session as a period of time when two or more members of a group are working together synchronously. The activities that take place for formulating the session, creating the shared workspaces or invoking other task-oriented activities, coordinating the members' activity during the session, etc. all require decisions and effort on the part of the group. The extent and manner by which the groupware system supports these activities determines the group's workload in setting up the session and in changing things as they go (e.g., adding new members, changing permissions, orchestrating group members' in engaging in the next discussion or activity). Session level activities are closely related to the natural "meeting management" activities we observed in unsupported face-to-face meetings [Ols92b].

## 7.2.1.4 ENVIRONMENT ACTIVITY

This activity cluster describes the relationship of the group and its activities to the broader environment. There are two possible ways in which a groupware system might relate to the broader environment: relating the group's shared workspace to each group member's personal workspace(s), and relating the group's work to the broader world. One important form of environmental activity is the importing and exporting of task objects to the world beyond the group's session, so individuals can perform their assigned tasks and bring them back to the next meeting. This kind of activity is closely related to "project management" as described in [Ols92b]. This category is where the characteristics that separate synchronous and asynchronous work would be articulated.

## 7.2.2 Linking

Linking is the mechanism which enforces relationships between characteristics of any object used by different group members. Having an object locked while someone else works on it (for concurrency control) is a very strict kind of linking. However, other types of linking are not so strict, where only a subset of attributes among objects are made to be similar, and perhaps only under certain circumstances. For example, sometimes users might want to view the same part of a document so they can discuss it. To do this, they invoke some mechanism to link their views. In concurrency control, users do not have any say over how and when it is enforced, but for view linking, they do. We define linking in a broad sense to include these two different sharing mechanisms and how they are controlled from the user's and system's perspective (see also [Dew92, Pat90]).

To make the idea more concrete, let's consider some extreme examples of the generic concept of linking. These first two examples do not involve groupware, whereas the next two do. For a group that is meeting in a conventional meeting room, information on a public display such as a white board is completely linked for all of the participants. Since the whiteboard is a single object and is fully available for all group members, any change in the whiteboard's content is immediately available for all group members. At the other extreme, suppose a group of coauthors each get a paper copy of the latest draft of their manuscript. They each go off to their offices and mark up the manuscript's paper copies. In this case, there is no linking. Changes made by one coauthor are not transmitted to any of the others until they get together and exchange comments.

It is easy to find corresponding examples with computer systems. A program like Timbuktu [Far91] allows Macintosh users to share any single-user application. It does so by running the single user application on one machine, and sharing the display, keystrokes, and mouse actions across a set of other users' machines. In this case there is only one program running, and every I/O event is shared by every user in exactly the same way. Both the data objects and the views are linked, much like the whiteboard above. At the other extreme, consider our set of coauthors now equipped with e-mail and word processors. A copy of the original manuscript is e-mailed to each coauthor, and they work on their own copies individually. While they started off with a common file, subsequent acts are not linked, much like the manuscript marking example above.

What makes the concept of linking interesting from the groupware perspective is that there are a number of intermediate cases, where attributes of objects can be linked in more subtle ways. Data objects can be linked more abstractly than having them be identical. For instance, various participants might be presented with summaries of objects (e.g., summary statistics or aggregate budget figures) that exist as detailed sets of individual objects for other users. Updates would consist not of the sharing of explicit objects but of attributes of collections of objects. This could be extremely useful in collaborative scientific applications or in managerial accounting in a hierarchical organization.

When interface objects are linked, the interface displays at various sites are identical, providing a What-You-See-Is-What-I-See (WYSIWIS) capability. But as Stefik, Foster, Bobrow, Kahn, Lanning & Suchman [Ste87] showed, various degrees of this linking are possible. Any or all of the interface attributes (e.g., window size, scroll position, color, font) might be shared, depending on the kinds of activity and differentiation that are important [Dew92, Pat90].

Within session activity, participants' permissions on different objects, or the history of the group's tasks within their sessions, might be linked to varying degrees. This could allow for the smooth flow of work between synchronous and asynchronous settings, and would permit things like global schemes and various inheritance hierarchies (e.g., style sheets) to operate across such information. This could be extremely useful in long-term projects or in large organizations with complex coordination needs. One specific example would be keeping track of changes and notifying users at later points in time that something they cared about had been modified. As another example, imagine how tedious it would be to set up a permission strategy on a shared document for a large group, and having to do this each time a different document is used. Even worse, if there are many objects with the same permission strategy, and the group wanted it to change, one would have to go back and change all of the objects. Linking the permission attributes would help to reduce or circumvent these types of problems [Dew92, Pat90]. Linking on session objects might also be very beneficial if there is a set of privileges, roles, applications, subgroups, etc. that are predefined that a session manager could use for an easy session configuration.

We believe that identifying a general concept of linking is beneficial for two reasons: (1) it broadens the idea of sharing in a groupware system so that the design options cover a wide set of possible links, and (2) it clarifies the notion that different attributes of the same object or related objects could, and maybe should, have different linking settings. It also raises the very interesting design option, namely, of having the control of the coordination shared between the system and the users. This will be discussed further later.

## 7.2.3 Awareness

Awareness is the ability of the group members to know the existence, state, and activities of others in the group. Awareness can be critical for effective coordination. In ordinary face-to-face settings, awareness is broad. If I pay attention I can always determine who said something, who wrote on the whiteboard, who had what facial expression, and so forth. While

I cannot know everything (e.g., those thoughts that people choose not to share), I at least know what the others are doing and saying. All of this *shared* activity is identifiable by person.

As soon as the shared activity starts passing through a computer system, the door is opened to varying degrees of awareness about who is doing what when. For example, group tasks such as brainstorming [Nun91] or voting could be anonymous. Designers have the option of supporting various levels and types of awareness. Here are some examples:

1. Who are the participants in the session?
2. How many participants are in the session?
3. What are the participants doing to the objects in the sessions?
4. Where are the participants working in the object?
5. Where are the participants located if they are distributed geographically?
6. Do any of the participants in the session have special roles or privileges?
7. What kinds of anonymity conditions are available and being used (e.g., for voting)?

Some of the most complex issues in the design of interfaces to groupware systems have to do with how to handle awareness. Existing systems tend to have very simple and sometimes intrusive means of handling this kind of information. Changes to the shared object are broadcast to all participants immediately. Participants have few or no controls over how this information is presented, or whether it is presented at all. Functions having to do with managing awareness include: (1) setting up different information channels to the users so they can be aware of aspects of the session, (2) offering various kinds of awareness options (e.g., anonymity), and (3) giving users control over how they are to be made aware --the flow and form of information to their interface. One reason this is such a difficult part of design is that awareness is handled subtly and in a variety of ways in traditional social situations and our experience with single-user applications does not inform us. There is little basis for experiencing various kinds of awareness in technology prior to actually designing and using groupware.

## 7.2.4 Reverting to Earlier States

Many single user applications have concepts like undo or revert that allow one to restore an earlier state through a single command. In such applications it is relatively unproblematic to define a state to which a user might want to return. However, in groupware, the issues are much more complex. With the possibility that different users may be carrying out concurrent streams of activity or may not be paying attention to the changes that others are making, it is less clear whether there is a set of states shared among the users that make an undo or revert an understandable or desirable event.

For instance, consider a multi-user editor where every editing action is applied to the document immediately, and everyone's copy is updated so that they all are always identical. What would undo mean under these circumstances? Do you undo the last editing action, regardless of who did it, or do you undo *your* last action if you are the person invoking the undo? Answers to these questions depend upon the tasks and applications a group is using, as well as the data/object management system.

Undo in the user interface means that a user could easily revert to a previous *view* in the interface. It is similar to undo for the task objects, but applies only to the view. If there is no linking of views across users, it could be simple to implement. When views are linked, the undo function becomes much more complex.

A broader sense of undo appears in a shared workspace tool called WeMet [Wol92]. WeMet keeps a history of all states that the users of the system have been in before through a time-stamped history of meeting events. This allows users to go back to earlier situations while not losing the later states that were created. The users could decide to use an earlier state as a point of departure for a new series of activities. This rich history keeping is an extension of the undo/revert idea, and as Wolf et al [Wol92] point out, this capability provided groups of users with the potential for both considerable power and confusion.

Every activity we describe is a candidate for revert or undo. In a few cases the analysis may be similar to single-user cases, but where there is any linking or shared awareness, matters become much more complex. Analysis of these issues is just beginning [Cho92, Pra92].

## 7.2.5 The Power of Groupware

What makes groupware such an interesting application domain is the wide range of possibilities for supporting intermediate levels of linking, awareness, and undo across the four activity clusters. Linking, awareness and undo are not necessarily sensible for all possible groupware functions, but they certainly apply to a large number of them. A variety of abstractions could be used to support such intermediate levels. Further, there is the prospect of interposing intelligent agents of various kinds who would adjust levels of linking or awareness as circumstances change.

## 7.3 DETAILED ACTIVITY DESCRIPTIONS

We developed our activity clusters by examining a wide range of groupware systems. These lists of activities are not exhaustive, but they show the wide range of functions that are in existing systems and the design literature. In this section, we describe in more detail the activities within each cluster, shown in Table 7.1. We use four different systems to help illustrate our descriptions: ShrEdit [Mcg92], Aspects [Gro90], GROVE [Ell91], and Timbuktu [Far91]. The first three are real-time, synchronous text editors, although Aspects also has a paint and draw editor which we will not refer to here, and GROVE only handles an outline structure. And, while Timbuktu allows any single-user application to be shared among a group of users, we consider it here only for the restricted case of sharing an editor.

## 7.3.1 Task Activities

Task activities fall into three broad clusters: change, locate, and set policies.

### 7.3.1.1 CHANGE

Changes are activities that modify the data objects in some way. The editing operations (i.e., create and modify) are defined as they would be in single user systems. Saving data objects can be somewhat complex for some of these systems. For ShrEdit and GROVE, there is only one file per session, so any command to save applies to the single file. With Aspects, when each user other than the session manager saves a file, it applies to their local copy only.

Controlling updates is the mechanism permitting the user to control the time at which changes from others are applied to his/her version of the shared workspace. All systems we know about apply updates literally and instantaneously. Other options are possible.

### 7.3.1.2 LOCATE

There are several ways one might want to navigate through a shared workspace. Search is implemented in single user systems through a function like Find. Find might include Boolean expressions and other powerful matching algorithms. Groupware introduces the additional complexity of managing objects that others have created. We suggest four dimensions on which navigation can operate; there may be more. Search can operate on the structure of the object, the content of the object, the history of its changes, and the participant's activity. The first two are applicable to single user systems as well as groupware systems. For example, navigating for *structure* would permit one to see all of the tables in a document. Navigating for *content* might allow a user to see all of the references to a particular design feature. In a group system, there are other things that one might search for: history and participation. One may wish to see all of the changes to the document that happened in the last two days or last two minutes. Or, one may wish to see where a person is working now, or all the edits that person made in the last hour. ShrEdit's Find and Track functions allow users to navigate to where another group member is currently working.

### 7.3.1.3 SET POLICIES

Setting permissions is a function for managing read, write, execute, and ownership capabilities to shared objects. GROVE allows users to set read and write permission for a shared view of various pieces of an outline object. The Aspects moderator can determine a work mode that could restrict write permissions to one, where all others are read-only, or a mode in which all have read-write permission. Controlling versions of the task objects is important when the group meets more than once, or works asynchronously. None of the editors examined here have explicit support for managing more than one version of the data objects except through file names that the user would provide.

## 7.3.2 Interface Activities

Interface activities are grouped into those that control joint attention, locate, and set policies.

### 7.3.2.1 CONTROL JOINT ATTENTION

Getting attention is the operation of bringing something to the attention of one, several, or all group members, while focusing attention is a mechanism to assist in attracting the group's attention to a particular object, or to guide the group through a particular task or set of tasks. Getting attention in synchronous work is an activity that interrupts the work flow or concentration of one or more group members. For example, Aspects uses centrally placed message boxes or bells to signal that someone is joining or leaving a session, or that someone has sent a message via the Chat Box. On the other hand, Aspects uses a more passive raised hand icon to inform the pen-holder that someone else wishes to type. A telepointer, a cursor that all can use, is often used for guiding attention from location to location, as described in [Cro90] and [Ols90]. Timbuktu has only a single cursor, which can be used for focusing on a location in the shared workspace. ShrEdit has no pointer, while Aspects offers a unique one for every user.

## 7.3.2.2  LOCATE

In multi-window systems, user interfaces can quickly get quite complex. When many windows are open on the desktop, it may be difficult to find a particular spot. There are several strategies for navigating the interface of groups. One might be based on content, for example on window name or type. Aspects provides a list of window names along with icons to distinguish the window type (e.g., draw, write, or paint). Another possibility might be to navigate via people's activity, such as activate the window that is currently active in someone else's view.

## 7.3.2.3  SET POLICIES

There are many functions one could use to control the way in which the underlying task objects are viewed by different users. Controlling the update of the representation in the user interface is different than controlling the update of the underlying data. Ellis, Gibbs & Rein [Ell91] describe an especially interesting metaphor for updates in the interface. In their system, as changes occur to the object in places other than where you are editing, but within your visual range (i.e., in the window in the screen), instead of seeing the actual changes made to the object, you see a cloud. The cloud indicates that the underlying data object is changing, but you are not being shown what those changes are. You can initiate the "cloud burst" at a time when you are ready to attend to its contents. The color of the cloud or some other feature could be set to indicate the amount of change, or who is making the change. None of the systems in our analysis offer this functionality.

Filter control and fidelity control permit the user to modify the *amount* of data presented in the interface. Filtering occurs in single user applications through the ability to turn on and off hidden text or symbols. Fidelity control would allow the user to choose the quality of presentation of the data. For example, in some multimedia systems, one can specify a frame rate for viewing video data.

Controlling the representation is the ability to change the way in which the data objects are presented. This could be as simple as allowing users to have different fonts for the same document. Or, one user might choose to have a pie chart representing the same data that another user wanted to see as a bar graph.

A related function is the degree of customizability allowed for such interface objects as windows. ShrEdit and Aspects permit one to change window attributes independently of the other users. Their tracking feature permits the linking of the user's scroll position even though window sizes and placements are different. In GROVE, one may only control the location of the window on the screen for all windows, and may only vary the scroll position for the window which is private (not public or shared). Finally, with Timbuktu, any action in the Timbuktu window is performed for all users; there is no ability for customization on any attributes.

### 7.3.3  Session  Activities

Session activities form three broad clusters: participation schemes, session structure, and session support.

#### 7.3.3.1  SET PARTICIPATION SCHEMES

Participation has to do with the various ways in which individuals can participate as part of a group in a session. Managing session enrollment defines who can join a session and when. The groupware may support various roles that could in turn shape the group process. Roles could include a facilitator, a scribe, an observer, an editor, a session manager and voters. All four systems allow users to enroll in a session at any time, though Aspects makes it possible for one person, the session moderator, to confirm or deny such an enrollment. GROVE, Aspects and Timbuktu provide support for different roles. Aspects has a moderator role, the person who sets the collaborative work mode (e.g., whether everyone can edit at the same time or if they have to take turns). Timbuktu offers two modes in which each participant merely observes or can fully participate by acting as well as seeing.

Some systems allow participants to work in parallel, whereas some allow only serial turn-taking. If there is turn-taking, there are various ways in which it can be controlled, either within the system or by social interaction, with either the current actor having to explicitly release control or the requester being able to seize control without permission. Aspects has a "free-for-all" parallel mode and a "one-at-a-time" mode that is set by the moderator but can change mid-session. In Aspects the system controls turn-taking on a first come first served basis within the one-at-a-time mode, in which the current holder of the pen must explicitly release it before the requester can begin to type.

Setting various access privileges, such as read and write to shared objects, could be very important when participants want to own their entries and changes. This could occur in heterogeneous groups or large groups. Privileges could also be linked with roles to be played in the group, where the scribe can read/write, whereas all others read only. For certain kinds of tasks or groups, it might be beneficial to have a mechanism for setting different awareness levels. The clearest example of this is allowing anonymity. Some idea generation methods use anonymous input to guard against some of the inhibiting effects of being in a group [Die87].

#### 7.3.3.2  SET SESSION STRUCTURE

In large groups, occasions may arise when groups wish to divide up, work in parallel for a while, then reconvene. We have called these "in room breakout sessions." Functions which allow participants to split and merge sessions solve this problem in a large grain. Forming and disbanding subgroups supports a more fluid change of access to work within a session. GROVE permits subgroups to form shared views of the common object; no other systems serve this kind of goal.

#### 7.3.3.3  SET SESSION SUPPORT

Managing task transitions, tracking tasks, and tracking session history are additional session activities. As the group changes its tasks, the groupware system might provide support, such as changing the application that the group uses from a brainstorming tool to a structuring one. We also think that the group might want to have two methods of tracking its progress: on a task level and on a session level, if there is more than one of either of these. These concepts are borrowed from standard project and meeting management procedures.

Session activities may prescribe the need for a communication channel for passing messages among group participants. We have defined two categories for this: direct and indirect. Direct communication is the ability for one participant to communicate to one other participant. It is a one-to-one communication channel. The other category, indirect, is defined as multicast communication where one participant can communicate with two or more, up to the entire group. Both are probably important to support in any group of three or more. Aspects offers a Chat Box as an explicit communication channel; video or audio channels for distributed participants would constitute another explicit channel.

Various kinds of configuring could be offered: those having to do with applications and those having to do with resources. Most groupware systems in the past have been standalone applications, and have not permitted the use of outside applications within their purview. However, recently, we have seen application programming interfaces and protocol suites appear which permit people to more easily build group computing environments. Therefore, we believe that this new generation of groupware systems will permit groups to use many different applications within a session. When doing that, the group may need to configure them appropriately to match their tasks. Similarly, we might want to configure session resources. This might include reserving a computational server or taking over the high priority channels on a network.

## 7.3.4 Environment Activities

Work during a synchronous session often must be related to the schedules and task assignments of both individuals and groups. One can imagine the usefulness of having the to-do list generated from a session connected to a group's project management system and individuals' calendars.

Importing and exporting data between the groupware system and other resources and applications is often important. Individuals might want to access their personal files, public files, or other resources like news feeds. Individuals might wish to bring their contributions to the group session in some electronic format or take them away at the end of a session. Aspects allows import/export from common single-user word processors, while ShrEdit allows cut and paste of ASCII text files from and to other applications.

## 7.4 THE MIX OF TECHNOLOGY AND USERS

In any group work situation, the coordination of a group's activities can occur in a variety of ways. For instance, in a face-to-face meeting, the group members coordinate their activities through spoken language, gestures, posture, proximity to others and to room features, and artifacts like whiteboards or paper and pencil. In designing technology to support group work, it is important to map the groupware functions we describe here onto the work situation, and to realize that many functions can be met outside of the groupware.

Support could occur at three levels:

- **explicit support** means that a particular function is embodied in the groupware through some specific interface object, set of actions, or other system component;
- **implicit support** means that there are means by which the system can support some function, even though it was not designed to do so;
- **social support** means the group accomplishes some coordination function entirely outside of the system.

Implicit support is probably the least clear; an example clarifies it. With a flexible groupware tool, users invent groupware functions within the range of capabilities that the system offers. Thus, with a shared text editor with instant updating of changes, several group processes were supported by techniques that different groups invented on the spot. For example, to implement voting, people assigned symbols to themselves and typed them next to the "thing" for which they were voting. To focus attention, a group created a pointer out of several dashes and an arrow (i.e.——> ). They used the cut and paste editing facility to move this ersatz telepointer to different locations. The person doing the telepointing asked the others to Track her so their views would be linked to hers as she explained her reasoning behind various items in the document. We characterize both of these as implicit support for an activity.

What needs to be supported by the system and what can be left to the context of use can vary greatly from situation to situation. Face-to-face meetings and distributed meetings require different support, since face-to-face carries physical channels that are absent in distributed situations. Appropriate design requires having a clear vision of what the usage context will be, or at the very least, providing flexibility so that users can adapt the tool to the context appropriate for themselves.

## 7.4.1  Situational Variables

Situational variables are important drivers of the success of any particular piece of groupware [Nun91]. In addition to the *system* itself, one has to take into account characteristics of the *group*, *task*, and *context*. From a design perspective, this means that the relative importance of various activity functions and the right mix of system and user handling of these functions can vary enormously in relation to these situational variables. Alternatively, given a set of groupware systems, potential users would want to select among them, ideally, by taking into account the match between the situational variables and the system characteristics. Let us briefly illustrate each of these classes of situation variables.

Groups vary in a number of ways that could determine support requirements and ultimate success [Hac87]. Small groups (3-10) need different kinds of support than large groups (more than 10). Groups can be homogeneous or heterogeneous by their levels in an organizational hierarchy, roles, profession, knowledge, etc. Coordination issues, the need for control to prevent chaos and to assure that important information is heard and understood by all, vary directly as a function of group size and composition.

There are many kinds of tasks that groups take on (design, strategic planning, negotiation, etc.). Many of these tasks involve different subtasks, such as understanding the goal, ideating, structuring, evaluating, selecting, implementing, and these occur in varying proportions.

Design tasks require a lot of ideation and evaluation, whereas policy meetings focus on understanding the goal, and negotiation meetings on evaluation and selection. Tasks also vary in their length and complexity: designing a new logo is very different than designing a space station.

The context in which groups work also varies widely. Organizations have different cultures and standard practices. This includes such things as reward structures, career trajectories, evaluative tone, time pressure, resources, and even the physical setting. Some explicitly teach meeting preparation and facilitation as well as project management. Some teach coordination practices through apprenticeships, testing budding managers by making them serve as project leaders. As Ishii [Ish90] has shown, the cultural assumptions that underlie a number of popular groupware programs developed in Europe and North America would fail in the typical Japanese company, where tasks like decision making are done in a very different way.

A feature that cuts across all of these situational variables is the nature of group work in a project context. Very few groups have tasks that can be completed in a single session of synchronous interactions. Much of a typical group's work is carried out by the members working on parts of their task alone. They may have multiple synchronous sessions, with varying numbers of participants. Synchronous interaction may be intermixed with asynchronous interaction. A large variety of tools may be needed to accomplish the many different parts of a complex task, with much shifting of material among these tools (e.g., e-mail text to a group editor to a rich word processor for formatting).

## 7.4.2 An Analysis Method

The feature list described in the previous section can serve as an analysis method for evaluating task-technology fit. This evaluation involves indicating for a particular task and context (group and situation) the way in which an activity is supported, either explicitly, implicitly, socially or not at all. We create a table that has all of the activities in Table 7.1 as row entries. We specify a series of technology by situation combinations that make up the columns. Then in each cell we evaluated whether what the system provides in this situation is appropriate, difficult or impeding for the group in doing the task in the specified situation. For small groups, for example, some activities might best be determined socially, with perhaps some flexibility in the software to support it implicitly. Turn-taking comes to mind. In a small face-to-face group, the turn taking often moves smoothly. Any explicit support would probably impede progress. In a larger group, however, where people do not know each other, support that is explicitly embedded in either social practice or technology is probably beneficial.

This analysis method then has two major steps -- 1) filling in a table of activities with indications of how the software would support that activity for that situation, and 2) evaluating these entries for whether that feature helps or hinders that task for that group. To date, we have progressed to realizing the value of the table itself, but have not progressed to making explicit how the second stage evaluation would take place. We believe that there are a number of research issues generated in this evaluation, and that the requisite research has not been done. So, although this method is not complete, at a minimum it provides the basis for a research agenda.

To better understand the usefulness of this analysis, we take as examples two specific systems and look at them in two specific situations. The two systems are ShrEdit and Aspects, with only the text editor portion of Aspects used. We picked tasks for which both systems provide a useful shared workspace, since they are both group editors with almost unlimited parallelism allowed. We contrast two working situations, one with a small group of peers who know each other well, the other with a large number of people with little familiarity with each other and with heterogeneous roles.

The entries in Table 7.2 reflect the way in which a particular activity is or could be supported under the work circumstances listed at the top of each column. The interpretation of each of the entries is:

- **E—explicit support:** the system provides an explicit command, tool, or feature that directly supports the activity
- **E-P—partial explicit support:** the system provides explicit support for a portion of a activity (e.g., Aspects provides explicit support for one particular meeting role, that of moderator, but not for any others)
- **I-E—implicit support, easy:** the system provides a means where, with social agreement, the users can find support for a specific activity easily (e.g., creating a shared pointer with cut-and-paste of a distinctive set of characters)
- **I-H—implicit support, hard:** the system provides a means by which a activity could be supported, but given the circumstances in which the system is being used it would be very difficult to do it
- **S—social support:** the system provides no support for the activity, but the members of the group could handle this activity socially under the given work circumstances
- **N—no support:** the system provides no support, nor could the users do it socially.

Table 7.2 shows in detail which activities these two systems offer in the two sample situations. An important caveat in looking over Table 7.2 is that we only show whether or not a function is offered, not whether the way in which it is handled is good or appropriate. Another important point is that there is no value judgment associated with whether the system or the people in the group bear the bulk of the burden in managing an activity. That judgment must come later.

Table 7.2 reveals several things about these systems. Both of them provide good coverage of the work situation for a small group of peers. This is because under these circumstances many of the activities that are not explicitly supported in the system can be easily managed by the group, either with the aid of the system's flexibility or socially. However, implicit support of activities is much more difficult when the groups are large in size and don't know each other as well. As a result, many of the I-E entries become I-H entries when we analyze the second of the two work situations. The fact that Aspects provides a wider range of explicit support for session activities suggests that it may be the more suitable groupware for the larger group. It might also suggest that using explicit support for an activity that can be managed well socially (such as turn-taking in a small group) could impede the group's progress.

## 7.5  GENERAL DISCUSSION

While our focus has been to develop a functional framework for groupware and we have illustrated it only in the context of synchronous work, the scheme can be used to analyze all forms of coordinated work. The various coordination functions that we describe can be met

**Table 7.2**   Comparison of Two Group Editors Used in Two Different Situations

| | | ShrEdit | | Aspects | |
|---|---|---|---|---|---|
| | group size | small | large | small | large |
| | specialized roles | equal | hetero-geneous | equal | hetero-geneous |
| | proximity | face-to-face | face-to-face | face-to-face | face-to-face |
| | task | design specs | strategic planning | design specs | strategic planning |
| **Task Object** | | | | | |
| | create | E | E | E | E |
| | modify | E | E | E | E |
| | save | E | E | E-P | E-P |
| | annotate | I-H | I-H | I-E | I-H |
| | update control | N | N | N | N |
| | navigate | E-P | E-P | I-H | I-H |
| | search | N | N | E | E |
| | sort | I-H | I-H | I-H | I-H |
| | compare | I-H | I-H | I-H | I-H |
| | set permissions | S | S | S | S |
| | version control | I-E | I-H | I-E | I-H |
| **Interface** | | | | | |
| | establish joint attention | S | S | E-P | E-P |
| | maintain joint attention | I-E | I-H | E-P | E-P |
| | navigate | S | S | E | E |
| | update control | N | N | N | N |
| | filter control | N | N | N | N |
| | fidelity control | N | N | N | N |
| | format control | E-P | E-P | N | N |
| | window attributes | E | E | E | E |
| **Session** | | | | | |
| | manage session enrollment | S | S | E | E |
| | set roles | S | S | E-P | E-P |
| | set access privileges | S | S | E-P | E-P |
| | control of turn taking | S | S | E | E |
| | set awareness levels | N | N | N | N |
| | serial vs. parallel | S | S | E | E |
| | split & merge sessions | S | S | S | S |
| | form & disband subgroups | S | S | S | S |
| | tracking tasks | I-E | I-E | I-E | I-E |
| | manage task transitions | S | S | S | S |
| | tracking session history | N | N | N | N |
| | provide comm. channels | I-E | I-H | E | E |
| | configure a set of applications | N | N | N | N |
| | configure session resources | N | N | N | N |
| **Environment** | | | | | |
| | personal & group scheduling | S | S | S | S |
| | task assignment | S | S | S | S |
| | import & export data | I-E | I-E | E-P | E-P |

either through software or through social practice. Humans have centuries of experience in working together, and where appropriate we should use our knowledge and communication skills to coordinate our work. We can also use this scheme to analyze coordinated work that uses other technologies. For instance, it is quite enlightening to examine how groups coordinate their work in a typical meeting room [Sch89], or how communication technologies like video can be used to support collaborative work [Ish91, Ish92, Tan90, Tan91]. We have used this kind of analysis to help us think of new interface metaphors for groupware [Ols92a].

This more general view of our enterprise fits in well with emerging theories of coordination. For instance, Malone & Crowston [Mal91] have described a hierarchy of coordination processes. In their scheme, our analysis is an attempt to describe the very lowest level of coordination processes. They point out that at this level coordination occurs through the perception of shared objects. This fits well with our analysis, and suggests that an object-oriented approach might well fit the building of coordination functionality in groupware. Because of the close ties between our analysis of the group functions of groupware and the emerging theories of coordination, we think of our clusters of activities as various areas of coordination activity.

The list of functions shown in Tables 7.1 and 7.2 are by no means complete. They arise from an analysis of the functions that are provided by current synchronous groupware or by design ideas that are technically feasible. We expect that the set of functions for synchronous and other groupware will evolve as we learn more about the design space of such software.

This analysis is of course only suggestive of the power of this scheme for aiding in the design of systems. It is also important to realize that while this analysis helps with identifying the profile of functions that should be available for a given situation, it says nothing about how these functions should be implemented, either at the level of architecture or interface. But it is an important step in the exploration of the design space, and one could imagine that it would provide a useful framework for cataloging the findings of studies that look into the impact of various functions in specific situations. This could in turn take us to the next stages in Card's evolution of systems, shown in Figure 7.1. We wish to move beyond building point systems to understand which features in an immense design space should go into groupware to support a particular work situation.

## ACKNOWLEDGMENTS

This work has been supported by the National Science Foundation (Grant No. IRI-8902930).

## REFERENCES

[Car91]   S. Card. The theories of HCI. Presentation at the NSF Workshop on Human Computer Interaction in Washington, D.C. July 1991.

[Cho92]   R. Choudhary and P. Dewan. Multi-user undo/redo. Manuscript. 1992.

[Cro90]   T. Crowley, P. Milazzo, E. Baker, H. Forsdick, and R. Tomlinson. MMConf: An infrastructure for building shared multimedia applications. *Proceedings of CSCW '90*, pages 329–342, Los Angeles, 1990.

[Dew92]   P. Dewan and R. Choudhary. A high-level and flexible framework for implementing multi-user user-interfaces. *ACM Transactions on Information Systems,* 10: 345-380, 1992.

[Die87]   M. Diehl and W. Stroebe. Productivity loss in brainstorming groups: Toward a solution of a riddle. *Journal of Personality and Social Psychology*, 53:497–509, 1987.

[Ell91]   C. A. Ellis, S. J. Gibbs, and G. L. Rein. Groupware: Some issues and experiences. *Communications of the ACM, 34*(1):38–58, 1991.

[Far91]   Farallon Computing, Inc. Timbuktu. 1987–1991.

[Gri88]   I. Grief and S. Sarin. Data sharing in group work. *ACM Transactions on Office Information Systems*, 5:187-211, 1988.

[Gro90]   Group Technologies, Inc. Aspects. 1990.

[Hac87]   J. R. Hackman. The design of work teams. In J. W. Lorsch, editor, *Handbook of Organizational Behavior*, pages 315–342. Prentice Hall, Englewood Cliffs, NJ, 1987.

[Ish90]   H. Ishii. Cross-cultural communication and computer-supported cooperative work. *Whole Earth Review*, pages 48–52, Winter 1990.

[Ish91]   H. Ishii and N. Miyake. Toward an open shared workspace: Computer and video fusion approach of TeamWorkStation. *CACM*, 34(12):37–50, 1991.

[Ish92]   H. Ishii, M. Kobayashi, and J. Grudin. Integration of inter-personal space and shared workspace: ClearBoard design and experiments. In *Proceedings of CSCW '92*, pages 33–42, Toronto, 1992.

[Lai88]   K.-Y. Lai, T. W. Malone, and K.-C. Yu. Object Lens: A "Spreadsheet" for Cooperative Work. *ACM Transactions on Office Information Systems*, 6:332–353, 1988.

[Lee90]   J. Lee and T. W. Malone. Partially shared views: A scheme for communicating among groups that use different type hierarchies. *ACM Transactions on Information Systems*, 8:1–26, 1990.

[Mal91]   T. W. Malone and K. Crowston. Toward an interdisciplinary theory of coordination. Technical Report 120, Massachusetts Institute of Technology, Center for Coordination Science, Cambridge, MA. April 1991.

[Mcg92]   L. McGuffin and G. M. Olson. ShrEdit: A shared electronic workspace. Technical Report #45, The University of Michigan, Cognitive Science and Machine Intelligence Laboratory. August 1992.

[Mcg84]   J. E. McGrath. *Groups: Interaction and Performance* . Englewood Cliffs, NJ: Prentice-Hall, 1984.

[Neu90]   C. M. Neuwirth, D. S. Kaufer, R. Chandhok, and J. H. Morris. Issues in the design of computer-support for co-authoring and commenting. In *Proceedings of CSCW '90* pages 183–195, Los Angeles, 1990.

[Nun91]   J. F. Nunamaker, A. R. Dennis, J. S. Valacich, D. R. Vogel, and J. F. George. Electronic meeting systems to support group work. *Communications of the ACM, 34*:40–61, 1991.

[Ols91]   G. M. Olson and J. R. Olson. User-centered design of collaboration technology. *Journal of Organizational Computing*, 1:61–83, 1991.

[Ols92a]  G. M. Olson and J. S. Olson. Defining a metaphor for group work. *IEEE Software*, 9(3):93–95, 1992.

[Ols92b]  G. M. Olson, J. S. Olson, M. Carter, and M. Storrøsten. Small group design meetings: An analysis of collaboration. *Human Computer Interaction.*, 7:347–374, 1992.

[Ols90]   J. S. Olson, G. M. Olson, L. A. Mack, and P. Wellner. Concurrent editing: The group's interface. In D. Diaper , editor, *INTERACT '90—Third IFIP Conference on Human-Computer Interaction.* Elsevier, 1990.

[Ols92c]  J. S. Olson, G. M. Olson, M. Storrøsten, and M. Carter. How a group editor changes the nature of group work as well as its outcome. *Proceedings of CSCW '92*, pages 91-98, Toronto, 1992.

[Ols93]   J. S. Olson, S. Card, T. Landauer, G. M. Olson, T. Malone, and J. Leggett. Computer-supported cooperative work: Research issues for the 90s. *Behavior and Information Technology*. In press.

[Pat90]   J. F. Patterson, R. D. Hill, S. L. Rohall, and W. S. Meeks. Rendezvous: An architecture for synchronous multi-user applications. *Proceedings of CSCW '90*, pages 317–328, Los Angeles, 1990.

[Pra92]   A. Prakash and M. Knister. Undoing actions in collaborative work. *Proceedings of CSCW '92* pages 273-280, Toronto, 1992.

[Sch89]  H. B. Schwartzman. *The meeting: Gatherings in organizations and communities*. Plenum, New York, 1989.

[Ste87]  M. Stefik, G. Foster, D. Bobrow, K. Kahn, S. Lanning, and L. Suchman. Beyond the chalkboard:  Computer support for collaboration and problem solving in meetings. *Communications of the ACM*, 30:32–47, 1987.

[Ste72]  I. D. Steiner, I. D. *Group Process and productivity*. Academic Press, New York, 1972.

[Tan90]  J. C. Tang. and S. L. Minneman. VideoDraw: A video interface for collaborative drawing. In *Proceedings of CHI '90*, pages 313–320. ACM, New York, 1990.

[Tan91]  J. C. Tang and S. L. Minneman. VideoWhiteboard:  Video shadows to support remote collaboration. In *Proceedings of CHI '91*, pages 315–322. ACM, New York, 1991.

[Wol92]  C. G. Wolf, J. R. Rhyne, and L. K. Briggs. Communication and information retrieval with a pen-based meeting support tool. In *Proceedings of CSCW '92*, pages 322–329. Toronto, 1992.

# 8

# Tools for Implementing Multiuser User Interfaces

**PRASUN DEWAN**
*Purdue University*

### ABSTRACT

A variety of tools can ease the difficult task of implementing multiuser user interfaces. In this paper, we identify them, classify them into different categories, motivate and describe the main concepts behind their design, point out the similarities and differences among the approaches implemented by them, outline the kind of multiuser interfaces they have been designed to support, and discuss the benefits and drawbacks of supporting each of these approaches. We provide a set of informal definitions for concepts that are common to these tools. We illustrate the tools by considering the implementation of an example multiuser user-interface using each of these tools. We evaluate them by considering how much automation they offer, how flexible they are, and how well they perform.

## 8.1   INTRODUCTION

Imagine two users, geographically dispersed, responsible for collaboratively testing a module and fixing the bugs. They use their workstations, which are connected by a network, to interact with a distributed application that supports their collaborative task. Figure 8.1 shows the windows created by the application on the workstations of the two users. The top pair of windows in the figure is created on the workstation of user A while the bottom pair is created on the workstation of user B. The application displays in "edit windows" created on both workstations (Figure 8.1, upper and lower right windows) the module to be tested. It allows either user to select one or more procedures for testing and underlines in "test windows" (Figure 8.1, upper and lower left windows) the parts of these procedures that are not covered by the test data.

The test windows display identical images–if one of the users, for instance, scrolls the

---

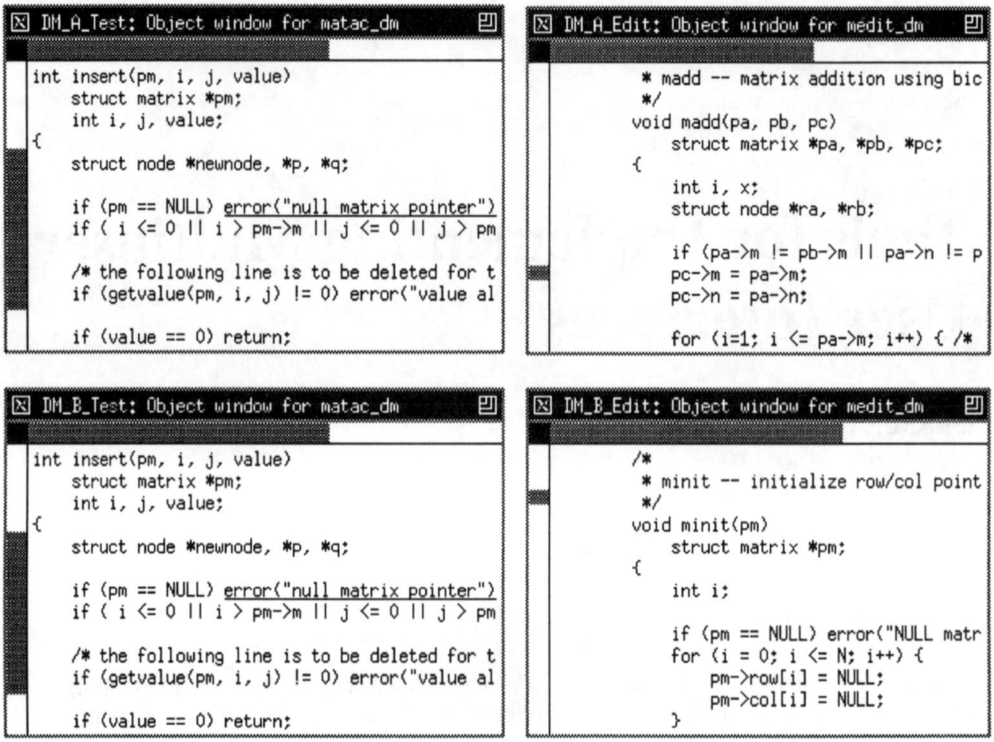

```
 DM_A_Test: Object window for matac_dm
int insert(pm, i, j, value)
    struct matrix *pm;
    int i, j, value;
{
    struct node *newnode, *p, *q;

    if (pm == NULL) error("null matrix pointer")
    if ( i <= 0 || i > pm->m || j <= 0 || j > pm

    /* the following line is to be deleted for t
    if (getvalue(pm, i, j) != 0) error("value al

    if (value == 0) return;
```

```
 DM_A_Edit: Object window for medit_dm
    * madd -- matrix addition using bic
    */
void madd(pa, pb, pc)
    struct matrix *pa, *pb, *pc;
{
    int i, x;
    struct node *ra, *rb;

    if (pa->m != pb->m || pa->n != p
    pc->m = pa->m;
    pc->n = pa->n;

    for (i=1; i <= pa->m; i++) { /*
```

```
 DM_B_Test: Object window for matac_dm
int insert(pm, i, j, value)
    struct matrix *pm;
    int i, j, value;
{
    struct node *newnode, *p, *q;

    if (pm == NULL) error("null matrix pointer")
    if ( i <= 0 || i > pm->m || j <= 0 || j > pm

    /* the following line is to be deleted for t
    if (getvalue(pm, i, j) != 0) error("value al

    if (value == 0) return;
```

```
 DM_B_Edit: Object window for medit_dm
    /*
    * minit -- initialize row/col point
    */
void minit(pm)
    struct matrix *pm;
    {
    int i;

    if (pm == NULL) error("NULL matr
    for (i = 0; i <= N; i++) {
        pm->row[i] = NULL;
        pm->col[i] = NULL;
    }
```

**Figure 8.1**   A multiuser user-interface allowing two users to collaboratively edit and test a module.

window, both windows are scrolled. As a result, the users can collaboratively browse through these windows. The edit windows, however, can display different images but display a common semantic state, that is, display the same set of procedures. As a result, the two users can independently browse through and modify the procedures displayed in their windows. These procedures are divided into private procedures, which can be modified by only one of these users, and shared procedures, which can be modified by both users. The application allows both users to modify the procedures they are authorized to edit. It broadcasts changes to a shared procedure as soon they are made and changes to private procedures only when they are committed. It provides concurrency control to ensure users do not simultaneously modify a shared procedure. It also provides users with a query language that allows them to determine which procedures are completely covered by test data. The two users carry out several iterations of collaboratively testing and fixing the module until they are satisfied.

This example illustrates the nature of multiuser applications– applications that interact with multiple users, possibly geographically dispersed. It also illustrates the power of such applications– it allows users to collaboratively carry out a complex task without having to leave their office or lose access to their workstations. Multiuser applications such as this one have the potential of automating a significant amount of cooperative work carried out at current organizations [Dem87]. As a result, several experimental multiuser applications have been implemented recently including the Colab [Stef87] and GROVE [Ell90] outline editors, the RTCAL appointment system [Sar85], the CES [Gre86], Quilt [Fis88], and PREP [Neu90] co-authoring systems, the MACE graphics editor [New91a], the ICICLE code inspector [Bro90], a cooperative air-traffic control system [Ben92], the EXPRES system for collaborative creation, submission, and review of research proposals [Ols90], and the FLECSE collaborative software development environment [Dew93c].

The example also illustrates the difficulty in implementing a multiuser application. Like a single-user application, a multiuser application must perform computation tasks such as testing a module for coverage and interaction tasks such as processing input commands and displaying results. In addition, it must efficiently and flexibly carry out several collaboration tasks such as dynamically making and breaking connections with possibly remote users, multiplexing input from and demultiplexing output to multiple users, informing users of input entered by other users, helping users coordinate their interaction, and providing concurrency and access control [Sar85] [Ell90]. For this reason, few multiuser applications have been developed so far despite the tremendous potential of these applications. Moreover, most of the projects that have implemented these applications from scratch have, typically, been multi-year, multi-person projects.

Today, however, multiuser applications do not have to be implemented from scratch, since a variety of tools exist that support the implementation of their user-interfaces. These tools can be classified into eight main categories:

- *Database systems,* which provide a relational repository of data that can be read/modified by multiple processes.
- *Distributed systems,* which allow programmers to implement distributed components of a multiuser application that are unaware of the low-level details of sending messages among each other.
- *Message servers,* which allow these components to be unaware of the identities of each other.
- *Shared object systems,* which support sharing of data among these components.
- *Shared window systems,* which are extensions of single-user window systems that support sharing.
- *Multiuser toolkits,* which offer predefined support for one or more collaboration functions and low-level facilities for customizing this support.
- *Multiuser UIMSs,* which are extensions of single-user UIMSs [Pfa85] (User Interface Management System) that support sharing.
- *Multiuser user-interface generators,* which are extensions of single-user user-interface generators that supports sharing.

In this paper, we motivate and describe the main concepts behind the design of these tools, point out the similarities and differences among the approaches implemented by them, outline the kind of multiuser user interfaces they have been designed to support, and discuss the benefits and drawbacks of each of these approaches. We evaluate each of these tools based on three main criteria:

- *Flexibility*: What is the range of multiuser user interfaces that can be supported by the tool?
- *Automation*: How much effort is required to implement/change the user interface?
- *Efficiency*: How well does the user interface perform?

In the next section, we give informal definitions of concepts used to describe these tools. We then discuss each of these tools in a separate section. In each of these sections, we illustrate the working and capabilities of the tool by considering how it could be used to implement the example user interface above. We first describe traditional database systems and then, in each of the subsequent sections, describe a tool that overcomes some of the limitations of the tool described in the previous section. However, the reader should not conclude that the tools are presented in order of superiority since a tool often overcomes limitations of a previous tool by sacrificing some of the advantages of the latter. Finally, we present conclusions and directions for future work.

A brief version of this discussion is given in [Dew92], which describes multiuser Suite, a multiuser tool developed by the author, and compares it with other multiuser tools to highlight its unique features. This paper is also related to a recent paper by Ellis et al [Ell90], which surveys the area of multiuser applications, describing the important issues raised by these applications and approaches to resolving them. Our paper complements this work by surveying the related area of multiuser tools. Furthermore, it complements the companion paper on multiuser applications by Olson et al [Ols93], which addresses the functionality of multiuser applications but not their implementation. Finally, it is important to note that several social issues must be resolved before multiuser applications are widely used. This paper does not address these issues and concentrates only on the technical barriers to implementing them.

## 8.2   DEFINITIONS

*Multiuser application*: An application that interacts with multiple users, that is, receives input from and/or displays output to multiple users. It may consist of multiple, distributed component processes.

   *Multiuser program*: A program executed by a multiuser application.

   *Multiuser user interface*: User interface of a multiuser application.

   *Independent/Coupled/Collaborative/Individual/WYSIWIS/WYSINWIS Interaction*: Interaction with multiuser applications can be classified into *independent interaction* and *coupled interaction* depending on whether or not the output seen by a user is a function of the input entered by another user. A time sharing system supports independent interaction since it allows its users to interact independently of each other while the example application supports coupled interaction since changes made by user A can be seen by user B. Coupled interaction can be further classified into *collaborative interaction* and *individual interaction* based on whether or not the interacting users depend on other users to perform their tasks. An airline reservation systems supports individual interaction since its users make reservations individually while the example application above supports collaborative interaction since a user may change a procedure in response to an action performed by another user to test the procedure. Individual interaction is similar to independent interaction except that the former allows users to compete for a shared set of resources. In this paper, we will focus mainly on the suitability of multiuser tools to support collaborative interaction. Finally, collaborative interaction can be classified into *WYSIWIS* (What You See Is What I See) [Stef87] interaction and *WYSINWIS* (What You See Is Not What I See) interaction based on whether or not the collaborating users see the same interaction state. The test windows of the example application support WYSIWIS interaction while the edit windows support WYSINWIS interaction.

   *Access control*– determines whether a user of a multiuser application is authorized to perform an action such as changing the procedure insert (Figure 8.1).

   *Concurrency control*– prevents users of a multiuser application from making concurrent inconsistent changes they are authorized to make such as concurrent changes to the shared procedure insert.

*Coupling*: The process by which coupled interaction occurs.

*Input multiplexing*–merging multiple input streams of different users.

*Output demultiplexing*–sending application output along the output streams of different users.

*Interaction function*: A user-interface function such as parsing of input or output of results that is common to both single-user and multiuser interfaces.

*Collaboration function*: A function such as access control or concurrency control that is specific to multiuser user interfaces.

*Single-user tool*: A tool supporting the implementation of one or more interaction functions.

*Multiuser tool*: A tool supporting the implementation of one or more collaboration functions.

*Basis*: A multiuser tool can be developed by extending a single-user tool. We refer to the latter as the *basis* of the former.

*Server/client*: A *server* is a runtime component of a tool that performs services for programmer-defined components, called *clients*, of an application.

*Interaction awareness*: A measure of the amount of code in a client of a single-user tool that defines interaction functions.

*Collaboration awareness*: A measure of the amount of code in a client of a multiuser tool that defines collaboration functions.

*Collaboration -aware/-transparent client* [Lau90]: A client that is aware/unaware it is interacting with multiple users, that is, a client that defines some/none of the collaboration functions.

*Call*: A procedure invoked by a client in a server.

*Callback*: A procedure invoked by a server in a client.

## 8.3  DATABASE SYSTEM

A database system is perhaps the first system that comes to mind when considering support for multiuser interaction. In this paper, we use the term "database system" for a traditional relational database system. The following two sections address some of the properties of "next generation systems" [Cac91]. Research in relational systems has shown that it is possible to create a tool that provides a repository of relational data that can be read and modified concurrently by multiple client processes executing on behalf of different users, allows its clients to group data accesses into transactions, provides concurrency control to ensure that transactions are executed atomically, offers access control to prevent unauthorized access, creates efficient data structures for storing large amounts of data, replicates data at distributed sites [Bha89], stores data in main memory [Leh86], and provides a relational query language for accessing and manipulating data.

Figure 8.2 shows how a database system can be used to develop a multiuser application. The multiuser application is composed of multiple database clients, each of which interacts with a particular user of the application and uses the database to store the data shared among the users (Figure 8.2). When one of the users commits changes to shared state, the corresponding client stores the new values in the database, from where the remote clients retrieve them and display them to their users. Figure 8.3 shows the main components of the program executed by the database client.

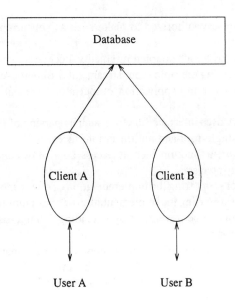

**Figure 8.2**   A Database System

```
declaration of data structures and procedures
--main steps
implement initial user interface
specify access control
do
    poll database to retrieve remote changes to shared state
    convert changes to internal represenation
    display changes to user
    get and parse input
    compute results
    display output
    convert local state changes to database representation
    store changes in database
until user quits
```

**Figure 8.3**   A Database Client

   There are several advantages in using a database system for developing multiuser applications. The system relieves its clients from implementing concurrency control. It also allows clients to make high-level access control specifications and provides the mechanisms required to implement these specifications. Furthermore, a database system can adopt the replicated approach to allow clients to read data without encountering network delays. Finally, unlike all the other tools discussed later, it provides efficient storage of large amounts of data and a predicate-based query language to access them. Our experience shows that implementing even simple queries can be a non-trivial task if a database system is not used [Dew93a].

   However, in comparison to some of the other tools discussed later, a database system has two main disadvantages. First, a database system and its clients use different representations of data. As a result, the database approach forces its clients to convert between different representations of data, which is referred to as the "impedance mismatch" problem [Atk87]. Impedance mismatch makes the overhead of developing multiuser applications high since programmers must write translation code that converts between the different representations. It also increases the response time of the applications because of the overhead of executing the translation code at runtime, which must perform costly join operations in case of structured data such as parse trees [Lin84]. Impedance mismatch is also a problem in single-user applications that use the database to store their persistent data. It is a more severe problem in multiuser applications developed using this approach since they use the database to also store shared, possibly non-persistent, data such as scrollbar positions.

Second, in highly collaborative tasks, users are often interested in receiving changes to shared data as soon as they are made available to them. Under this approach, such collaboration can only be supported if each client listening for changes frequently polls the database system for the changes, thereby making the client more difficult to program and, more important, drastically degrading the performance of the system [Dew90b]. The cost of polling together with the cost of impedance mismatch makes this technology unsuitable for highly concurrent collaborative tasks.

**Implementing the example user-interface:** To make the discussion concrete, consider implementation of the example user-interface (Figure 8.1) using a database system. A separate client is created for each user, which creates the two windows displayed on the user's workstation, processes input events generated by the workstation, and generates output requests for the workstation. The shared data such as the semantic state of the edit windows and the complete state of the test windows is kept in the database. The clients specify the rights of the different users to the edit procedures and other shared data–the database system provides the access control procedures required to implement these specifications. The database system also provides concurrency control procedures required to ensure that changes to a shared datum are not made concurrently by different clients. Furthermore, it provides a predicate-based query language for retrieving coverage and other information from the database. The parse trees of edit procedures and other shared data are represented internally in clients using some general purpose programming language. The clients translate between the programming language and database representations of these data. The overhead of polling and performing this translation makes it unsuitable to use this application to support highly collaborative interaction such as one in which the procedures in the edit windows are changed frequently or the test windows are scrolled frequently.

Several of the drawbacks of database systems arise because they were designed to support individual interaction and not collaborative interaction. We discuss below tools that are more appropriate for implementing collaborative interaction.

## 8.4   DISTRIBUTED SYSTEM

Some of the problems of a database system can be overcome if the clients interacting with different users directly exchange information with each other. Two kinds of tools have been developed to provide high-level support for communicating information among distributed clients: *Distributed RPC (Remote Procedure Call) systems* such as Cedar [Bir84], which allow a client to invoke procedures in remote clients and *distributed constraint systems* such as the Mercury attribute grammar system [Kai87], which allow programmers to define constraints among the data maintained by different distributed clients. An application programmer can

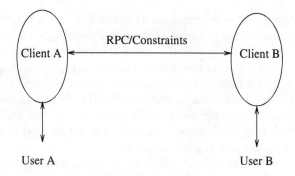

**Figure 8.4**   Distributed RPC and Constraint Systems

```
declaration of data structures and procedures
--main steps
implement initial user interface
use RPC to inform peers about identity
do
     receive from new peers their identities
     receive from existing peers remote changes to shared state
     display changes to user
     get and parse input
     implement access and concurrency control
     implement querying of state
     compute results
     display output
     for each remote peer
          use RPC to send to peer local changes to shared state
until user quits
```

**Figure 8.5**   An RPC Client

implement a multiuser application using either of these systems by creating a local client for each user of the application and using RPC/constraints to communicate information among the clients (Figure 8.4). Figure 8.5 outlines the structure of the program executed by a client of an RPC system. A distributed constraint system would be used similarly except that the implementation would be defined declaratively instead of procedurally.

These distributed tools do not suffer from the drawback of polling–distributed RPC systems explicitly inform a client of remote changes in which it is interested (by invoking appropriate procedures in the client) and distributed constraint systems automatically update the remote states. Moreover, these systems automatically convert between internal and external representations of data, thereby relieving programmers from the task of implementing this function. Furthermore, this code does not involve relational joins and can be generated at compile time. Finally, these systems offer the advantage of flexible sharing and communication since a client can determine which parts of its state are shared with others and when changes to it are communicated to them.

On the other hand, they do not offer several other benefits of the database approach. They do not address efficient storage of data or querying of it. Moreover, they do not know which parts of the clients' state are shared data structures and simply provide a high-level scheme for communicating information among the clients. As a result, these systems cannot automatically offer concurrency control or access control, which have to be implemented by the clients.

These drawbacks arise because these systems were designed to enable clients to share changes to related data and not different versions of the same data. We discuss later tools such as shared object systems designed to explicitly handle the (more restricted) latter case. Another important drawback of these tools is that they require a client interacting with a user to be aware of the identities of the clients interacting with other users and the parts of the local state in which the remote users are interested. As a result, the programmer of a client must write code that establishes communication with other clients and determines which part of the local state should be transmitted to the other clients. More important, this code must be tediously changed if unanticipated kinds of clients and communication patterns are desired later. In the next section, we discuss tools that allows clients to be unaware of these details.

**Implementing the example user-interface:** Consider implementation of the example user-interface using an RPC system. As in the previous section, each of the clients creates the two windows displayed on its user's workstation, processes input events generated by the workstation, and generates output requests for the workstation. The clients directly communicate among themselves changes to the shared data such as the semantic state of the edit windows and the complete state of the test windows. They are not responsible for converting the internal representation of parse trees and other shared data structures to an external representation since the RPC system automates this task. On the other hand, they manually ensure that their users make only authorized changes to edit procedures and other shared state. Moreover, they manually implement concurrency control and querys retrieving coverage information. Finally, each of the clients is aware of the identities of its peers and the state it shares with them. As a result, the clients must be tediously changed if, for instance, their users decide that they wish to completely share the edit windows and such sharing was not anticipated when the clients were coded.

Distributed RPC and constraint systems differ mainly in the style of programming they offer–distributed RPC systems offer procedural programming while distributed constraint systems offer declarative programming. A comparison of these two styles of programming is beyond the scope of this paper.

## 8.5   MESSAGE SERVER

Message servers such as Field [Rei90], YEAST [Kri91], and the CB Message Bus [Kap92] allow a client to exchange messages with remote clients without being aware of the identities of the remote clients or the messages in which they are interested. Each client sends to the message server messages regarding all possible changes to its state that other clients may be interested in. In addition, it registers message patterns with the server that describe the specific set of messages from other clients in which it is interested. The message server forwards a message sent by a client to all other clients who have registered patterns matching the message. A client is not aware of the patterns registered by other clients or even the identities of these clients. Figure 8.6 shows the architecture of a multiuser application developed using a message server and Figure 8.7 shows the main steps performed by a client.

**Implementing the example user interface**: Each client sends to the message server messages announcing all changes to the state of both windows. Moreover, it registers patterns with

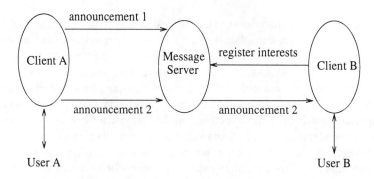

**Figure 8.6**   Message Servers

```
declaration of data structures and procedures
--main steps
implement initial user interface
register patterns with message server
do
    receive from message server remote changes to shared state
    display changes to user
    get and parse input
    implement access and concurrency control
    implement querying of state
    compute results
    display output
    announce to message server changes to shared state
until user quits
```

**Figure 8.7**   Client of a Message Server

the server that request messages regarding changes to the complete state of the test windows and the semantic state of the edit windows. Thus, the message server forwards to a client messages regarding changes to the scrollbars of the remote test windows but not the edit windows. If one of the clients wishes to not share the positions of scrollbars of a remote test window, it only has to register a new pattern with the message server. It does not have to directly communicate with the remote client, which is unaware of its interests. As a result, it is easy to change the sharing between two clients. Moreover, it is easy to add new users to the application since their clients have to communicate only with the message server and not the existing clients.

A message server combines benefits of database systems and distributed systems by allowing clients to exchange data without polling or being aware of each other. It does not, however, combine all the benefits of the previous two tools. In particular, like distributed systems, it does not provide concurrency control or access control since it has no notion of shared state. Moreover, it does not relieve clients from all details of communicating with each other since they must register patterns and process incoming messages. Perhaps the biggest drawback of using it is that all communication among clients must be routed through a single process. As a result, the message server is unsuitable for clients that are distributed across slow networks or share state such as scrollbar and pointing device positions that change frequently. Message

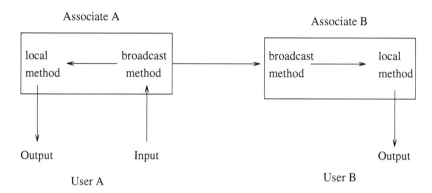

**Figure 8.8**   Colab Associates. Input entered by user A invokes a broadcast method in both associates. Each broadcast method invokes a local method to display the output to its user.

servers have been designed to support loosely-coupled processes communicating using a local area network.

## 8.6   SHARED OBJECT SYSTEM

Colab [Stef87] offers an approach to implementing multiuser applications that combines features of the three previous tools. Like a database system, it supports the notion of data that can be shared by multiple clients and replicated on multiple sites. However, unlike the former, it knows about the clients sharing the data and replicates the data in the address spaces of these clients. Like a distributed system, it provides mechanisms to automatically notify a client of remote changes to the shared state stored in its address space. Moreover, like a message server, it allows a client to be unaware of the identities of the other clients sharing data with it.

In Colab, the clients interacting with the users of a multiuser application execute the same application program. Colab offers a programmer the abstraction of an *association* to implement the application program. An association is an object declared in an application program whose state can be shared among the clients executing the program. In each one of these clients, a representation of the object called an *associate* is created. An association can define special methods called *broadcast methods* that are invoked on all of its associates (Figure 8.8). An application program can ensure that a particular part of the state of an association is shared by declaring methods that change that part as broadcast methods. Figure 8.9 shows the structure of an application program executed by a Colab client.

**Implementing the example user interface:** The example is implemented using Colab by writing a single Colab program, which is executed by clients interacting with both users. The program consists of a set of Colab objects, which encapsulate both semantic state such as procedures and user-interface state such as scrollbar positions. Methods that change shared state such as scrollbars of test windows are made broadcast methods.

Colab combines benefits of all three tools described above. By replicating the clients, it allows users to view the output of their clients without encountering network delays. Moreover, it does not suffer from the drawback of polling since methods are explicitly invoked in clients to inform them of changes to shared state. In addition, it is built on top of an RPC mechanism and thus allows programmers to define a single representation of objects and automatically converts between this representation and the network representation. Finally,

```
declaration of objects
specification of broadcast methods
--main steps
implement initial user interface
do
     get and parse input
     implement access and concurrency control
     implement querying of state
     compute results
     display output
until user quits
```

**Figure 8.9**   A Colab Client

it requires application programmers to be aware of very few details of sharing since they are responsible only for specifying which methods in the original single-user program are broadcast methods. Colab takes care of the details of starting and terminating clients at the workstations of users and broadcasting messages to them.

Colab also has its drawbacks. The task of selecting broadcast method can be non-trivial since the programmers must carefully identify which methods modify the shared state and ensure that a broadcast method invoked in a client does not invoke other broadcast methods. Programmers who have used Colab report that this task was simple for the applications they developed [Stef87]. However, Colab applications support sharing of (almost) the complete state of the clients executing a Colab multiuser program. It is not clear if this task would be as simple if less sharing was to be supported.

Moreover, Colab fixes the sharing among the different clients at compile time. As a result, it does not allow, for instance, the two users of the example application to couple the scrollbars of their edit windows while modifying shared procedures and later uncouple them while modifying private procedures. It also does not support the notion of a "multicast method"– a method invoked in a subset of the clients executing the multiuser program. Thus, it does not allow the two users of the example application to share the scrollbars of their test windows without requiring the other users to also do so. Furthermore, it does not support the concept of user-controlled transactions– remote invocations of a broadcast method occur as soon as the local invocation occurs. Thus, the Colab example implementation above does not exactly implement the example user-interface of Figure 8.1, since the user-interface requires that changes made by users to private procedures be made immediately on their screens but at commitment time on the screens of other users. Colab also has the drawback of the replicated window architecture discussed later. Finally, it also does not offer concurrency control or access control, which have to implemented by application programmers.

Some of the these drawbacks arise because Colab was designed to support only WYSIWIS interaction. Colab programmers found that in these applications the communication overhead is so high that it may not be possible to add concurrency control overhead without making the response times of the applications unacceptable. Moreover, Colab users found that in these applications, it is less useful to implement concurrency control since each user is aware of all the actions of the other users and can immediately take corrective actions in response to conflicts [Stef87]. We discuss below tools explicitly designed to support looser collaboration and concurrency control.

None of the tools discussed so far is bound to any single-user tool. This can be considered an advantage since the collaborative applications they support are free to use the single-user tools that best support their interaction functions. For instance, a Colab application is free to choose a window system, a toolkit, or a UIMS to process its input and display its output. Nonetheless, much of the recent work in multiuser tools has focussed on developing multiuser tools that are extensions of existing single-user tools and allow sharing of the state maintained by their basis. There are two main reasons for taking this approach:

- A single-user tool often maintains state information for a client that the latter is not aware of and may not be able to access. In particular, a high-level single-user tool maintains a large amount of such state to reduce the interaction awareness in its clients. For instance, a single-user tool may maintain state representing window scrollbars, which its clients may not need to be aware of and may not be able to access. This approach allows sharing of this state among multiple users. Other approaches such as the Colab approach (which allow sharing of only the client data) either do not allow sharing of this state (if the state is inaccessible to the client) or require that the client become more interaction aware by loading this state into its data structures.
- This approach can be used to develop a multiuser tool that offers the same programming interface as its basis. Such a tool can support collaboration-transparent multiuser programs. In particular, it can allow sharing of existing single-user applications developed using the basis.

In [Dew93b] we give general principles of designing a multiuser tool using this approach. In the remainder of the paper, we discuss and compare specific multiuser tools that have been developed using this approach.

## 8.7 SHARED WINDOW SYSTEM

A *shared window system* such as VConf [Lan86] and Rapport [Ens88] is like a shared object system except that it supports sharing of windows rather than sharing of arbitrary objects. It offers its clients the abstraction of a *shared window*, which is a single logical window physically replicated on the screens of all users of the application. The system allows a client to be completely unaware that it is interacting with multiple users– the client is aware of only the logical window and receives input events from and sends output requests to this window. The shared window system is responsible for creating the physical replicas of this window and keeping them consistent.

Two main architectures have been used in shared window systems: the *centralized* and *replicated* architectures. Under the centralized architecture, a single, central client is created for the multiuser application, which receives input events from the workstations of all users and broadcasts output requests to all of them (Figure 8.10). Under the *replicated* architecture, a separate replica of the application is created on each workstation, which executes the application code and sends output to only the local user. To ensure that the different replicas remain synchronized, input from all workstations is sent to each replica and mechanisms are used to ensure that the replicas process inputs from different users in the same order (Figure 8.11).

**Implementing the example user-interface**: The programmer would define a single application program, which would be responsible for creating and updating the two logical windows

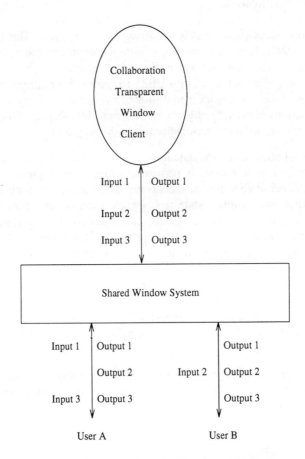

**Figure 8.10** Shared Window System: Centralized Architecture. A single process receives input from both users and broadcasts output to both of them.

shown in Figure 8.1. The shared window system would be responsible for creating physical replicas of these windows on the screens of both users of the application and keeping them consistent. Under the centralized approach, a single process would be created for the program (Figure 8.10) and under the replicated approach a replica would be created for each of the two users of the program (Figure 8.11). Like the Colab implementation, this implementation would be an approximation of the example user-interface because of limitations of shared windows systems discussed below.

There are several benefits of using shared window systems to develop multiuser applications. Unlike the previous tools, they support collaboration-transparent application programs. Moreover, it is possible to create a shared window system by extending an existing single-user window system. Such a window system can be used to create multiuser interfaces to existing clients of the single-user window system. These clients would not only include direct clients of the window system but also indirect clients, that is, clients of the single-user tools built on top of the window system. For instance, a shared X window system can be used to create multiuser user-interfaces to not only direct clients of the X window system but also the clients of the large number of toolkits and user interface management systems developed on top of the window

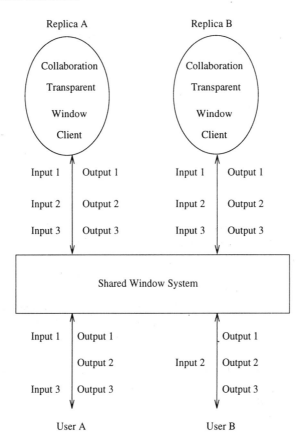

**Figure 8.11**  Shared Window System: Replicated Architecture. Each replica receives input events from both users in the same order and displays output to its local user.

system. Finally, since they manage the shared data structures, they can provide concurrency control to ensure multiple users do not submit input to a shared window simultaneously.

However, these systems have been designed mainly to allow existing single-user applications to be shared in the WYSIWIS mode. As a result, they have several disadvantages that make them unsuitable tools for general multiuser applications. Since they do not know the structure of the data displayed by the windows, the only concurrency control mechanism they can support is coarse-grained floor control, which allows only one user (the user with the floor) to enter input at any time. Continuing with the example, a shared window system can either allow both users to make arbitrary concurrent changes to the displayed procedures or allow only one of them to edit a procedure at any one time. Moreover, they cannot allow sharing of data without also sharing of the associated screen images created for displaying these data. For instance, they cannot allow users of the example application to share the procedures displayed in the edit windows without sharing the complete contents of the windows. Furthermore, like Colab, shared window systems do not support user-controlled transactions– users immediately see the effects of commands invoked by others.

Finally, both the centralized and replicated shared window approaches have important drawbacks. The centralized architecture creates a central bottleneck that broadcasts potentially large

```
declaration of data structures and procedures
--main steps
implement initial user interface
do
     get and parse input
     implement querying of state
     compute changes to state
     display output
until user quits
```

**Figure 8.12**    A Client of a Shared Window System

amounts of output [Lan86]. The replicated architecture does not suffer from this performance problem since the output for a workstation is produced by a local workstation. (It does require the shared window system to broadcast user input but input data are, typically, small in size.) On the other hand, it executes semantic operations multiple times, once for each replica of the application. This is not always desirable since multiple invocations of a semantic operation may perform computationally expensive operations multiple times, attempt to read the same file simultaneously, attempt to write the same data to a file multiple times, access files that are not available at all workstations, and send a mail message multiple times [Lan86] [Lau90] [Cro90]. For instance, if the example application program mails a message whenever a module is fixed, the message will be sent by each replica created by the shared window system. Thus, in several situations, shared window systems either do not give the desired performance or desired semantics. These drawbacks also apply to the Colab system since a broadcast method can invoke semantic actions.

## 8.8   MULTIUSER TOOLKIT

The tools discussed in this section overcome some of the limitations of shared window systems by allowing collaboration-aware programs to customize various aspects of collaboration using a low-level toolkit of collaboration functions. MMConf [Cro90] supports the replicated architecture and allows a replica to determine whether an input event generated by its user should be broadcast to other replicas. This facility allows the different "replicas" to become separate logical entities with separate states. Moreover, it allows an operation with side effects to be executed by a single replica. Like shared window systems, MMConf supports floor control but allows the client to explicitly lock and unlock the floor, thereby allowing it to determine the floor-control policy. Figure 8.13 shows the structure of an MMConf client program.

**Implementing the example user-interface**: The implementation is similar to the implementation in the previous example except that the client broadcasts input events that change scrollbars of test windows and other shared state but not those that change scrollbars of edit windows and other private state.

DCS [New91b] provides conference management facilities for applications while allowing them to implement their own methods for sharing, concurrency control, and access control. All application programs developed using DCS must provide a special interface for interacting with the system. DCS automatically starts these programs in response to user requests, provides

```
declaration of data structures and procedures
--main steps
implement initial user interface
do
     get and parse input
     implement querying of state
     broadcast input if it changes shared state
     specify floor-control policy
     implement access control
     compute changes to state
     display output
until user quits
```

**Figure 8.13**   An MMConf Client

them with a mechanism to vote on various issues, manages the files created by a multiuser application, provides mechanisms to control which users can vote and access the files it manages, and shows the users status information regarding the conference such as the names of their collaborators. A DCS program is like an MMConf program except that it has to implement concurrency control manually.

GroupKit [Ros92] is an extension of a single-user toolkit that offers support for sharing. It has been designed to support the replicated architecture, access control, and overlaying of cursors and annotations on displays created by single-user applications. It offers several predefined classes to transform a single-user application developed using the single-user toolkit to a multiuser application. These classes can be used directly by a programmer or subclassed to provide application-specific functionality including application-defined access control. A GroupKit program is like a DCS program except that it can use predefined classes implementing multiple concurrency and access control policies and create subclasses of these classes.

All three tools allow programmers to customize some of the aspects of collaboration that are automatically managed by shared window systems. However, they provide low-level facilities for customizing collaboration. The next two tools, which were developed independently about the same time, provide higher-level customization facilities.

We have so far seen two kinds of tools for sharing state:

- *Data Sharing Tools*: Tools such as database systems and shared object systems that have a model of application data structures and allow sharing of these data structures.
- *User-Interface Sharing Tools*: Tools such as shared window systems and GroupKit that have a model of user-interface data structures such as windows and widgets and allow sharing of user-interface state.

The next two tools manage both application and user-interface state, thereby overcoming some of the disadvantages of the tools above.

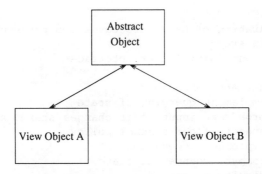

**Figure 8.14**   Rendezvous Abstract and View Objects

## 8.9   MULTIUSER UIMS

A UIMS separates semantic values from their screen representations. It is possible to use this separation in a multiuser UIMS to provide high-level abstractions for supporting sharing of both semantic values and their screen representations, as illustrated by the work on Rendezvous [Pat90] [Pat91]. Like Colab, Rendezvous assumes that the state of a multiuser application is encapsulated in objects and supports sharing of these objects. In addition, it offers a constraint system, which can be used to keep related objects consistent. (Unlike a distributed constraint system, the Rendezvous constraint system relates data stored within a single process.) Rendezvous also allows programmers to define rules, which can modify object state and are fired in response to input and other events. Rules can be associated with guards, which determine the conditions under which they fire.

Rendezvous distinguishes between *abstract objects* and *view objects*, which correspond to Smalltalk models and views, [Kra88] respectively. The former define semantic data while the latter define how these data are viewed and manipulated by users (Figure 8.14). Rendezvous supports three degrees of sharing: i) *semantic sharing*: sharing of abstract objects, ii) *image sharing*: sharing of view objects, and iii) *complete sharing*: sharing of views and access rights to these views. An abstract object is shared among a group of users by creating a view object for each of these users and defining constraints that keep the abstract object consistent with its view objects. Views of an abstract object are shared by making the associated view objects replicas of a special *sharing object*. The access rights to the views of a sharing object are shared by making guards that authorize actions independent of the identity of the user who invokes the actions. The Rendezvous constraint mechanism can be used by programmers to implement other kinds of sharing among view objects. Figure 8.15 shows the main components of a Rendezvous program.

For each multiuser program, Rendezvous creates a single *abstract process*, which stores the abstract objects defined by the program. Moreover, for each user of the multiuser program, it creates a *view process*, which stores all of the view objects created for that user. The abstract process and the view processes created for a multiuser program are lightweight processes that execute as part of a single heavyweight process.

**Implementing the example user-interface**: The application programmer would define abstract objects to encapsulate semantic values such as procedures and coverage information, view objects for defining their screen representations, and constraints for keeping view objects consistent with the underlying abstract objects. The programmer would create separate view objects for each user of the abstract objects displayed in edit windows but a single logical set

```
declaration of abstract and view objects
rules that implement initial user interface
rules that get and parse input
rules that perform computations
rules that display output
rules that process queries
guards that implement concurrency and access control
constraints that relate abstract and view objects
declaration of shared views as sharing objects
```

**Figure 8.15** Components of a Rendezvous Multiuser Program

of sharing view objects for the abstract objects displayed in the test windows. Rendezvous would automatically create a separate replica of the sharing view object for each user of the application and ensure that these replicas are always kept consistent. All abstract objects would be stored in a single abstract process while the view objects created for different users would be kept in different view processes. Access and concurrency control would be implemented by associating appropriate guards with rules that get input.

Unlike the other tools discussed so far, Rendezvous provides high-level support for three useful kinds of sharing: semantic sharing, image sharing, and complete sharing. Some of the other tools discussed so far such as shared windows systems support only one kind of sharing while others such as message servers enable arbitrary kinds of sharing but provide low-level facilities for implementing them. The constraint mechanism of Rendezvous also supports arbitrary sharing.

On the other hand, Rendezvous has all the performance drawbacks of the centralized window architecture since the abstract process and the associated view processes all execute at a central site. Moreover, like Colab, it does not provide high-level support for maintaining state shared by only a subset of the users of a multiuser application, dynamically changing the sharing, or flexible communication of changes to shared data. Finally, it does not automatically support concurrency control or access control.

## 8.10 MULTIUSER USER-INTERFACE GENERATOR

By a user-interface generator, we mean a UIMS that automatically generates views of abstract data from high-level descriptions of these views. Examples of user-interface generators include ADE [Row85], which supports form-filling interfaces; and single-user Suite [Dew90a], which supports generalized editing interfaces [Dew90c]. Multiuser Suite [Dew92], which is an extension of single-user Suite, illustrates the benefits of extending a single-user user-interface generator to support multiuser applications.

Single-user Suite offers near automatic generation of single-user editing interfaces. It supports the abstraction of active variables and interaction variables. An *active variable* is an application variable whose value is displayed to the user and can be changed by him via an interaction variable. An *interaction variable* is a user's local version of an active variable of an object, which is automatically created by the system when the user connects to the object. It can be updated by the client to show a result, edited by the user to input a new value, and

```
declaration of data structures
specification of active variables
specification of interaction attributes
specification of sharing attributes
specification of communication attributes
specification of access attributes
specification of concurrency control attributes
implementation of validate callbacks
implementation of update callbacks that change semantic state
implementation of update callbacks that process queries
```

**Figure 8.16**  Components of a Suite Multiuser Program

committed by the user to update the value of the corresponding active variable. An interaction variable is associated with *interaction attributes*, which determine interaction properties of the variable such as the format used to display it. The system invokes *validate callbacks* in a client to ask it to validate user changes to interaction variables and *update callbacks* to inform it of committed changes to these variables.

Multiuser Suite extends single-user Suite by displaying active variables to multiple, possibly distributed users, and allowing multiple users to manipulate the displays and the underlying variables. It provides a default collaboration scheme including a default sharing, communication, and concurrency control scheme, which can be used to create multiuser interfaces to collaboration-transparent Suite clients. It also defines a variety of high-level *collaboration attributes*, which are based on the editing model of interaction and can be used by application programs and users to dynamically specify alternate collaboration schemes. These attributes include sharing attributes, communication attributes, access attributes, and concurrency-control attributes.

*Sharing attributes* [Dew91] support the semantic, image, and complete sharing schemes discussed above. In addition, they support other kinds of sharing such as sharing of selected regions and cursor positions. *Communication attributes* [Dew91] determine when changes made by a user are communicated to other users. They support, for instance, communication of changes as they are made or when they are explicitly committed. Both the sharing and communication attributes can refer to arbitrary groups of users, thereby allowing a user to share and communicate differently with different sets of users. *Access attributes* [She92] are used to specify access rights and *concurrency control attributes* determine the granularity of locking.

The system also defines *collaboration calls* and *collaboration callbacks*, which can be used by clients to implement their own collaboration schemes. In particular, it provides primitives to multicast a call to a variety of groups of users. Figure 8.16 shows the main components of a Suite multiuser program.

Figure 8.17 shows the architecture of Suite. It creates a single copy of the application, and for each user of the application, it automatically creates a system-defined dialogue manager which manages the user's interaction with the object. An application and its dialogue managers communicate with each other to keep their states consistent. They execute in separate address spaces and can reside on different computers. In particular, a user's dialogue manager can execute on the local workstation.

**Implementing the example user-interface:** The application program specifies the parse

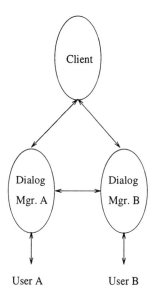

**Figure 8.17** The Suite Hybrid Architecture

tree and other data structures displayed to users, callbacks for receiving changes to these data structures and implementing queries, and collaboration attributes that specify, for instance, that the complete state of test windows should be shared between users A and B, these changes should be communicated incrementally, only the semantic state of edit windows should be shared between these users, and only user A should be allowed to edit the madd procedure (Figure 8.1).

Multiuser Suite combines the benefits of a variety of tools. It offers collaboration-transparent programs, fine-grained concurrency and access control, high-level support for specifying semantic, image, and complete sharing, and collaboration calls and callbacks for implementing application-specific collaboration schemes. In addition, it provides high-level support for other kinds of sharing methods, specifying the communication scheme, dynamically changing the collaboration scheme, and allowing selected groups of users to share parts of the application state.

Moreover, its architecture is designed to keep network traffic low while executing semantic operations once. The architecture can be regarded as a combination of the centralized and replicated architectures since it supports a central semantic component (application) and local user-interface components (dialogue managers). Under this architecture, semantic actions are executed once in the central application component and user-interface tasks are performed locally. Since the semantic tasks are performed remotely, a user has to wait for communication delays involved in receiving results but not their displays, which are formatted locally by dialogue managers. Preliminary experience shows that these delays are not perceptible since (a) the size of a result is typically small in comparison to its display and, more important, (b) results are produced infrequently since users execute long transactions before they commit their input values.

Multiuser Suite has two important drawbacks. First, it is tied to single-user Suite and thus cannot offer multiuser versions of single-user interfaces that cannot be supported by single-user Suite. Second, unlike a database system, it does not address efficient access of large data structures or a relational query language, since the shared data structures it supports are defined and managed by a conventional programming language.

## 8.11   USING MULTIPLE MULTIUSER TOOLS

As shown above, each of the multi-user tools we have considered has important advantages and drawbacks. Therefore, it would be useful if a single application could use the services of multiple tools to to support sharing of different parts of its data. However, currently, there are several barriers to using more than one of these multiuser tools together:

- A client cannot simultaneously use multiuser tools supporting different architectures. For instance, a Suite client cannot also be a Colab client since the former assumes that a single version of the client is created while the latter assumes that multiple versions of it are created.
- Current shared window systems do not support partial sharing–all windows created by a client are made shared windows. Thus, a client cannot use both a shared window system and another multiuser tool since the latter will provide redundant sharing.
- Tools that are bound to different programming languages cannot be used together by a single client. Thus, Colab, Rendezvous, Mercury, and multiuser Suite, cannot be used together by a single client since they are bound to different programming languages, and more important, different programming styles.

On the other hand, it is possible for a client of one of these multiuser tools to also be a client of a database system, an RPC system, or a message server since these tools have been designed to accommodate multiple application and machine architectures, programming languages, and operating systems. Thus, it is possible to create a multiuser application as a set of cooperating processes that communicate with each other using a database system, RPC system, or a message server, as illustrated by Figure 8.18.

**Implementing the example user-interface**: Consider implementation of the example user-interface using a message server, RPC, Colab, and Suite (Figure 8.18). Each user of the application would interact simultaneously with a Suite dialogue manager, which would manages the edit window, and a Colab client, which would manage the test window. Colab broadcast methods would be used to define the WYSIWIS coupling among the test windows and the Suite coupling attributes would be used to define the semantic coupling among the edit windows. The coupling among test and edit windows would be implemented by the Suite and Colab clients, which could communicate with each other using RPC, a message server, and/or a database system.

Naturally, this approach is not ideal since it requires that logical components of a multiuser application that needs the services of different incompatible tools be made separate processes, thereby increasing the cost of starting the application and communicating among these components. However, it is the only practical approach until these tools are made more interoperable.

## 8.12   CONCLUSIONS

Three main conclusions can be drawn from this paper:

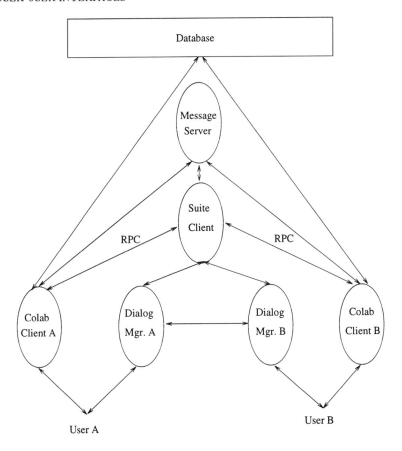

**Figure 8.18**   Using Multiple Tools

- A variety of tools can be used to support the implementation of multiuser applications. Some of them such as shared object systems extend programming language abstractions, others such as distributed RPC systems extend communication abstractions, while still others such as shared window systems, GroupKit, Rendezvous, and multiuser Suite extend user-interface abstractions such as windows, widgets, views, and active variables, respectively.
- Each of these tools has both important advantages and disadvantages. More important, each one of them offers some benefits that are not offered by other tools and thus supports some class of applications better than the others. Database systems offer efficient querying of large data structures and are thus suitable for traditional applications such as airline reservation systems that support independent multiuser interaction. Distributed RPC and constraint systems provide a high-level mechanism for keeping arbitrary relationships among distributed data and are thus suitable for applications such as the Mercury multiuser module editor, which allows users to make consistent changes to related, distributed modules. Message servers provide flexible mechanisms that allow clients for different users to be unaware of each other. GroupKit supports extensible multiuser interfaces to applications developed using an existing single-user toolkit. Rendezvous provides high-level support for sharing of both semantic data and their screen representation while making no assumptions about how the screen representations are generated. Multiuser Suite provides high-level and

efficient support for a variety of sharing, concurrency control, communication, and access control schemes, and allows users and applications to change these schemes dynamically.

- The approach of using a single-user tool as a basis for a multiuser tool must be taken to support collaborative interaction requiring sharing of interaction state that is not stored in client data structures. It is for this reason that almost all of the current work in multiuser tools is being carried out by the user-interface community.

In this paper, we have considered only a subset of the collaboration functions to compare the automation, flexibility, and performance of multiuser tools. It is necessary to also consider other important collaboration functions such as support for multimedia [Man91], undo/redo [Cho92], and navigation [Jef92] in multiuser applications. It would be also useful to consider other criteria for comparing these tools such as how easy it is to use the applications supported by them.

One of the important conclusions of this paper is that each of these tools has important advantages and drawbacks. We see two future approaches for solving this problem. One approach is to make these tools "open", that is, allow a single client to use the services of multiple tools, thereby allowing the application to use different multiuser tools to share different parts of its data. A second, more difficult and challenging, approach is to build an integrated system that offers the benefits of all of these tools. By describing the main concepts behind the design of these tools and pointing out the similarities and differences among the approaches implemented by them, this paper has taken a first step towards this goal.

## ACKNOWLEDGMENTS

Gregory Abowd and the anonymous referees provided insightful suggestions towards improving the form and content of this paper. This research was supported in part by National Science Foundation grants IRI-9015442 and IRI-9208319 and in part by grants from the Software Engineering Research Center at Purdue University, a National Science Foundation Industry/University Cooperative Research Center (NSF Grant No. ECD-8913133).

## REFERENCES

[Atk87]    Malcolm P. Atkinson and O. Peter Buneman. Types and persistence in database programming languages. *ACM Computer Surveys*, 19(2), June 1987.

[Ben92]    Richard Bentley, Tom Rodden, Peter Sawyer, and Ian Sommerville. An architecture for tailoring cooperative multi-user displays. *Proceedings of the ACM Conference on Computer Supported Cooperative Work*, pages 203–209, Nov 1992.

[Bha89]    Bharat Bhargava and John Riedl. The Raid distributed database system. *IEEE Transactions on Software Engineering*, 15(6):726–736, June 1989.

[Bir84]    Andrew D. Birrel and Bruce Jay Nelson. Implementing remote procedure calls. *ACM TOCS*, 2(1), February 1984.

[Bro90]    L. Brothers, V. Sembugamoorthy, and M. Muller. ICICLE: Groupware for code inspection. *Proceedings of the ACM Conference on Computer Supported Cooperative Work*, pages 169–181, October 1990.

[Cac91]    CACM. Special issue on next-generation database systems. *CACM*, 34(10), October 1991.

[Cho92]    Rajiv Choudhary and Prasun Dewan. Multi-user undo/redo. Technical report, Software Engineering Research Center, Purdue University, 1992.

[Cro90]     Terrence Crowley, Paul Milazzo, Ellie Baker, Harry Forsdick, and Raymond Tomlinson. MMConf: An infrastructure for building shared multimedia applications. *Proc. of ACM Conference on Computer Supported Cooperative Work*, pages 329–342, October 1990.

[Dew90a]    Prasun Dewan. A tour of the Suite user interface software. *Proceedings of the 3rd ACM SIGGRAPH Symposium on User Interface Software and Technology*, pages 57–65, October 1990.

[Dew90b]    Prasun Dewan and Rajiv Choudhary. Experience with the Suite distributed object model. *Proceedings of IEEE Workshop on Experimental Distributed Systems*, pages 57–63, October 1990.

[Dew90c]    Prasun Dewan and Marvin Solomon. An approach to support automatic generation of user interfaces. *ACM Transactions on Programming Languages and Systems*, 12(4):566–609, October 1990.

[Dew91]     Prasun Dewan and Rajiv Choudhary. Flexible user interface coupling in collaborative systems. *Proceedings of the ACM CHI'91 Conference*, pages 41–49, April 1991.

[Dew92]     Prasun Dewan and Rajiv Choudhary. A high-level and flexible framework for implementing multiuser user interfaces. *ACM Transactions on Information Systems*, 10(4):345–380, October 1992.

[Dew93a]    Prasun Dewan. Designing and implementing multi-user applications: A case study. *Software-Practice and Experience*, 23(1):75–94, January 1993.

[Dew93b]    Prasun Dewan. Principles of designing multi-user user interface development environments languages. *Proceedings of the 1992 IFIP TC2/WG 2.7 Working Conference on Engineering for Human-Computer Interaction, Ellivuori, Finland*, to appear.

[Dew93c]    Prasun Dewan and John Riedl. Toward computer-supported concurrent software engineering. *IEEE Computer*, 26(1), to appear in January 1993.

[Dem87]     T. DeMarco and T. Lister. *Peopleware: Productive Projects and Teams*. Dorset House Publishing Co., New York, 1987.

[Ell90]     Clarence A. Ellis, Simon J. Gibbs, and Gail L. Rein. Design and use of a group editor. *Proceedings of IFIP WG2.7 Working Conference on Engineering for Human Computer Communication, August 1989*, pages 13–28, 1990.

[Ens88]     J.R. Ensor, S.R. Ahuja, D.N. Horn, and S.E. Lucco. The Rapport multimedia conferencing system: A software overview. *Proceedings of the 2nd IEEE Conference on Computer Workstations*, pages 52–58, March 1988.

[Fis88]     R. Fish, R. Kraut, M. Leland, and M. Cohen. Quilt: a collaborative tool for cooperative writing. *Proceedings of ACM SIGOIS Conference*, pages 30–37, 1988.

[Gre86]     Irene Greif, Robert Seliger, and William Weihl. Atomic data abstractions in a distributed collaborative editing system. *Conference record of POPL*, January 1986.

[Jef92]     Kevin Jeffay, Douglas E. Shackelford, John B. Smith, and F. Donelson Smith. A distributed graph storage system for artifacts in group collaborations. *Proceedings of CSCW'92*, Nov 1992.

[Kai87]     Gail E. Kaiser, Simon M. Kaplan, and Josephine Micallef. Multiuser, distributed language-based environments. *IEEE Software*, 4(6):58–69, November 1987.

[Kap92]     Simon M. Kaplan, William J. Tolone, Douglas P. Bogia, and Celsina Bignoli. Flexible, active support for collaborative work with conversationbuilder. *Proceedings of CSCW'92*, Nov 1992.

[Kra88]     Glenn E. Krasner and Stephen T. Pope. A cookbook for using the model-view-controller user interface paradigm in smalltalk-80. *Journal of Object-Oriented Programming*, 1(3):26–49, August/September 1988.

[Kri91]     Balachander Krishnamurthy and David S. Rosenblum. An event-action model of computer-supported cooperative work: Design and implementaion. *International Workshop on CSCW*, pages 132–145, 1991.

[Lan86]     Keith A. Lantz. An experiment in integrated multimedia conferencing. *Proceedings of Conference on Computer-Supported Cooperative Work*, pages 267–275, December 1986.

[Lau90]     J.C. Lauwers and K.A. Lantz. Collaboration awareness in support of collaboration transparency: Requirements for the next generation of shared window systems. *Proceedings of ACM CHI'90*, pages 303–312, April 1990.

[Leh86]     T. Lehman and M. Carey. Query processing in main memory database systems. *Proceed-*

*ings of 1986 SIGMOD conference*, pages 239–250, May 1986.

[Lin84] Mark A. Linton. Implementing relational views of programs. *Proceedings of the ACM SIGSOFT/SIGPLAN Software Engineering Symposium on Practical Software Development Environments*, pages 132–140, April 1984.

[Man91] M. Mantei, R. M. Backer, A. J. Sellen, W. A.S. Buxton, T. Milligan, and B. Wellman. Experiences in the use of a media space. *Proceedings of CHI'91*, pages 203–208, April 1991.

[Neu90] Christine M. Neuwirth, David S. Kaufer, Ravinder Chandok, and James H. Morris. Issues in the design of computer support for co-authoring and commenting. *Proceedings of ACM Conference on Computer Supported Cooperative Work*, pages 183–195, October 1990.

[New91a] R.E. Newman-Wolfe and H. Pelimuhandiram. The Mace fine-grained concurrent text editor. *Proceedings of ACM/IEEE Conference on Organizational Computing Systems (COCS 91)*, pages 240–254,, November 1991.

[New91b] R. E. Newman-Wolfe, C. L. Ramirez, H. Pelimuhandiram, M. Montes, M. Webb, and D. L. Wilson. A brief overview of the DCS distributed conferencing system. *Proceedings of the Summer Usenix Conference*, pages 437–452, June 1991.

[Ols90] Gary Olson and Dan Atkins. Supporting collaboration with advanced multimedia electronic mail: the nsf expres project. *In Intellectual Teamwork: Social and Technological Foundations of Cooperative Work. J Galegher, R. Kraut, and C. Egido (Eds).*, 1990.

[Ols93] Gary M. Olson, Lola J. McGuffin, Eiji Kuwana, and Judith S. Olson. Designing software for a group's needs: A functional analysis of synchronous groupware. *Trends in Software: User Interface Software*, trends 1, 1993.

[Pat90] John F. Patterson, Ralph D. Hill, Steven L. Rohall, and W. Scott Meeks. Rendezvous: An architecture for synchronous multi-user applications. *Proceedings of the Conference on Computer-Supported Cooperative Work*, pages 317–328, October 1990.

[Pat91] John F. Patterson. Comparing the programming demands of single-user and multi-user applications. *Proceedings of the 4th ACM SIGRAPH Conference on User Interface Software and Technology*, pages 79–86, November 1991.

[Pfa85] G. Pfaff. *User Interface Management Systems*. Springer Verlag, Englewood Cliffs, NJ, 1985.

[Rei90] Steven P. Reiss. Connecting tools using message passing in the Field environment. *IEEE Software*, 7(4):57–66, July 1990.

[Ros92] Mark Roseman and Saul Greenberg. Groupkit: A groupware toolkit for building real-time conferencing applications. *Proceedings of the ACM Conference on Computer Supported Cooperative Work*, November 1992.

[Row85] Lawrence A. Rowe. 'Fill-in-the-form' programming. *Proceedings of VLDB*, pages 394–404, 1985.

[Sar85] Sunil Sarin and Irene Greif. Computer-based real-time conferencing systems. *IEEE Computer*, 18(10):33–49, October 1985.

[She92] Honghai Shen and Prasun Dewan. Access control for collaborative environments. *Proceedings of the ACM Conference on Computer Supported Cooperative Work*, November 1992.

[Stef87] Mark Stefik, Gregg Foster, Daniel G. Bobrow, Kenneth Kahn, Stan Lanning, and Lucy Suchman. Beyond the chalkboard: Computer support for collaboration and problem solving in meetings. *CACM*, 30(1):32–47, January 1987.

# 9

# Multimedia Computing: Applications, Designs, and Human Factors

Scott M. Stevens

*Software Engineering Institute*[1]
*Carnegie Mellon University*

### ABSTRACT

Computer input and output has evolved from teletypewriters to text oriented CRTs to today's window oriented bit mapped displays. Beyond text and images, multimedia input and output must be concerned with constant rate continuous media such as digital video and audio. Today's multimedia applications are just beginning to explore the capabilities of multimedia computing. There is a growing understanding of the functionality required by multimedia application domains such as intelligent interfaces, collaboration environments, visualization systems, and virtual reality environments. Advanced applications dynamically operate on and modify multimedia objects, providing possibilities previously unavailable for human computer interaction. This chapter discusses some of these advanced multimedia paradigms through examples of today's nascent multimedia applications. With an understanding of multimedia's full capabilities, large, quantum improvements in the usefulness of applications are possible.

## 9.1 Introduction

Modes of communication, interfaces, between humans and computers have evolved from teletypewriters to text oriented CRTs to today's window oriented bit mapped displays. One of the next steps in this evolution, multimedia, affords the interface designer exciting new

---

[1] This work supported by the U.S. Department of Defense

*User Interface Software*, Edited by Bass and Dewan

channels of communication. However, the definition of multimedia is indistinct and rapidly evolving.

A graphical simulation of a falling body, such as a ball, associated with a text on Newton's Laws certainly seems to fit within the domain of multimedia. If each image of the simulation is a three dimensional perspective view of the falling ball, does the application continue to fit what we call multimedia or is it an animation [Sta93]? Is it multimedia, animation, or virtual reality if we create perspective views from two different locations and look at the same simulation through immersive displays [Esp93]? In a short chapter such as this it is impossible to survey every aspect of what may fit under the heading of multimedia. Instead, I will focus on one of the most talked about and probably least understood areas of multimedia, digital video and audio.

The distinction between digital and analog video is an important one. Over the years there have been many interesting, useful demonstrations employing analog video technology. Such projects span more than a decade from the Aspen project, a "multimedia" tour of Aspen, Colorado [Lip80], continuing to current efforts such as ClearBoard, using analog video in support of collaboration [IK92]. In each case, these high quality, high functionality analog video-computer systems have in common expensive, one-of-a-kind, complicated hardware. With the introduction of all digital video and audio systems application and interface designers have access to increased functionality at a fraction of the cost.

Having video and audio as another manipulable, digital data type afford the opportunity to create new interfaces and applications never before possible. Moreover, it becomes both easier and more important to design these applications so they conform to the needs of the user, rather than force the user to conform to the design of the system.

This chapter begins by describing the characteristics of digital video (it is a constant rate continuous time medium). It then illustrates the difficulties and the opportunities, both social and technical, of designing applications for this new medium through two prototypical application domains (multimedia electronic mail, and networked digital video conferencing). While there are great opportunities in multimedia, there is a danger in the rush to incorporate multimedia in today's computing environment. Some of the problems associated with low fidelity implementations of multimedia are discussed in Section 9.5. Finally, a broad hint at how multimedia applications may evolve is given in the concluding section.

## 9.2   Digital Video: Continuous Time Multimedia

Early interface designers certainly did not and perhaps could not anticipate the capabilities of today's computing environments. In a teletypewriter or CRT, synchronization and control issues were mainly ones of, "is the output device ready to receive the next character?" and "should each line send a line feed, carriage return, or both?" Today's typical multimedia applications ask synchronization questions such as "how should audio stream A and video stream B be synchronized with each other?" and "should video C, graphic image D, or both be presented on the display of text E?" The complexities and flexibility of today's multimedia systems go beyond placing a video window of arbitrary size on a computer screen. It is now possible to operate on video as a data type in order to conform the system to the needs of the user.

In an emerging, complex field such as multimedia, it is not surprising that most of today's applications have failed to take full advantage of the information bandwidth, much less the capabilities of a multimedia, digital video and audio environment. Today's designs typically employ a VCR/VideoPhone view of multimedia. In this simplistic model, video and audio can be played, stopped, their windows positioned on the screen, and, possibly, other simple events such as the display of a graphic synchronized to a temporal point in the multimedia object. This is essentially the traditional analog interactive video paradigm developed almost two decades ago. Rather than interactive video, a much more appropriate term for this is "interrupted video."

Today's interrupted video paradigm views multimedia objects more as text with a temporal dimension [HSA89, YHMD88]. Researchers note the unique nature of motion video. However, differences between motion video and other media, such as text and still images, are attributed to the fact that time is a parameter of video and audio.

Every medium has a temporal nature. It takes time to read (process) a text document or a still image. However, in traditional media each user absorbs the information at his or her own rate. One may even assimilate visual information holistically, that is, to come to an understanding of complex information all at once. Even the creative process is subject to such "Ah ha!" experiences. Mozart said that he conceived of his compositions in their entirety, in one instant, not successively [Had45]. Yet, time is an intrinsic part of music that to most of us cannot be separated from pitch, melody, etc. Even though Mozart created and "saw" a whole composition at once, the temporal aspect of the music must have been present to him in that same instant.

Comparing the scrolling of text to viewing a motion video sequence illuminates the real difference between video and audio and other media. Let us assume a hypothetical application designer performs extensive human factor testing and determines that a mythical average user reads at exactly 400 words per minute. This designer then develops an electronic encyclopedia that continuously presents its text at 400 words per minute. Clearly, a user that reads at even 401 words per minute would soon be out of synch with the text. Even our designer's canonical reader will undoubtedly find text that, because of complexity, vocabulary, or interest, requires more time to read. It is unlikely that anyone would argue for fixed text presentation rates.

However, to convey almost any meaning at all video and audio must be played at a constant rate, the rate at which they were recorded. Granted, a user might accept video and audio played back at 1.5 times normal speed for a brief time. However, it is unlikely that users would accept long periods of such playback rates. In fact, studies described in Section 9.5, show that there is surprisingly significant sensitivity to altering playback fidelity. Even if users did accept accelerated playback, the information transfer rate would still be principally controlled by the system.

The real difference between video or audio and text or images is that video and audio have **constant rate** outputs that cannot be changed without significantly and negatively impacting the user's ability to extract information. Video and audio are a constant rate continuous time media. Their temporal nature is constant due to the requirements of the viewer/listener. Text is a variable rate continuous medium. Its temporal nature only comes to life in the hands of the users.

## 9.2.1 Searching Continuous Time Multimedia

Searching for information highlights one of the more significant differences between constant rate continuous time and variable rate continuous media. The human visual system is adept at quickly, holistically viewing an image or a page of text and finding a desired piece of information while ignoring unwanted information (noise). This has been viewed as a general principle of selective omission of information [Res89] and is one of the factors that makes flipping through the pages of a book a relatively efficient process. Even when the location of a piece of information is known a priori from an index, the final search of a page is aided by this ability.

On the other hand, objects that have intrinsic constant temporal rates such as video and audio are difficult to search. There are about 150 spoken words per minute of "talking head" video. One hour of video contains 9,000 words, which is about 15 pages of text. The problem is acute if one is searching for a specific piece of a video lecture, or worse yet from audio only. Even if a comprehensible high playback rate of 3 to 4 times normal speed were possible, continuous play of audio and video is a totally unacceptable search mechanism. This can be seen by assuming the target information is on average half way through a one hour video file. In that case it would take 7.5 to 10 minutes to find! Certainly no user today would accept a system that took 10 minutes to find a word in 15 pages of text.

Detailed indexing can help. However, users often wish to peruse video much as they flip through the pages of a book. Unfortunately, today's mechanisms are inadequate. Analog videodisc scanning, jumping a set number of frames, may skip the target information completely. To be comprehensible, scanning every frame such as in a VCR's fast forward, often takes too much time. Accelerating the playback of motion video to, for instance, twenty times normal rate presents the information at an incomprehensible speed. And it would still take six minutes to scan through two hours of videotape!

Even if users could comprehend such accelerated motion, finding a specific piece of video would be difficult. A short two second scene would be presented in only one tenth of a second. With human and system reaction times easily adding to a second or more, significant overshoots will occur as the user tries to stop the video when the desired segment is found.

Playing audio during the scan will not help. Beyond 1.5 or 2 times normal speed audio becomes incomprehensible as the faster playback rates shift the frequencies to inaudible ranges [DMS92]. Digital signal processing techniques are available to reduce these frequency shifts. At high playback rates, these techniques present sound bytes much like the analog videodisc scan. Listening to a Compact Disc audio scan is convincing proof that even without frequency distortion, rapid scanning of audio fails to be a practical search mechanism for large volumes of data.

Tools have been created to facilitate sound browsing where visual representations of the audio waveform are presented to the user to aid identification of locations of interest. However, this has been shown to be useful only for audio segments under three minutes [DMS92]. When searching for a specific piece of information in hours of audio or video other mechanisms will be required.

The Advanced Learning Technologies (ALT) project at CMU's Software Engineering Institute developed a multidimensional model of multimedia objects (text, images, digital video, and digital audio). With this model, variable granularity knowledge about the domain, content, image structure, and the appropriate use of the multimedia object is embedded with the object. In ALT an expert system acts as a director, behaving intelligently in the presentation of image, digital audio, and digital video data. Based on a history of current interactions (input and output) the system makes a judgment on what and how to display multimedia objects [CS92, Ste89].

Techniques using such associated abstract representations have been proposed as a mechanism to facilitate searches of large digital video and audio spaces [Ste92]. In this scheme, embedding knowledge of the video information with the video objects allows for scans by various views, such as by content area or depth of information. When video objects are imbued with knowledge about their content, then partitioning them into many separate small files permits first pass searches to retrieve a small segment of one to two minutes of video. Continuous play of extended sequences is accomplished by seamlessly concatenating logically contiguous files.

Another aid to searching is found in compression schemes for digital video. Since significant image changes affect the compression and decompression algorithms, identification of visual information changes is relatively easy. Thus, scans of small digital video files can be performed by changes in visual information, such as by scene changes. This can be an improvement over jumping a set number of frames, since scene changes often reflect changes in organization of the video much like sections in a book. And in cases where this is not efficient, embedded knowledge about the content of scenes or even individual frames can substitute. In the end, appropriate application of these techniques will permit information-based scanning of multimedia material much like noticing chapter and section headings in a book while flipping pages.

The search and presentation of information stored as motion video and audio is the essence of today's interrupted video paradigm. Emerging multimedia applications move somewhat beyond this by the combination of presenting text, images, animations, and interrupted video. The structures of these paradigms are due to the historical fact that the first marriage of video and the computer was the combination of analog video with the computer's video output.

In these early systems, the analog video was presented on one screen while the computer output was on a second screen. Until the advent of digital video the only integration between video and computer output was through key color mixing. Here, computer graphics could be overlaid on the video image. But the analog video was still effectively separated from the computer and could not be affected by the computer, other than starting, stopping or covering it with graphics.

Even though today's digital video integrates the video and audio completely with other digital data, the interrupted video paradigm remains. This is in part due to current multimedia developers' lack of experience and limited number of more advanced models to emulate. It may also be due to the fact that video and audio are constant rate continuous time media. Yet just because video and audio have a constant rate does not mean they cannot be manipulated by the system or the user. The following sections investigate the limitations of simple multimedia paradigms and suggest the possibilities for human computer interaction afforded by state of the art multimedia designs.

## 9.3  Multimedia Electronic Mail

One of the simplest applications of multimedia is electronic mail. Most users appreciate the advantage of hearing a message and seeing the face of the speaker. Factors such as being more personal and eliminating the need to rely on punctuation to impart messages with affect are cited as benefits of multimedia email.

Multimedia email will impact business, professional, and personal communications. In each domain, multimedia email will afford similar advantages and potential disadvantages. Highlighting one application domain will serve to illustrate the complex social issues raised by combining multimedia with electronic mail.

It is hard to imagine an area in greater need of technological tools than education and training. The nation's schools and industry together spend between \$400 and \$600 billion per year on the business of education and training. Ninety-three percent of this expense is labor-intensive, approximately two times that of the average business, with no change in teacher productivity since the 1800s [Per90].

Advantages of multimedia email for education and training seem obvious. Clearly it is difficult for students to gain individual attention in today's classroom. An instructor has lecture time for a few questions at best. And those questions are usually posed by the most aggressive or outspoken students. The average student may wait until an office hour to ask a question, or more typically, ask another student, or never ask the question at all. In the classroom of the future students will be able to send their instructor a multimedia email question. The general hypothesis is that students will then have greatly increased access to their instructors.

But this hypothesis is based on the assumption that multimedia email is isomorphic to textual email with respect to how users will interact with it. Underlying multimedia email is constant rate continuous time media. Neither the audio nor the video will be able to be played back at a significantly greater speed than the speed they were recorded. Textual email is variable pace continuous media. This may produce some unexpected consequences.

For example, a hypothetical lecture has one hundred and twenty students. If each student were to ask only one multimedia email question per week with an average length of one minute, the instructor will spend a minimum of two hours per week just listening to the questions. Individual two minute answers from the instructor will add another four hours to the task. The six hours to listen and respond to students' questions assume no time was necessary to think out the answers or to interact with the video email interface! At a minimum, the instructor will need to edit responses. What will be the best form for this editor? No matter how easy a multimedia email system is to use, the time to listen to a question and compose a response will be more than the total time of the messages. Few faculty will appreciate trading one hour recitation and two office hours for six to ten hours of multimedia email.

Granted, numerous questions will be asked repeatedly. This will permit the instructor to prerecord his or her responses, helping reduce the time to respond to these questions. But we have seen that the time to listen to the multimedia email cannot be significantly reduced.

Moreover, it is not clear if this will be an improvement over today's system. Will a generic response miss nuances of a student's question? Might it then misdirect the student? Instructors will without a doubt create catalogs of answers to frequently asked questions (FAQ), just as there are FAQs for today's network news groups. All too many instructors today give lectures from notes that are used year after year. It will be difficult for the most conscientious instructors to keep their multimedia email responses up to date, much less those who continually reuse their lecture notes.

When multimedia FAQ answers are saved for years, how will students react to their instructor, appearing years younger, giving a canned answer in his out of style leisure suit? If a student asks more than one question in a single message and the instructor composes a response from two separate files how will the discontinuity affect the user? Section 9.5 in this chapter reports on questions of fidelity in multimedia. It will be seen that changes more subtle than these can have significant effects on users' understanding.

Technical solutions can help. For a classroom environment the students' multimedia email questions can be tied to a passage under study or a problem being solved in an electronic text. Knowledge about the content area that generated the question can be automatically attached to the students question in a machine readable form. Prospective prerecorded responses can then be brought to a local information space for easier perusal and retrieval by the instructor. Creation dates can be checked by the system and messages that are too old, defined by some agreed to convention, can be flagged to encourage re-recording. Innovative tools are being developed to help manage this type of information flow in text form [LM91]. Still, the potential is great for creating an environment that fosters mindless responses, using stale recordings.

These issues carry over to professional and business multimedia electronic mail as well. Managers high on the organizational tree may become inundated with time consuming messages and create "one size fits all" responses. What is the legal liability of a physician who sends a prerecorded response to a colleague that is not absolutely up to date? Certainly there are analogs to these issues in paper environments. But how much more prevalent they may be when multimedia computing aids the process is unknown.

Multimedia email as a solution to current communications problems raises many questions. It will not be a panacea for reducing the time it takes to communicate. The advantages of seeing and hearing the tone of an author will likely outweigh the potential problems. But the issues raised by such a seemingly straightforward application as multimedia email are suggestive of the power and complexity of multimedia applications for human computer interaction.

## 9.4   Networked Digital Video Multimedia Conferencing

When it becomes interactive and real-time, multimedia email evolves into digital video conferencing. Although teleconferencing and analog video conferencing have both been available for decades, new difficulties and opportunities arise when multimedia computing solutions are brought to bear on this old problem.

Today's analog teleconference can be multiple simultaneous telephone connections, more than one person using a speaker phone, or some combination. And a video conference may be effected between two or more remote sites each with the capability of receiving and transmitting both video and audio. (It is interesting to note that up to now common usage of the term "video conference" is often applied to the case of two parties making what might more appropriately be called a video phone call. As technology changes to permit every phone call to be a video call, the term video conference will no doubt be applied differently than it is today. AT&T and MCI's 1992 introductions of video phones that permit real time compressed video to be transmitted over standard phone lines are the beginning of this change.)

Unlike a conference call wherein all audio signals are mixed, today's analog video conference uses a separate monitor for each video feed. Usually, when more than one person at one of the sites is participating in a video conference the camera and furniture are arranged so that all of the collocated participants are simultaneously framed in the video. Some video conference facilities have multiple cameras. When several people are involved in the conference from such a site, one camera is trained on each participant and then switched by an operator. A single video feed is then distributed to the other sites.

In successful collaborative meetings participants have specific roles [Off85]. These roles have titles such as facilitator, scribe, and reader. But beyond the participants and their roles, researchers have found the physical arrangement of the seats in the room to be important to meeting success [SS88].

In this respect analog video teleconferencing schemes have significant disadvantages. Probably the most obvious consequence of analog video schemes is what I call "The Brady Bunch Effect." In the opening sequence to the TV series the Brady Bunch each of the actors was placed in postage stamp fashion in a portion of the screen as they are in today's video conferencing systems (See Figure 9.1).

**Figure 9.1**    Brady Bunch 2x2 video meeting screen

With the type of visual presentation illustrated in Figure 9.1, problems with perceived social dominance or lack thereof, due to arbitrary spatial locations of images arise. Xerox PARC's Media Space and its successors such as CAVECAT (Computer Audio Video Enhanced Collaboration And Telepresence) exemplify an interrupted, analog video paradigm and illustrate this older paradigm's limitations with respect to visual organization of a meeting space:

> ...CAVECAT changed social status relationships due to the loss of the usual spatial and nonverbal cues which convey status information. In face-to-face meetings, the seating of the people in the room is usually indicative of a hierarchy with higher status people occupying more central positions or "head of the table" locations. The design of CAVECAT unintentionally introduced its own social status cues. In meetings of four individuals, CAVECAT arbitrarily positioned participants' images in a 2X2 grid. CAVECAT also configured the video images for a meeting based on who requested the meeting. This meant that if meetings were reconvened after a short break by a different person, the result was a different image configuration. This was highly disconcerting to the participants. It was as if everyone had left the room and returned to take new positions around the table [MBS+91].

It is unfortunate that this type of artifact has been needlessly carried to networked computer/video conferencing designs. An obvious and simple solution to the problem of random image placement is to allow screen placement of meeting participant's images to be determined by their role. When a meeting is continued at a later time, no matter by whom, the same arrangements for each user would be reconstructed. This is not to say that each viewer sees the same scene. In fact, that would be most unlike a face to face meeting where each person sees the room from own visual perspective.

This type of facility has been argued against, not on human factors grounds, but on erroneous technical grounds. The argument chain begins with the see yourself "mirror" window of systems such as Xerox's Media Space and CAVECAT. In the 2x2 meeting screen of Figure 9.1 one of the images is your own. This permits each user to insure that they have framed themselves in the camera properly and to point to other screen objects. Novice users are immediately struck by the fact that their image is in fact not a mirror image. The consequence of this is that visual cues in the media space's "mirror" are precisely backward from what the user expects. So that unlike an optical mirror, if you point to the left you see your image point to its left (your right). But what the user really needs to see is an image that is pointing in the same absolute direction as he or she is pointing (see Figure 9.2).

It has been argued that after a period of time users adapt to the situation. This is undoubtedly true. As part of a workshop on the development of intelligent digital video simulations, university faculty are put through similar experiences [SFC89]. Participants perform a number of writing tasks in a device that permits them only a mirrored view of their hand and paper. The purpose of this task is to give attendees personal experience in the accommodation of cognitive processes. During the one-half to one hour experience some people never accommodate. However, frequently someone will experience a gestalt shift and begin to write perfectly well in the mirror system. A frightening experience for some of these people is that after this, and sometimes for several hours, they cannot write normally without the mirror.

Arguing for the not mirroring the user's own view of their image in a media space is analogous to defending any design by saying users adapt. In other words, it is the Marie Antoinette 'Let them eat cake' school of human factors design. In a digital video, multimedia environment one's own image can be mirrored locally and sent non-mirrored to external recipients. Thus, images, such as text, that were placed in front of the camera in such a system would not be mirrored for the other participants. Manipulations such as these are trivial in a digital video environment, but very difficult in an analog video environment.

The question arises whether this will cause a new problem: in such a system when a user points to another person in the media space, another quadrant on the screen, the rest of the participants would see the first user pointing in the wrong direction (see Figure 9.3). As can be seen in these figures, if placement of the images is arbitrary, the direction of pointing will be incorrect (see Figure 9.4). However, in a digital video multimedia paradigm there is no reason why the placement cannot be tailored for each user.

Moreover, the work of Stone and others suggests that the placement of these images should not be arbitrary but associated to some convention. Thus, in the simplest case the screens could be arranged as in Figure 9.5 where it is seen that each user sees a unique but basically correct representation of the meeting and the participants. In this design, not only would each user have a natural image of themselves (i.e. actually mirrored), but there would be consistent screens for reconvened meetings and effectively arranged "meeting chairs."

Since you do not see yourself in real meetings, it may in fact be preferable to have a small, inconspicuous image of the user presented locally. The principal use of the your own image is then for centering (framing) your self in the camera's field of view, not pointing to locations in the media space. In this case, if the user wishes to point to a location in the media space, rather than their own hand, a digital pointer can be made available.

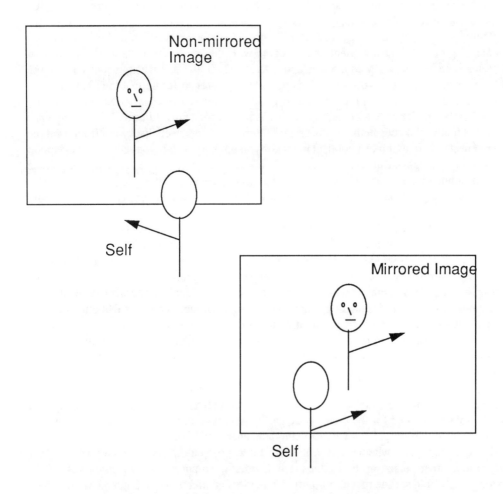

**Figure 9.2**   Effect of non-mirrored images on user gesticulation

Still more advanced representations of meeting spaces are possible. Figure 9.6 is an image from a simulation of a meeting [CS92, Ste89]. This image is actually made from five different images blended to form a single seamless scene (see Figure 9.7). While these images are prerecorded, there is no impediment to performing this type of synthesis live. With luminance keying users need not be seated in a "Chromakey blue" space. Thus, with few special architectural constraints placed on their offices, users could be placed in a virtual meeting space.

While digital video in multimedia computing permits natural, user centered designs, many questions remain. Can and should a system automatically frame the subject in the camera's field of view? What is the effect of camera angles on users' perception? How should subjects

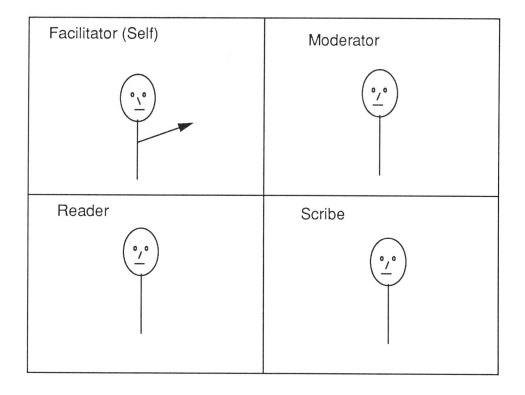

**Figure 9.3**   What user sees in a mirrored self image video conference

be properly lighted? Although the new questions generated by multimedia are complex, technologies suggesting solutions are available today.

At the consumer end of the scale $150 camcorder tracking devices are available that can keep subjects framed. At the high end of the scale NHK has developed SYNTHEVISION. Foreground and background images are coupled in SYNTHEVISION. Using data from the foreground image a background image is derived with appropriate perspective, taking into consideration panning, tilting, focusing, zooming, and dollying of a camera tracking the foreground image [NHK91]. This allows for users to be electronically placed in any arbitrary physical space with a totally convincing visual presentation.

The effect of camera angles and lighting on viewers' comprehension perception is well studied [Kra87, Kra88]. Mechanisms for capturing that expertise and automatically applying

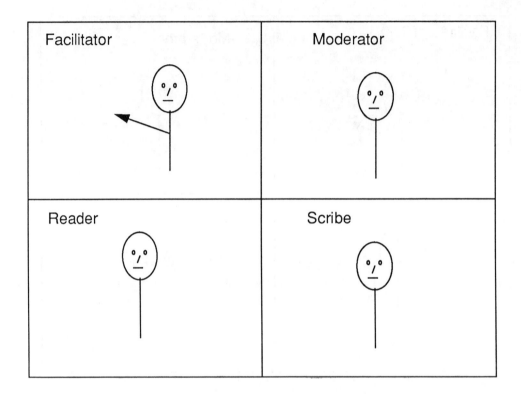

**Figure 9.4**  What others would see when the non-mirrored image is sent to others.

it in multimedia computing systems have been demonstrated [SFC89]. With capabilities such as these, multimedia meeting spaces can ultimately be as comfortable and productive as a well designed conference room.

## 9.5  Fidelity

So far this chapter has equated multimedia with digital video and implied that any video is better than no video. But is that really true? Are there differences between the closeness to reality (fidelity) of the design of a multimedia space? How much fidelity is enough? Does frame rate of video matter?

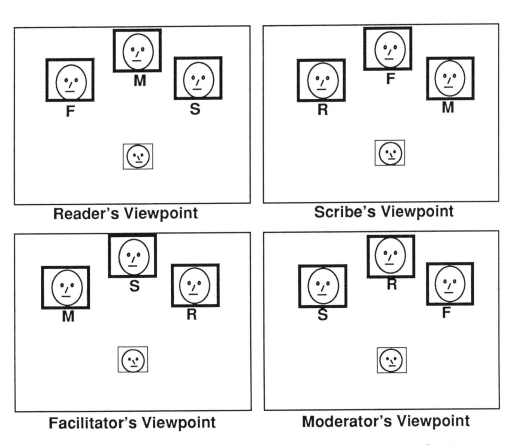

**Reader's Viewpoint** **Scribe's Viewpoint**

**Facilitator's Viewpoint** **Moderator's Viewpoint**

F = Facilitator, M = Moderator, R = Recorder, and S = Scribe

**Figure 9.5** Variable placement of participants allows each user a unique scene

### 9.5.1 Design Fidelity

Michael Christel studied users of a virtual reality workspace for learning and experience software inspections [Chr91]. Two methods of navigating through the world were evaluated, one a direct manipulation point and click floor plan of the space, and the other a surrogate travel interface where the user "walks" through the space and into the desired sub-world (see figure 9.8). Both groups of users liked, or disliked, the interfaces equally and used them in equivalent fashions to navigate the world. In itself this is surprising as one would expect the direct point and click interface to permit the users more freedom to move between sub-worlds. This is especially true as the surrogate travel interface took considerably more time to perform the equivalent task (moving the user from one sub-world to another).

More interesting than the fact that the users navigated between sub-worlds equivalently was

**Figure 9.6**   High visual fidelity simulation of a conference

their attitudes after the experience. Users with the surrogate travel interface came away from the experience with more positive opinions about the subject under investigation! While the surrogate travel interface was more cumbersome and slower, its users were more completely brought into the virtual world and developed better attitudes because of it.

Earlier evidence from a study of an interactive videodisc laboratory simulation also supported the view that more realistic interfaces had positive effects on users [Ste85]. That study showed that by creating a more visually abstract yet easier to use interface (analogous to the floor plan above), users tended to act as if the visually salient features of the interface were to be operated on rather than the functions those features represented.

Since the virtual conference room, multimedia meeting place described in Section 9.4 has yet to be implemented, the formal assertion that it is preferable to a "Brady Bunch" design

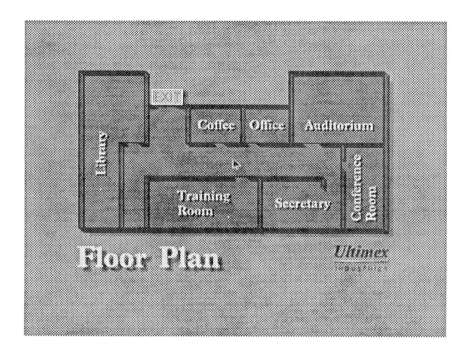

**Figure 9.7**   Component multimedia objects used to create the conference simulation

cannot yet be made. However, the work cited above suggests that in general a design will have positive effects if it more closely resembles a real-world environment. Such design fidelity more closely maps to users' day to day world and allows them to more naturally enter the computer's world.

### 9.5.2   Motion Fidelity

Besides design fidelity, multimedia applications must be concerned with spatial (resolution) and especially frequency (temporal or motion) fidelity. A simple view of resolution is that it is a function the number of lines per image and pixels per line. Assume a 1,000 by 1,000 pixel image completely fills a monitor. Now, if one cuts the number of lines and pixels per line each in half, there is one fourth of the information. However, if you display the new image on the same monitor, it looks like a smaller but equally clear image. Such operations in the frequency domain are not so benign. If we loose three out of four frames of thirty frame per second video there is no masking the effect. Until recently, how great an effect motion fidelity has was unknown.

Without special hardware many of today's multimedia operating systems and networks are incapable of thirty frame per second motion digital video. From an application's perspective these operating systems may make seemingly arbitrary presentation decisions, for example trading frame rate for resolution or synchronization. Is this lower motion fidelity, lower frame

**Figure 9.8**   Point and click surrogate travel interfaces

rate video effective? Do differing levels of fidelity matter? Are four frames per second fast enough? Twenty-five frames? Thirty frames?

There are compelling reasons to believe that high frame rates are more than frills. In the same experiment cited above, Christel presented one group of users with thirty frame per second full motion video and audio in the various sub-worlds. Another group had the same experience except identical, but sequential still images, one every four seconds taken from the video, with audio. The users with the full motion video retained significantly more information even though the information tested on was contained in the audio.

In a second experiment, we compared five frame per second video to full motion video. The subjects were graduate students in a course on software engineering. The students were required to use the virtual workspace as part of the course requirements. With their consent, they participated in the experiment and were randomly assigned to one of two groups. One group's system presented full motion, thirty frame per second video. The second group had the same virtual workspace with identical video, except that the video was presented at five frames per second.

Seven out of ten users subjected to the five frame per second video refused to finish the experiment! Typical of the responses was one user's: "What did I do wrong in life that I had to go through this hell?" Such reactions should not be surprising. Photic stimulation in the one to eighteen cycle per second range has been shown to produce effects from migraines and epileptic seizures to resonances of EEGs and induced visual imagery [FBK90, Gli87, RM90, WW49].

Even with text, a user's performance can be adversely affected when text is presented at less than fifteen characters per second [TAD85]. With video, users will not accept a "wait" of over one thirtieth of a second (or, according to PAL video standard advocates, one-twenty-fifth of a second) for the presentation of the next image.

The lesson seems to be clear. It is one thing to watch a 30 second QuickTime or Indeo movie running at five frames per second on a personal computer with no special hardware to improve multimedia performance. It is something quite different to sit for three hours viewing video presented at such a frame rate. In short, motion fidelity is critical. If a comfortable frame rate is not possible with the available hardware, users are better served with still images and audio. Beyond this, it is not just motion fidelity or design fidelity that makes a high quality multimedia application. Success comes from an understanding of users' needs, human factors, and system capabilities.

## 9.6   Outlook

There is a growing understanding of the appropriate design and functionality required by multimedia applications. Along with many other factors, developers must consider the complexity inherent in multimedia objects, create high fidelity designs, and factor in the temporal nature of multimedia.

In the future, multimedia applied to collaboration environments will permit multi-person workspaces that greatly enhance distributed groups' creativity and productivity. Beyond video conferences, multimedia computing will impact virtually every facet of human computer interaction. In each new domain, multimedia applications must be designed with a deep knowledge of both multimedia capabilities and human factors.

A seemingly simple multimedia object such as audio may be used or misused. In the analog world video is relatively difficult to mix. This has led to the Brady Bunch video interface even though in the digital world video is easily manipulated. Conversely, most digital audio components of multimedia systems make mixing digital audio difficult if there is only one DAC or DSP. Requiring participants of a multimedia audio conference to "take the floor" before talking will certainly alter the meeting. There is no technical constraint that would require this. Digital audio data can be combined in an algorithmic fashion by the multimedia platform. Just because digital audio may be more difficult to mix is not sufficient justification to constrain the user. Developers must look to the requirements of the user.

Multimedia technology is becoming widely available and it can deliver more information, more effectively than any scheme developed to date. But more than just delivering information, effective design of multimedia systems will require a deep understanding of the roles of interaction with huge volumes of information, simulation, learning, and even virtual reality. Ultimately, multimedia computing will allow communication, access to information, and learning to become more active and compelling.

Both aiding other applications and as applications in their own right, multimedia visualization and presentation systems will intelligently present information based on users needs, human factors, and even cinematic principles [CS92, DSP91, Ste89]. Artificial intelligence applied to multimedia will permit intelligent interfaces, agents, guides, and anthropomorphic systems [Lau86].

This chapter has just begun to scratch the surface of multimedia computing's role in human computer interaction. Advanced multimedia applications require much more of developers and computing systems than do today's interrupted video. Rather than develop the multimedia equivalent of a teletypewriter I/O paradigm, there is today an opportunity to avoid the mistakes of the past. Through a creative, multi-disciplinary approach, a new multimedia paradigm will emerge that provides a quantum leap beyond today's GUIs.

## References

[Chr91]    M. G. Christel. *A Comparative Evaluation of Digital Video Interactive Interfaces in the Delivery of a Code Inspection Course*. PhD thesis, Georgia Institute of Technology, Atlanta GA, 1991.

[CS92]     M. B. Christel and S. M. Stevens. Rule base and digital video technologies applied to training simulations. In *Software Engineering Institute Technical Review 92*. Software Engineering Institute, Pittsburgh, PA, 1992.

[DMS92]    L. Degen, R. Mander, and G. Salomon. Working with audio: Integrating personal tape recorders and desktop computers. In *Proceeding of ACM CHI '92 Conference on Human Factors In Computing Systems*, 1992.

[DSP91]    G. Davenport, T. Smith, and N. Pincever. Cinematic primitives for multimedia. *IEEE Computer Graphics and Applications*, July 1991.

[Esp93]    C. Esposito. Virtual reality: Perspecitves, applications, and architectures. In Bass and Dewan, editors, *User Interface Software*, Trends in Software Series. Wiley, 1993.

[FBK90]    A. I. Fedotchev, A. T. Bondar, and V. F. Konovalov. Stability of resonance eeg reactions to flickering light in humans. *International Journal of Psychophysiology*, 9, 1990.

[Gli87]    J. Glicksohn. Photic driving and altered states of consciousness: An exploritory study. *Cognition and Personality*, 6(2), 1986–87.

[Had45]    J. Hadamand. *The Psychology of Invention in the Mathematical Field*. Princeton University Press, Princeton, NJ, 1945.

[HSA89]    M. E. Hodges, R. M. Sasnett, and M. S. Ackerman. A construction set for multimedia applications. *IEEE Software*, January 1989.

[IK92]     H. Ishii and M. Kobayashi. Clearboard: A seamless medium for shared drawing and conversation with eye contact. In *Proceeding of ACM CHI '92 Conference on Human Factors In Computing Systems*, 1992.

[Kra87]    R. Kraft. The influence of camera angle on comprehension and retention of pictorial events. *Memory and Cognition*, 15(4), 1987.

[Kra88]    R. Kraft. Mind and media: The psychological reality of cinematic principles. In D. Schultz and C.W. Moody, editors, *Images, Information and Interfaces: Directions for the 1990's*. Human Factors Society, New York, NY, 1988.

[Lau86]    B. Laurel. Interface as mimesis. In D. Nomran and S. Draper, editors, *User Centered System Design*, chapter 4. Lawrence Erlbaum Assoc., 1986.

[Lip80]    A. Lippman. Movie-maps: and application of the optical videodisc to computer graphics. *Computer Graphics*, 14(3), 1980.

[LM91]     K-Y. Lai and T.W. Malone. Object lens: Letting end-users create cooperative work application. In *Proceeding of ACM CHI '91 Conference on Human Factors In Computing Systems*, 1991.

[MBS+91]   M. M. Mantei, R. M. Baecker, A. J. Sellen, W. A. S. Buxton, and T. Milligan. Experiences in the use of a media space. In *Proceedings of ACM CHI'91 Conference on Human Factors In Computing Systems*, 1991.

[NHK91]    NHK. *1991 Technology Open House*. NHK Engineering Services, Inc., Tokyo, Japan, 1991.

[Off85]    Xerox Corporation's Quality Office. *Leadership Through Quality; Mining Group Gold; A Guide Providing Facilitation Techniques, Tips, Checklists and Guidesheets*. Multinational Customer and Service Education Reprographic Business Group, Xerox Corporation,

Rochester, NY, July 1985.

[Per90]    L. J. Perelman. A new learning enterprise. *Business Week*, December 10 1990.

[Res89]    H. L. Resnikoff. *The Illusion of Reality*. Springer-Verlag, New York, NY, 1989.

[RM90]     A. Richardson and F. McAndrew. The effects of photic stimulation and private self-consciousness on the complexity of visual imagination imagery. *British Journal of Psychology*, 81, 1990.

[SFC89]    S.M. Stevens, R. G. Fuller, and M. G. Christel. *Workshop on Intelligent Tutoring Systems and Digital Video*. American Association of Physics Teachers and Software Engineering Institute, Pittsburgh, PA, 1989.

[SS88]     D. Stone and A. Stone. The seat of power. *Carnegie Mellon Magazine*, Winter 1988.

[Sta93]    J. Stasko. Animation in user interfaces: Principles and techniques. In Bass and Dewan, editors, *User Interface Software*, Trends in Software Series. Wiley, 1993.

[Ste85]    S.M. Stevens. Interactive computer/videodisc lessons and their effect on students' understanding of science. In *National Association for Research in Science Teaching: 58th Annual NARST Conference*, Columbus, OH, 1985. ERIC.

[Ste89]    S. M. Stevens. Intelligent interactive video simulation of a code inspection. *Communications of the ACM*, July 1989.

[Ste92]    S. M. Stevens. Next generation network and operating system requirements for continuous time media. In R.G. Herrtwich, editor, *Network and Operating System Support for Digital Audio and Video*. Springer-Verlag, New York, NY, 1992.

[TAD85]    J. W. Tombaugh, M.D. Arkin, and R. F. Dillon. The effect of vdu text-presentation rate on reading comprehension and reading speed. In *Proceedings of ACM CHI '85 Conference on Human Factors In Computing Systems*, 1985.

[WW49]     V.J. Walter and W.G. Walter. The central effects of rhythmic sensory stimulation. *Electroencephalography and Clinical Neurophysiology*, 1, 1949.

[YHMD88]   N. Yankelovich, B. J. Haan, N. K. Meyrowitz, and S. M. Drucker. Intermedia: The concept and the construction of a seamless information environment. *IEEE Computer*, January 1988.

# Index

*Index compiled by Geoffrey C. Jones*